Faculty as Global Learners

OFF-CAMPUS STUDY LEADERS AT LIBERAL ARTS COLLEGES

Joan Gillespie

Lisa Jasinski

Dana Gross

**LEVER
PRESS**

Lever Press (leverpress.org) is a publisher of pathbreaking scholarship. Supported by a consortium of liberal arts institutions focused on, and renowned for, excellence in both research and teaching, our press is grounded on three essential commitments: to be a digitally native press, to be a peer-reviewed, open access press that charges no fees to either authors or their institutions, and to be a press aligned with the ethos and mission of liberal arts colleges.

The complete proposal and manuscript of this work were subjected to a partly closed ("single blind") review process. For more information, please see our Peer Review Commitments and Guidelines at https://www.leverpress.org/peerreview

DOI: https://doi.org/10.3998/mpub.11923682
Print ISBN: 978-1-64315-019-2
Open access ISBN: 978-1-64315-020-8

Library of Congress Control Number: 2019954803

Published in the United States of America by Lever Press, in partnership with Amherst College Press and Michigan Publishing

Contents

Member Institution Acknowledgments

Lever Press is a joint venture. This work was made possible by the generous support of Lever Press member libraries from the following institutions:

Adrian College	Denison University
Agnes Scott College	DePauw University
Allegheny College	Earlham College
Amherst College	Furman University
Bard College	Grinnell College
Berea College	Hamilton College
Bowdoin College	Harvey Mudd College
Carleton College	Haverford College
Claremont Graduate	Hollins University
University	Keck Graduate Institute
Claremont McKenna College	Kenyon College
Clark Atlanta University	Knox College
Coe College	Lafayette College Library
College of Saint Benedict /	Lake Forest College
Saint John's University	Macalester College
The College of Wooster	Middlebury College

Morehouse College
Oberlin College
Pitzer College
Pomona College
Rollins College
Santa Clara University
Scripps College
Sewanee: The University of the South
Skidmore College
Smith College
Spelman College
St. Lawrence University
St. Olaf College

Susquehanna University
Swarthmore College
Trinity University
Union College
University of Puget Sound
Ursinus College
Vassar College
Washington and Lee University
Whitman College
Willamette University
Williams College

Figures and Tables

FIGURES

TABLES

Foreword

Milton Reigelman

The tectonic plates that underlie assumptions about private residential liberal arts colleges have shifted dramatically in the past
45 years. In 1975, liberal arts schools were thought of as places in a
fixed geographical location, with distinct and obvious boundaries,
consisting of brick-and-mortar buildings, students, faculty, and
staff. For many, the image that came first to mind was an ivory
tower existing on a tree-lined plot away from large cities and the
hurly-burly world. For four years students could read and listen—if
sometimes inertly—to academic lectures from learned professors
(à la Matthew Arnold) about "the best that has been thought and
said" in their own culture before returning to take their proper
place in that culture.

Today that conception has become an anachronism. The walls
separating a liberal arts college from the world have become porous,
the border crossings open, no visa required either way. Colleges are
no longer ivy-clad towers but observation posts from which students not only observe but interact with the outside world in various ways. The protective college bubble has burst. The alma mater,
affectionately called "mother college," that nurtured students for

four years has also become the "mother ship" that transports them to new spaces for active exploration. Just as experiencing the different gravitational pull and physical environment of Mars would deepen and expand the ways travelers thought about and understood their own gravity and environment, living in a foreign country (or even a different part of the United States) deepens and expands the ways students think about and understand their own society and culture. As Aristotle said as he strolled through Athenian groves 2,350 years ago, one comes to a deeper understanding of something through comparison with different things.

What brought about this change in liberal arts colleges? One might point to new approaches in the traditional academic disciplines (in my own, literature, structuralism and post-colonial studies, e.g.) or to the new disciplines that emerged (computer science and environmental studies, e.g.) or to Thomas L. Friedman's "flat," interconnected world. Whatever the causes, one obvious marker of the change can be summed up in two words: study abroad.

Let's begin with some numbers. During the 1973–1974 academic year, about 3% of the students at my institution, Centre College, studied abroad. Today, 45 years later, *more than 11 times as many students,* about 34%, study abroad each year. By the time our seniors graduate, about 85% have studied abroad at least once, 30% two or more times. This exponential growth is not uncommon in liberal arts institutions, almost all of which now include "global learning" or "global citizenship" or "cross-cultural learning" in their mission statements.

The correlation between the very top colleges in the *U.S. News & World Report* rankings and those with the highest study abroad percentages in the annual Institute of International Education (IIE) Open Doors report is not accidental. Only about 4% of students leaving high school today end up at residential liberal arts colleges. One of the most important things that draws them to our institutions—and differentiates us from their other good options—is our study abroad programs. This sea change has affected not only students but faculty, pedagogy, and budgets as well.

Faculty who've taught students abroad often say their experiences have transformed them. In 1979–1980, as a youngster who was comfortable, even pleased, with the evaluations from his U.S. American literature courses, I was a most unlikely prospect for any transformation. As a Fulbright lecturer, I looked forward to wowing students at the University of Warsaw with one of my favorite books, Faulkner's *The Sound and the Fury*. My best-laid plans went quickly astray. I'd never had to think about, much less answer, the questions my Polish students peppered me with almost immediately. Could the African American speech of Faulkner's Dilsey and Luster be translated into Polish as Yiddish? We spent the next class talking about differences between Faulkner's 1920s Mississippi Black characters and the Polish Jews living contemporaneously in the Warsaw ghetto. When I returned to Eastern Europe a few years later, Gorbachev's *perestroika* and *glasnost* had emboldened many in the satellite countries, but nothing could have emboldened my students at Kiev State University like Emerson's "Self-Reliance," Thoreau's "Civil Disobedience," and Whitman's *Song of Myself*. Though I'd had an intellectual understanding of those canonical U.S. American texts, nothing could have prepared me for the emotional, almost visceral power they exerted on those students. Those beloved old chestnuts burst the bounds of literary analysis and exploded, emotionally, into politics, economics, history, sociology, religion, etc. I never taught them the same way again.

Something of the same thing happened while later teaching in semester programs in France and England. From the very first sentence of Henry James's *Portrait of a Lady,* we were led into a lively discussion about the differences between U.S. American and English assumptions about manners, the class system, entertainment, leisure, even beverages: "Under certain circumstances there are few hours in life more agreeable than the hour dedicated to the ceremony known as afternoon tea." Trying to parse this Jamesian precision to U.S. students tied to their iPhones in Danville, Kentucky, would have been beyond difficult; doing so while they were discovering life in London's Bloomsbury district seemed perfectly natural. They soon wondered why James and T. S. Eliot moved to England in the first place, and then why Hemingway, Fitzgerald, and a host of other U.S. American writers and painters and musicians gravitated to Paris in the 1920s. Teaching any subject matter in a new environment puts it in a brighter, fuller light.

The personal reflections (Faculty Voices) that the three authors wisely include in this volume are a testament to the profound influence that teaching in an off-campus program has in transforming faculty's understanding of their students and of global learning—as well as expanding and enriching their pedagogical practices.

When students are off-campus trying to understand a different culture, the siloed walls between sociology and economics, politics and religion, or history and literature become weakened. Off-campus teachers inevitably find themselves using what the American Association of Colleges & Universities calls high-impact practices: collaborative projects, learning communities, writing-intensive projects, and capstone experiences.

Here's one example of an assignment rare on home campuses but perfectly natural when students are in a new environment. A class of 21 students is split up into seven groups. Each group of three is assigned some aspect of the new environment for intensive study that includes examining original on-site documents, spending time in a certain institution or neighborhood until they become comfortable, and interviewing selected or random people. The small groups then present their findings to the class and prepare a written document such as "The Political Landscape of Seven London Neighborhoods" or "How Science Is Taught in Seven Shanghai Elementary Schools." Chapter 3 of this volume highlights some of the changes in pedagogy that faculty adopt while away— and continue once they return to the home campus.

Faculty behavior is not the only important thing that undergoes a change. Parents have told me about the subtle but enormously important difference they note after their sons or daughters have studied abroad, away from the relative luxuries many campuses now provide, including dining commons featuring various specialty "stations" and, yes, even those infamous climbing walls. Simply put, when they study away, students tend—as one of my colleagues likes to put it—"to grow up!" Having overcome the challenges of adapting to a totally new environment and a new group of students, they have an expanded sense of the possible. They return to their home campuses with a new confidence and the desire to continue their adventure by seeking out new challenges, including internships, research, and service-learning.

But what about cost? Colleges with the very highest endowments and longest lines of students waiting to be admitted have the financial capacity to offer their students a wide range of study abroad options around the globe run by the best third-party providers. The drawback of such an ideal situation, however, is that faculty may not be significantly involved, as they should be, before, during, or following the student experience, and the off-campus study becomes more disconnected from on-campus education than it needs be.

Slightly less wealthy institutions are able to offer all students a semester off-campus with no additional cost by using third-party providers only to fill in gaps, using their own faculty to set up and run their largest programs.

Student exchanges with foreign universities are difficult to set up, but they can be an excellent option, even on the smallest scale. Such exchanges efficiently internationalize a campus by both exporting and importing students with little additional cost to either institution. If students on both campuses continue to pay their home institution whatever they would pay if they remained there, the problematic institutional decisions about how much need-based and merit aid is "transportable" is completely—and happily—avoided.

Partnerships with other U.S. institutions can be attractive not only because they widen the pool of faculty experts and interested students but also because outside funding is available, especially for planning and coordination. The Mellon Foundation recently funded a three-college partnership (Centre, Rhodes, and Sewanee) to set up a joint New York internship program and then joint programs in Africa and other underrepresented areas. To be sure, institutional partnerships are difficult to sustain. The Associated Colleges of the Midwest is eliminating its admirable and ambitious, but expensive, overseas programs, and the Associated Colleges of the South earlier canceled its consortial Turkey program. We all know where the devil resides. Chapter 4 in this volume may help institutions avoid or at least navigate some of the devilish problems inherent in any institutional partnership.

Faculty members who have directed and taught students away know how much more effort it takes off-campus than it does on-campus to meet classes and do the other expected things. While off-campus they feel responsible 24/7 and may find themselves standing-in for the academic advisor, the student life support staff, nurse, public safety officer, bursar, and/or chaplain. Institutions, therefore, should send abroad only faculty who are committed, well prepared, and know the site thoroughly through experience. At institutions with strong study abroad programs, finding such people is not as difficult as it may seem: the best and most enterprising faculty applicants, like the best students, apply. If you build it, they will come. As argued in chapter 2 of this volume, proper institutional support during the planning stage and once faculty arrive on-site will increase both their effectiveness and long-term job satisfaction. Chapter 5 identifies how two liberal arts colleges have recently undertaken significant efforts to elevate the status and place of global learning through structures of shared governance.

Of the changes that have taken place in liberal arts schools over the past 45 years, none is as important for their future viability as their study abroad/away programs, which prepare students for our increasingly interconnected and interdependent world—and gives them the worldview and confidence to thrive in that world.

This volume provides private, residential liberal arts schools the latest study abroad/away research as well as vivid, firsthand scouting reports from the field. This military image is not haphazard: there are political leaders today who mistakenly think of higher education as a battle between practical, STEM training for jobs in the "real world" and airy liberal arts education that takes place in isolated ivory towers disconnected from that world. This is, of course, a false dichotomy: nothing could be further from the truth. There is no better way to educate and prepare students today than a liberal arts education that allows them—whether classics or STEM majors—to understand and appreciate different ways of thinking and their own culture more deeply and fully through quality study abroad/away programs. Because liberal arts colleges are now expanding and strengthening these programs, this volume will be particularly relevant. It could not come at a better time.

EXECUTIVE SUMMARY

Opportunities and Strategies to (Better) Support Leaders of Off-Campus Programs

Dana Gross, Lisa Jasinski, and Joan Gillespie

This executive summary provides a concise overview of the five chapters and 17 Faculty Voices essays that compose this book. We hope that these key findings and recommendations stimulate conversations among administrators, faculty, and staff about concrete actions they can explore and steps they can take on their campuses to both support faculty leaders of off-campus programs and advance strategic institutional goals for global learning.

CHAPTER SUMMARIES

Chapter 1 builds on Faculty as Global Learners, a collaborative, multi-institution survey of more than 200 faculty members who led off-campus study programs at 27 selective liberal arts colleges (Gillespie, Glasco, Gross, Jasinski, & Layne, 2017). The scale and scope of that foundational survey allowed us to capture a chorus of faculty voices in a systematic, credible, and persuasive way. Participant responses guided us toward topics meriting further investigation and led us to imagine policies and practices to (better) support

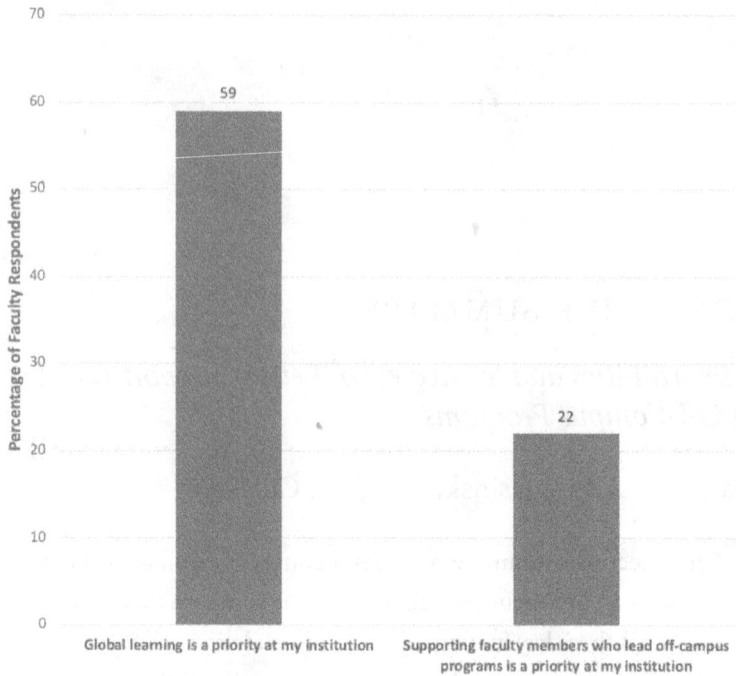

Figure 1. Percentage of Faculty Respondents Who Agree "to a Great Extent" Regarding Institutional Support of Global Learning and Off-Campus Faculty Leaders

Note: Adapted from *Faculty as global learners: Enhancing the transformative impact of leading off-campus study programs,* by J. Gillespie, S. Glasco, D. Gross, L. Jasinski, & P. Layne, 2017, paper presented at Forum on Education Abroad Annual Conference, Boston, MA.

faculty program leaders. As shown in Figure 1, the survey surfaced key issues: faculty members' perceptions of institutional practices and their view that liberal arts colleges are not doing enough to support the outcomes they say they value.

This disconnect is explored further in chapter 2, which notes that although an increasing number of colleges place a high value on global learning and internationalization, the majority of baccalaureate institutions have not supported these goals by investing in strategic faculty hiring, review, and development (Helms, 2015; Helms, Brajkovic, & Struthers, 2017).

- Only 6% of baccalaureate institutions report that they frequently hire faculty with international background, experience, or interests in fields that are not explicitly international/global.
- The vast majority (93%) of baccalaureate institutions do not specify international work or experience as considerations in faculty promotion and tenure decisions.
- Faculty development is often a significantly lower institutional priority for global learning and internationalization than activities such as recruiting international students, increasing U.S. student mobility, and creating partnerships abroad (as shown in Figure 2).

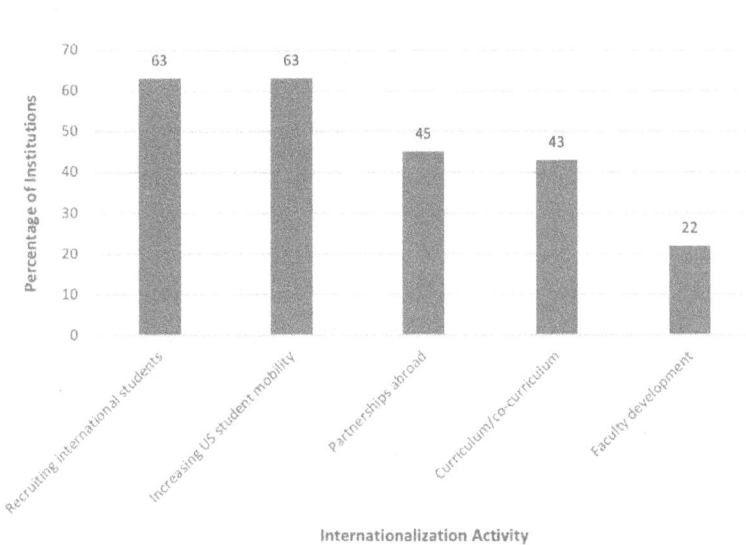

Figure 2. Baccalaureate Institutions Reporting Internationalization Activities Among Their Top Three Priorities
Note: Adapted from *Mapping internationalization on U.S. campuses: 2017 edition,* by R. M. Helms, L. Brajkovic, & B. Struthers, 2017, Washington, DC: American Council on Education.

In order to address the perceived deficiencies, chapter 2 asserts that one of the most effective ways that liberal arts colleges can maximize students' global learning is by synergistically investing in faculty program leaders in ways that provide immediate support for off-campus programs and also cultivate long-term job satisfaction and career success among the faculty. As illustrated in Figure 3, effective support must be holistic in nature and also meet instructors' immediate needs before, during, and after an off-campus study program, including practices such as:

- providing program development travel allowances to enable instructors to meet with site partners in advance;
- offering sufficient administrative support for tasks such as student recruitment and reconciling expense reports;
- fostering the continuing education of program leaders, encouraging faculty members to convert their program experiences into new areas of research, including expanding their disciplinary research to new regions or advancing research about effective practices in international education; and
- targeting the specific needs and preferences of the populations served—creating customized approaches for early, mid-career, and senior scholars while keeping in mind the generational preferences of baby boomers, Gen Xers, and a forthcoming wave of millennial faculty members.

The distinctive pedagogical features of off-campus study programs at liberal arts colleges are the focus of chapter 3. Evidence from in-depth interviews and syllabi demonstrates that instructors regularly incorporate recognized high-impact practices from the Association of American Colleges & Universities (Kuh & Schneider, 2008) into their off-campus study courses. Many characteristics of off-campus study programs—a flexible daily schedule, the ability to interact with students in both formal learning settings and less structured outings, and a propensity to incorporate active learning

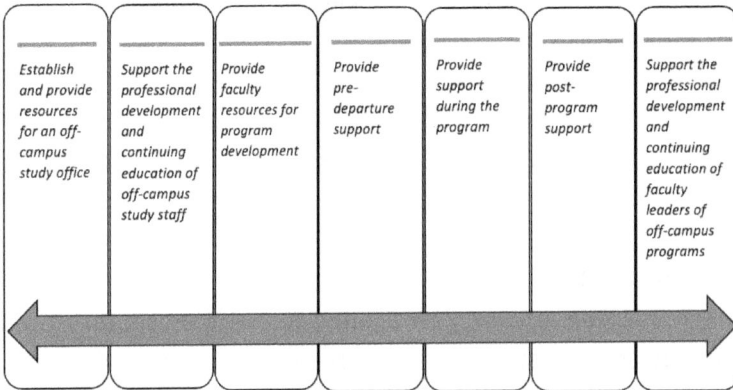

| Establish and provide resources for an off-campus study office | Support the professional development and continuing education of off-campus study staff | Provide faculty resources for program development | Provide pre-departure support | Provide support during the program | Provide post-program support | Support the professional development and continuing education of faculty leaders of off-campus programs |

Figure 3. Synergistic Investments in Faculty Leaders of Off-Campus Programs Support Immediate and Long-Term Strategic Goals for Global Learning and Internationalization

assignments—resulted in instructors embracing creative, interdisciplinary, and flexible teaching strategies and other elements of good practice in undergraduate education (Chickering & Gamson, 1987). Other pedagogical characteristics include the following:

- Concentrated blocks of time during the academic year, lasting for a period of weeks rather than months, create "mini-mester" opportunities for studying off-campus.
- Daily interactions in an off-campus setting allow faculty and students to pursue forms of interdisciplinary and experiential learning that are difficult to achieve during a "normal" weekly academic semester.
- Distinct phases before, during, and after a program allow faculty to make strategic use of time and employ different types of assignments and structured interactions to achieve overall program goals.
- Student-faculty contact during off-campus programs is qualitatively different from contact with students on campus,

offering opportunities for greater understanding, intimacy, and empathy.

- Academic rigor characterizing off-campus programs includes space for guided reflection about experiential learning.
- Off-campus programs encourage faculty to be more flexible, creative, and interdisciplinary.

Preparing and leading an off-campus study program is a time- and energy-intensive endeavor for faculty. For their efforts, faculty are rewarded with high student engagement and personal insights about how best to teach. When faculty engage in these creative and impactful forms of teaching, liberal arts colleges fulfill their missions to become more globally engaged and student centered. Given the perceived benefits, merit and promotion reviews should reward explicitly this work.

Chapter 4 explains how small liberal arts colleges have leveraged partnerships and consortium relationships to achieve sustainable off-campus study programs. Not only do multi-institution partnerships benefit from larger pools of prospective program leaders and participating students, but also the long-term commitment demanded to sustain a collaborative program lends itself to regular assessment and continuous improvement. Program leaders and administrative professionals reap additional benefits from belonging to a community of practice associated with an affiliated program. Whereas a faculty member may be the only person on an individual campus interested in a particular topic or a region, a partnership arrangement surrounds each faculty member with like-minded collaborators and thought partners. Chapter 4 uses vivid examples to illustrate that when small colleges participate in collaboratively managed faculty-led off-campus study programs, they affirm liberal arts values, such as student-centeredness and a commitment to interdisciplinary approaches, while also benefiting from the economies of scale usually associated with larger institutions. The chapter reviews high-level characteristics of a successful partnership, then makes recommendations for translating these ideals into action, including roles assigned to senior leadership, faculty members, and administrative staff. Tables 1, 2, and 3 identify practical recommendations for colleges establishing new partnerships, including the following:

- taking time during the exploratory phase to conduct an audit or inventory of recent and existing collaborations in order to find the right partner(s);
- utilizing a checklist of current activities and performance indicators of quality during the program development phase to articulate the mission and goals for the partnership; and
- creating an assessment process and plans for a review by institutional participants in the partnership.

The discussion is particularly directed to senior administrators and faculty who already are charged with the designated authority to plan and implement academic initiatives, including institutional partnerships and off-campus study programs, and to those who aspire to centralize strategic international engagement with clear processes and protocols in order to further their educational mission.

Some private liberal arts colleges—led jointly by senior administrators and faculty leaders—have reinvented themselves in the arena of global learning by increasing student access to off-campus study, using strategic planning to formalize ambitious goals, adopting new curricular elements and graduation requirements, and crafting marketing messages to reflect underlying changes. Chapter 5 presents in-depth case studies of ongoing internationalization initiatives at Susquehanna University and Grinnell College and discusses five strategies for institutional transformation (Eckel & Kezar, 2003):

Table 1. Parties and Tasks During the Exploratory Phase in Off-Campus Program Partnerships

RESPONSIBLE PARTY	EXPLORATORY PHASE
President	Appoint senior administrator or faculty to lead partnership initiative, with appropriate committee or task force support
Provost or dean*	Direct feasibility study and audit of existing partnerships & programs; establish partnership criteria with Education Abroad; establish mission statement and goals for partnership; establish partnership approval process; draft policies and structures for managing partnerships
Academic departments/ faculty**	Identify academic needs for majors; propose cross-disciplinary curricular theme(s)
Office of Education Abroad	Identify gaps in current programming for students; establish partnership criteria with provost or dean
Finance	Prepare criteria for cost analysis of potential program
Legal	Review internal regulatory frameworks
Education Abroad Advisory Committee	Potential support for leadership initiative

Note: Adapted from *Comprehensive internationalization: Institutional pathways to success* (p. 65), by J. K. Hudzik, 2015, Abingdon, UK: Routledge; "Partnering for success," by L. Sternberger, 2005, *International Educator, 14*(4), p. 20; "The changing landscape of international partnerships," by S. B. Sutton & D. Obst, in S. B. Sutton & D. Obst (Eds.), *Developing strategic international partnerships: Models for initiating and sustaining innovative institutional linkages* (pp. xvii–xviii), 2011, New York, NY: Institute of International Education.
*Office appointed to lead partnership initiative.
**May overlap with Education Abroad Advisory Committee.

- senior administrative support;
- collaborative support;
- flexible vision;
- staff development; and
- visible action.

The chapter ends by identifying two key facets of campus internationalization that remain most overlooked by colleges—aligning

Table 2. Parties and Tasks During the Program Development Phase in Off-Campus Program Partnerships

RESPONSIBLE PARTY	PROGRAM DEVELOPMENT
Provost or dean*	Synthesize data from various sources; make site visits; assess potential partners per criteria; identify faculty champions; draft implementation plan
Academic departments/ faculty**	Outline potential curriculum based on student learning goals; make site visits; observe teaching practice and assess capabilities to teach curricular themes; advise provost or dean on strengths and weaknesses of potential partners
Office of Education Abroad	Propose potential partners based on data from various sources; plan and lead site visits; assess partner capabilities for academic and student life; advise provost or dean on strengths and weaknesses of potential partners; guide potential program through approval process
Finance	Conduct cost analysis of potential partners and program
Legal	Analyze regulatory frameworks of potential partners (labor law, contracts, banking, insurance, etc.)
Dean of students	Assess housing options at potential sites
Registrar	Analyze credit and grade conversion scales
Education Abroad Advisory Committee	Continuing support for initiative, as needed

Note: Adapted from "Partnering for success," by L. Sternberger, 2005, *International Educator*, *14*(4), p. 20; "The changing landscape of international partnerships," by S. B. Sutton & D. Obst, in S. B. Sutton & D. Obst (Eds.), *Developing strategic international partnerships: Models for initiating and sustaining innovative institutional linkages* (pp. xvii–xviii), 2011, New York, NY: Institute of International Education.
*Office appointed to lead partnership initiative.
**May overlap with Education Abroad Advisory Committee.

stated university priorities with reward and recognition systems and fulfilling a diversity and inclusion imperative. After reading chapter 5, senior administrators and faculty leaders will be better positioned to envision, plan for, and initiate transformative change on their own campuses.

Table 3. Parties and Tasks During the Program Implementation Phase in Off-Campus Program Partnerships

RESPONSIBLE PARTY	IMPLEMENTATION
President	Review recommendation from leadership; guide recommendation through final approval
Provost or dean*	Secure resources (staffing, financial aid, etc.); oversee management of partnership and program, per existing policies and procedures; develop program assessment plan; set regular calendar of communications, meetings
Academic departments/ faculty**	Advise students; participate in program management, per institutional policy
Office of Education Abroad	Coordinate with management team on marketing & recruiting, application and approval process, student pre-departure preparation; finalize on-site details with partner
Finance	Arrange financial transactions
Legal	Create Memorandums of Understanding (university, on-site providers for housing, travel, etc.)
Dean of students	Review housing contract with partner
Registrar	Confirm transcript process with partner
Education Abroad Advisory Committee	Approve program for credit transfer

*Office appointed to lead partnership initiative.
**May overlap with Education Abroad Advisory Committee.

SUMMARY OF FACULTY VOICES

The authors of the Faculty Voices essays describe how leading an off-campus study program led to rich pedagogical insights and personal growth. Their reflections about traveling and learning alongside their students include a diverse range of experiences, approaches, and disciplinary and geographic vantage points, as seen in Table 4. Table 5 provides an overview of the key issues highlighted across these essays: debriefing and reflection; faculty self-awareness; integrative, interdisciplinary learning; mentoring student research projects; navigating challenges and crises; off-campus partnerships; site-based learning; and time use.

Table 4. Summary of Faculty Voices Contributors

Contributor(s)	Chapter	Primary Discipline(s)	Institution(s)	Destination(s)	Issue(s) Highlighted
Emily Margaretten	2	Anthropology	Ripon College	Tanzania	• faculty self-awareness
Kylie Quave & Chuck Lewis	4	Anthropology and English	The George Washington University & Beloit College	Peru	• off-campus partnerships • integrative, interdisciplinary learning
Verna Case	3	Biology	Davidson College	Zambia	• off-campus partnerships
James J. Ebersole	3	Biology and Ecology	Colorado College	Tanzania	• mentoring student research projects
Linda D. Horwitz	5	Communication	Lake Forest College	Florence and Chicago	• faculty self-awareness • site-based learning
Christine S. Cozzens	3	English	Agnes Scott College	Ireland	• site-based learning
Susan Jaret McKinstry	1	English	Carleton College	Florence and London	• faculty self-awareness • site-based learning
Amanda M. Caleb	4	English	Davidson College & Misericordia University	Poland	• off-campus partnerships • debriefing and reflection
Nancy K. Barry	2	English	Luther College	London	• navigating challenges and crises
William G. Moseley	4	Geography	Macalester College	Botswana	• off-campus partnerships • debriefing and reflection
Marcy Sacks	5	History	Albion College	Boston	• mentoring student research projects
Michael A. Schneider	1	History	Knox College	Japan	• faculty self-awareness • site-based learning
Stephen Volz	2	History	Kenyon College	Botswana	• navigating challenges and crises
Shiwei Chen	5	History	Lake Forest College	China	• navigating challenges and crises
Brian Caton	4	History	Luther College	India	• time use
Claudena Skran	1	Political Science	Lawrence University	West Africa	• off-campus partnerships
L. DeAne Lagerquist	3	Religion	St. Olaf College	Greece and Turkey	• time use

Table 5. Overview of Issues Highlighted in Faculty Voices Essays

Issues Highlighted	Contributor (Chapter)
Debriefing and reflection	Amanda M. Caleb (4), William G. Moseley (4)
Faculty self-awareness	Susan Jaret McKinstry (1), Michael A. Schneider (1), Emily Margaretten (2), Linda D. Horwitz (5)
Integrative, interdisciplinary learning	Kylie Quave & Chuck Lewis (4)
Mentoring student research projects	James J. Ebersole (3), Marcy Sacks (5)
Navigating challenges and crises	Nancy K. Barry (2), Stephen Volz (2), Shiwei Chen (5)
Off-campus partnerships	Claudena Skran (1), Verna Case (3), Amanda M. Caleb (4), William G. Moseley (4), Kylie Quave & Chuck Lewis (4),
Site-based learning	Susan Jaret McKinstry (1), Michael A. Schneider (1), Christine S. Cozzens (3), Linda D. Horwitz (5)
Time use	L. DeAne Lagerquist (3), Brian Caton (4)

Christine S. Cozzens of Agnes Scott College discusses the power of reading poetry and prose aloud in Ireland, and anthropologist Emily Margaretten describes a hard-learned lesson leading her students through an unexpectedly harrowing hike in Tanzania. While the experiences of Cozzens and Margaretten could not have been more different, participating in off-campus study programs had a significant effect on their professional careers, prompting them to develop a greater awareness of how site-based learning impacts students and their personal responsibilities as instructors.

Many Faculty Voices authors explain how they navigated a "teachable moment," which frequently entailed having to guide students through a setback or challenge while being attentive to their own personal and emotional needs. When traveling in Greece and Turkey with St. Olaf College students, L. DeAne Lagerquist shares a memory of how students drew from their sensory and aesthetic experiences—an explicit focus of her teaching—to make the most of an unexpected travel delay. Many Faculty Voices authors demonstrate nimbleness and resourcefulness in moments of uncertainty or even crisis. Faced with student protests and a strike at the University of Botswana, Stephen Volz (Kenyon College) describes his efforts to ensure student safety while revising the program schedule to minimize disruptions to students' learning. Nancy K. Barry of Luther College describes her response during a student's mental health crisis in London. Faced with the prospect of a public health emergency unfolding in real time, Shiwei Chen of Lake Forest College decided to shift the focus of his team's research project to examine the response of the Chinese government to the H1N1 virus. In all of these cases, instructors took advantage of an unplanned turn of events and provided a rich learning experience for students.

Several Faculty Voices essays address how consortia and other partnerships contribute to off-campus study programs. William G. Moseley of Macalester College describes an experience leading a study abroad program in Botswana, a program that was managed by the Associated Colleges of the Midwest and enrolled students from many liberal arts colleges. In dialogue with each other, Kylie Quave (The George Washington University) and Chuck Lewis (Beloit College) leveraged their interdisciplinary connections to promote integrative learning during a three-week summer program in Peru. Biologist Verna Case spent decades building relationships with Zambian partners to help Davidson College students better understand the role of Western medicine and traditional healers within the community. Similarly, Claudena Skran, political scientist, writes about how students' perspectives about chiefdoms in tribal communities in West Africa changed when they visited a rural village and realized the importance of the chief's leadership following the Ebola outbreak. In "Lessons from Auschwitz: Education and Outreach," Amanda M. Caleb (Misericordia University) describes the immediate and extended impact of a short-term program that she led for her alma mater, Davidson College.

This non-credit program, developed with donor funds to provide Davidson student-athletes with an off-campus study experience, illustrates what can be achieved through the creative collaboration of a number of different parties, in this case, an alumna, a coach, and a Holocaust survivor.

While Faculty Voices authors share perceptions of how off-campus study experiences positively impacted their students, the authors further explain how leading such programs left them changed for the better. As a result of traveling with students to a concentration camp outside of Berlin, Michael A. Schneider of Knox College reconsidered his unwillingness to take students to Hiroshima during a Japan program he regularly led. Informed by her experiences leading a semester-long program in Florence, Linda D. Horwitz at Lake Forest College developed a new experiential course exploring the material culture of Chicago, reflecting her newfound commitment to site-based learning.

Implicit in these essays are ways that campus policies and support structures enabled (or inhibited) the goals of off-campus study programs. Skran describes how she used Lawrence University's required pre-departure orientation meetings to begin to scaffold students' learning about traditional healers. As a result of having been introduced to the topic months before arriving in Africa, students were prepared to interrogate and often reframe their previous assumptions in the field. Not all institutional policies and structures proved to be as valuable. Marcy Sacks of Albion College identifies how implicit bias in selection criteria may prevent students from diverse backgrounds from participating in beneficial high-impact practices like mentored undergraduate research. Keeping the principles of equity and inclusion in mind, Sacks encourages colleges to more closely examine the unintended consequences that might result from their application and selection processes.

CONTINUING THE CONVERSATION WITH FACULTY

To accompany the release of this book, the authors have created a limited podcast called *Postcard Pedagogy* to continue and broaden the conversation about the role of faculty-led study abroad and study away programs at private liberal arts colleges. The series highlights the experiences of faculty program leaders and other academic leaders in "postcard"-sized 10-minute installments. Each episode showcases innovative teaching strategies, memorable lessons learned in the field with students, or suggestions to promote institutional change in the area of global learning. Consistent with the claim that faculty voices should play a more prominent role in promoting off-campus study as a form of transformative learning, the podcast creates a space for continued dialogue between the authors and many of the individuals profiled and described in the book. This free series is available on Apple Podcasts.

CONCLUSION

As the co-authors and co-editors of this book, we seek to amplify the good work being done by our colleagues at small private liberal arts colleges. Although each chapter and essay emphasize a different stakeholder perspective on off-campus study programs, the contributors share the common understanding (shown in Figure 4) that effective global learning and internationalization depend on explicit institutional strategic goals and policies; opportunities for student mobility; global partnerships; and faculty background, interest, and training. A supportive institutional context makes a significant difference—college leaders must continue to remove obstacles and limit the barriers that hinder faculty members from achieving excellence in their off-campus study programs.

There is compelling evidence that month-long "mini-mesters" have facilitated high levels of student participation in study abroad at Centre, Washington and Lee, Elon, Agnes Scott, St. Olaf, and

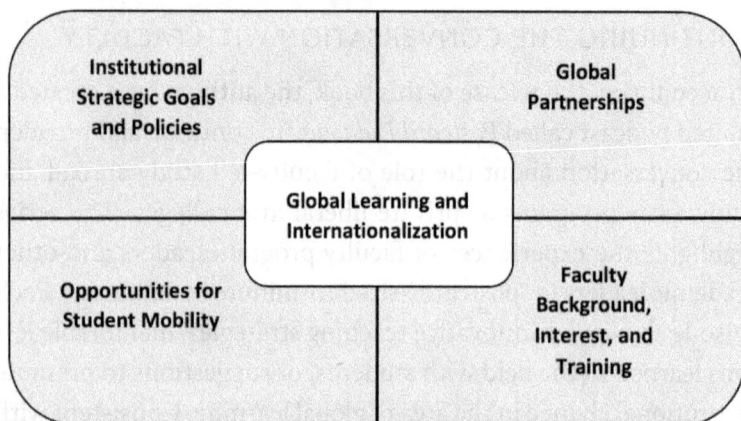

Figure 4. Global Learning and Internationalization Depend on Synergistic Relationships and Activities in Both the Short and Long Term

elsewhere. A study of the Great Lakes Colleges Association (Baker, Lunsford, & Pifer, 2017) identified topics meriting additional faculty development, including the expansion of active learning pedagogies and strategies that help instructors meet their college's goals for diversity, equity, and inclusion. Consortia and other regional partnerships of liberal arts colleges—like the Claremont Colleges, the Quaker Consortium in Philadelphia, and the Five College Consortium in Western Massachusetts—demonstrate how small institutions have joined forces with their geographic neighbors to swap best practices and leverage their individual strengths. From these exemplars, we see how relatively small, inexpensive, and symbolic gestures can result in a big impact, be it through course development seed grants, efforts to formally recognize the work of program leaders, or intra-campus conversations between faculty members who study similar regions. We strongly recommend, therefore, that colleges strive toward greater alignment between what they say they value and what they do—especially in the policies, practices, and reward structures that directly impact faculty program leaders in the name of global learning.

Throughout this book, we have offered evidence-based, empirical research about the experiences of faculty members who lead off-campus study programs at liberal arts colleges and practical recommendations about what colleges can do to better support them. To create change on their campuses, it is essential for senior administrators to initiate dialogue about the status and place of global learning as a high-impact practice; to build bridges across disciplines; to make intentional, targeted investments in faculty development to advance institutional priorities; to affirm the place of diversity and inclusion; and to align rhetoric with action. We believe it is just as important to engage in discussions about the change process itself. With this in mind, we suggest the following questions to frame and inform this important work:

- What roles do administrators, faculty, and professional staff play in determining campus priorities and policies related to off-campus study and study abroad? What structures ensure open lines of communication, shared governance, and effective decision-making?
- How might we begin a process to ensure that global learning and participation in off-campus study programs are given appropriate weight in criteria for hiring, performance reviews, and tenure and promotion decisions? How much should these contributions "count" relative to other worthy activities (e.g., publications, mentoring student research, committee service)? How might a synergistic mindset enable us to regard off-campus study as an avenue for enhancing these other significant areas?
- How can we leverage our alumni and parent networks, donors, and other potential partners to achieve our goals related to internationalization?
- Who else needs to be "at the table" to elevate the status and place of global learning at our college?
- How will we determine whether our off-campus study programs are accessible and inclusive?

- What is the legacy we seek to create for a new generation of global learners?

REFERENCES

Baker, V. L., Lunsford, L. G., & Pifer, M. J. (2017). *Developing faculty in liberal arts colleges: Aligning individual needs and organizational goals.* New Brunswick, NJ: Rutgers University Press.

Chickering, A., & Gamson, Z. (1987). Seven principles for good practice in undergraduate education. *AAHE Bulletin, 39*(7), 3–7.

Eckel, P. D., & Kezar, A. J. (2003). *Taking the reins: Institutional transformation in higher education.* American Council on Education/Praeger series on higher education. Westport, CT: American Council on Education/Praeger.

Gillespie, J., Glasco, S., Gross, D., Jasinski, L., & Layne, P. (2017). *Faculty as global learners: Enhancing the transformative impact of leading off-campus study programs.* Paper presented at Forum on Education Abroad Annual Conference, Boston, MA.

Helms, R. M. (2015). Internationalizing the tenure code: Policies to promote a globally focused faculty. Washington, DC: American Council on Education.

Helms, R. M., Brajkovic, L., & Struthers, B. (2017). *Mapping internationalization on U.S. campuses: 2017 edition.* Washington, DC: American Council on Education. Retrieved from https://www.acenet.edu/Documents/Mapping-Internationalization-2017.pdf

Hudzik, J. K. (2015). *Comprehensive internationalization: Institutional pathways to success.* Abingdon, UK: Routledge.

Kuh, G. D. (2008). *High-impact educational practices: What they are, who has access to them, and why they matter.* Washington, DC: Association of American Colleges & Universities.

Sternberger, L. (2005). Partnering for success. *International Educator, 14*(4), 12–21.

Sutton, S. B., & Obst, D. (2011). The changing landscape of international partnerships. In S. B. Sutton & D. Obst (Eds.), *Developing strategic international partnerships: Models for initiating and sustaining innovative institutional linkages* (pp. xiii–xxiii). New York, NY: Institute of International Education.

INTRODUCTION

Joan Gillespie

Liberal arts colleges in the United States join the balancing act in higher education worldwide with every decision they face; resources dictate priorities for the academic mission, student support services, facilities, and the hiring and retention of administrative staff and faculty members. This reality applies to initiatives for off-campus study programs, particularly those planned and led by faculty members. The conversation draws strong opinions from opposite sides, reflecting the broader discussion among senior higher education administrators and faculty about the institutional sponsorship of these programs and their relative value.

- Faculty-led off-campus programs are a low priority, particularly given the third-party provider options for students, *versus* faculty-led programs are a high priority, meeting institutional goals for internationalization, addressing students' academic interests and needs, and contributing to long-term faculty job satisfaction.
- Only tenured faculty are eligible to lead programs, and non-tenured faculty should focus on research that moves them

closer to tenure status *versus* all faculty should be given the chance to lead programs, making available to a diverse group such benefits as developing new pedagogical and administrative skills that accrue to the campus community when they return.

- The most important job for a faculty program leader is risk management, and teaching is secondary *versus* faculty program leaders need training and broad administrative support so they can do what they do best: teach.

These conflicting opinions and others that are expressed in the related discussions about faculty development, global learning, study away–study abroad programming, and resource allocation suggest either/or solutions. This book seeks to add to this discussion the perspective of faculty who have led off-campus programs, with data-informed recommendations. It argues that these experiences offer profound learning and development to all faculty members and, by extension, to their students and the campus community at large. Furthermore, strategies for pooling resources through institutional partnerships to reduce risk and realize the benefits are proposed. The book's specific focus is global learning, equally applicable to faculty and students, characterized as the gradual formation of one's identity as a citizen with intersecting national and international responsibilities and knowledge of and respect for the countries, regions, and cultures of the world (Hovland, 2014).

The book advances a holistic and integrated argument for paradigmatic change in the way liberal arts colleges think about and support off-campus study programming and the faculty who lead and teach these programs in the context of limited resources and competing institutional priorities. The authors emphasize concrete suggestions and examples for senior academic administrators who share responsibilities for faculty development, campus internationalization, curriculum development, and international and off-campus domestic programming about how to better support faculty members and student learning and development.

BACKGROUND OF THE FACULTY AS GLOBAL LEARNERS STUDY

Student participation in study abroad continues to grow, from 304,467 students in 2013–2014 to 341,751 students in 2017–2018, marking a 12.2% increase. Students enrolled in short-term programs, defined as a summer program or fewer than eight weeks, represent the largest segment of that population, 64.6% in 2017–2018 (Institute for International Education, 2019). Many of these programs are led by faculty.

The upward trend of off-campus study programming and enrollment served as the framework for a seminar on global learning in the context of the study of teaching and learning (SoTL), sponsored by Elon University Center for Learning and Engagement, that drew together a number of researchers, including the authors of this book. The impetus for the focus on faculty was driven by the high strategic value of faculty-led study abroad and study away programs and the concurrent high opportunity costs. Researchers sought to examine and understand the impact on faculty members' teaching, research, service, and overall well-being as program leaders to inform university policies and practices for professional development. This collection builds upon the original research, a multi-institution survey of more than 200 faculty members who led study away and study abroad programs at 27 selective liberal arts colleges. Researchers intentionally adopted an inclusive definition of off-campus programming that included both study abroad (international) and study away (domestic) programs (Sobania, 2015).

Most research that investigates the effects of participating in off-campus study programs concerns students, but in our case, faculty members were identified as the research subjects. Our project limited the subject pool to faculty at private liberal arts institutions in the United States. Faculty members who have led off-campus study programs have been the subject of recent articles and doctoral dissertations (Davis, 2014; Goode, 2008; Rasch, 2001), but we aimed to help shape the direction of future research by focusing on faculty experiences within liberal arts colleges. While geographically disparate, the institutions included in the survey share many traits, including low student-to-faculty ratios, residential campuses, liberal arts curricula, moderate to high student selectivity, and small undergraduate enrollments (1,000 to 5,000 students). The rationale for this choice of research subjects was twofold: first, scarce attention has been paid to the impact on faculty of leading or teaching in off-campus study programs, compared to studies of the outcomes of these experiences on students; second, liberal arts colleges present a unique model in higher education, combining creative pedagogical practices with holistic student development, which are also the hallmarks of best practice in off-campus study.

NOTABLE FINDINGS

The Faculty as Global Learners survey captured faculty experiences and their self-reported learning in a systematic, credible, and persuasive way, in all stages of their planning and on-site teaching and program management. A number of specific findings stood out as worthy of further examination and discussion. One such finding is the intrinsic motivation of faculty leaders to do this work; many describe these programs in terms of value to their own professional and personal development as well to their students' development. One finding that could undermine this personal value is the faculty perceptions of a gap between institutional support for global learning as a priority for students and support for faculty who lead off-campus study programs. Faculty also call for revised tenure and promotion policies that recognize and reward international work.

This data points to the opportunity for a new area of scholarship, extending beyond the existing studies that focus on pedagogical, logistical, and legal advice for practitioners (France & Rogers, 2012; Young, 2014).

An analysis of the survey findings identified a number of other topics that drove this book and intersect with ongoing conversations on college campuses.

- Demographic data showed that program leaders were more or less equally distributed between men and women but weighed heavily toward tenured, White faculty members, with policy implications for diversity and equal opportunity in international mobility.
- A majority of faculty respondents reported incorporating additional AAC&U-recognized high-impact practices (HIPs) into their off-campus study programs—including undergraduate research, service-learning, and internships—presenting implications for on-campus teaching and curricular offerings.
- Faculty respondents described the importance of—or a need for—pre-program mentorship and training, including a scouting trip to the proposed destination, on-site administrative support, and a post-program debriefing with a community of practice.

The research presented in this volume thus extends beyond the scope of the Faculty as Global Learners survey to include policies set by senior administrators, department chairs, and faculty members who are involved in institutional governance and institutional change.

OVERVIEW OF CHAPTERS

This collection uses broadly accepted social scientific research methods—survey research, case studies, and qualitative interviews—to examine pedagogical and administrative practices in liberal arts colleges related to off-campus study. Each chapter seeks to explore the implications for off-campus study programs through the lens of stakeholders, namely, campus leaders, faculty developers, and the faculty members who design and deliver these programs.

Chapter 1, "Faculty as Global Learners," describes the context of liberal arts education and the central place of off-campus study programs on many liberal arts college campuses. It presents recent research on the role of faculty and their training and development related to on-campus internationalization initiatives and off-campus study programs. The details of the research methodology are followed by the demographics of faculty leaders of off-campus study programs at liberal arts colleges, program locations, and a discussion of the five major findings. The final section reviews the various definitions of global learning, including those written by faculty who participated in the research.

Chapter 2, "Synergistic Approaches to Global Learning: Effective Institutional Support for Faculty Leaders of Off-Campus Study Programs," offers ideas that provosts and academic deans, as well as directors of off-campus study offices and teaching-and-learning centers at liberal arts colleges, can use to provide effective, continuous support for faculty leaders of off-campus study programs. The chapter, written by Dana Gross, emphasizes the value of investing resources that both enhance the immediate effectiveness of program leaders and contribute to their long-term job satisfaction and career success.

In chapter 3, "The World Is My Classroom: The Distinctive Pedagogies of Off-Campus Study Programs at Liberal Arts Colleges," Lisa Jasinski explains how liberal arts college faculty members employ innovative and effective pedagogical strategies to enhance student learning. Research findings indicate that a majority of faculty respondents incorporated recognized high-impact practices into their off-campus study programs, including research, intensive writing, and collaborative projects. Follow-up interviews were conducted with a number of faculty members who responded to the surveys and indicated their willingness to continue to be involved in the research; they provide case studies to demonstrate how they incorporated these practices into programs.

In chapter 4, "Pooling Resources for Off-Campus Study Programs Through Institutional Partnerships: Benefits, Challenges, and Guidelines," Joan Gillespie draws from examples and faculty reports to describe the benefits and challenges to faculty and their institutions in partnering with other higher education institutions in the United States and abroad to design and manage off-campus study programs. Using a number of sources, the chapter outlines steps in researching, developing, and implementing institutional partnerships and presents a model for the roles played by senior administrative staff and faculty members at each stage. Examples from liberal arts colleges demonstrate the possibilities and potential of these partnerships.

In chapter 5, "Strategic Leadership for Off-Campus Study: How Colleges Reimagine the Place of Global Learning," Lisa Jasinski uses two case studies, Susquehanna University and Grinnell College, to illustrate strategies that propelled the institutions toward internationalization goals and global learning initiatives. It establishes a link between the resulting positive changes, diversity and inclusion, and the need for institutions to consider policies for promotion and tenure in the context of internationalization.

Following each chapter are personal narratives written by faculty leaders of off-campus study programs. Most, but not all, of the 17 essays were written by faculty participants from the Faculty as Global Learners survey who indicated a willingness to contribute further to the study. These brief essays are drawn from their experiences and present specific examples of a single event or cumulative events that changed the faculty leaders' thinking or approach in order to provide stronger support to student learning and development. Most essays are accompanied by a photograph that illustrates the event or concept described. Taken together, these Faculty Voices offer direct evidence of the impact of leading off-campus programs and constitute a profound statement of teaching practice learned at an off-campus study site.

The authors extended the conversation with some of the faculty members who contributed essays to this publication with a series of interviews about program leadership and teaching experiences in off-campus study. These personal accounts of strategies tested in the field, lessons learned, and recommendations are designed as brief *Postcard Pedagogies*. The series has been edited as 10-minute podcasts and is available on Apple Podcasts.

RESOURCES

This Faculty as Global Learners survey was conducted in conjunction with the research seminar Integrating Global Learning with the University Experience: Higher-Impact Study Abroad and Domestic Off-Campus Study hosted by the Center for Engaged Learning at Elon University. Research team members were Joan Gillespie, Independent Scholar; Sarah Glasco, Associate Professor of French, Elon University; Dana Gross, Professor of Psychology, St. Olaf College; Lisa Jasinski, Special Assistant to the Vice President for Academic Affairs, Trinity University; and Prudence Layne, Associate Professor of English, Elon University.

Descriptions of the survey and findings in the introduction and chapter 1 originally were presented by research team members at conferences in 2017 and 2018. Complete citations are listed below in references.

REFERENCES

Davis, Y. (2014). *University faculty contribution to study abroad programs: What do we know about their motivation?* Ann Arbor, MI: ProQuest Dissertations Publishing.

France, H., & Rogers, L. (2012). Cuba study abroad: A pedagogical tool for recon-structing American national identity. *International Studies Perspectives, 13*(4), 390–407.

Gillespie, J., Glasco, S., Gross, D., Jasinski, L., & Layne, P. (2017a). *Faculty as global learners: Enhancing the transformative impact of leading off-campus programs.* Paper presented at Associated Colleges of the Midwest Directors' Workshop, Chicago, IL.

Gillespie, J., Glasco, S., Gross, D., Jasinski, L., & Layne, P. (2017b). *Faculty as global learners: Enhancing the transformative impact of leading off-campus study pro-grams.* Paper presented at Forum on Education Abroad Annual Conference, Boston, MA.

Gillespie, J., Glasco, S., Gross, D., Jasinski, L., & Layne, P. (2017c). *Faculty as global learners: Strategies to enhance the transformative impact of leading off-campus programs.* Paper presented at Association for the Study of Higher Education Annual Conference, Houston, TX.

Gillespie, J., Glasco, S., Gross, D., Jasinski, L., & Layne, P. (2017d). *Faculty as global learners: The transformative impact of leading off-campus programs.* Paper pre-sented at Associated Colleges of the Midwest Conference on Integrating Off-Campus Study and On-Campus Learning, Chicago, IL.

Gillespie, J., Glasco, S., Gross, D., Jasinski, L., & Layne, P. (2017e). *Faculty as global learners: The transformative impact of leading off-campus programs.* Paper pre-sented at Texas Higher Education Symposium, Austin, TX.

Gillespie, J., Glasco, S., Gross, D., Jasinski, L., & Layne, P. (2017f). *Faculty as global learners: The transformative impact of leading study away and study abroad pro-grams.* Paper presented at Elon University Symposium on Integrating Global Learning with the University Experience, Elon, NC.

Gillespie, J., Glasco, S., Gross, D., Jasinski, L., & Layne, P. (2017g). *Global learning at liberal arts colleges: Investing in faculty leaders of study abroad–study away.* Paper presented at Association of American Colleges & Universities Global Learning Conference, New Orleans, LA.

Gillespie, J., Glasco, S., Gross, D., Jasinski, L., & Layne, P. (2017h). *Liberal arts faculty self-assess the transformative impact of leading study abroad.* Paper presented at Wake Forest University Workshop on Intercultural Skills Enhancement, Winston-Salem, NC.

Gillespie, J., Glasco, S., Gross, D., Jasinski, L., & Layne, P. (2017i). *Supporting faculty as global learners.* Paper presented at Association of International Education Administrators Annual Conference, Washington, DC.

Gillespie, J., Glasco, S., Gross, D., Jasinski, L., & Layne, P. (2017j). *Using faculty voices to support practice: Improving global learning at liberal arts colleges.* Paper presented at Association of American Colleges & Universities Global Learning Conference, New Orleans, LA.

Gillespie, J., Glasco, S., Gross, D., Jasinski, L., & Layne, P. (2018). *Faculty as global learners: The impact of leading study away programs.* Paper presented at Forum on Education Abroad Annual Conference, Boston, MA.

Goode, M. (2008). The role of faculty study abroad directors: A case study. *Frontier: The Interdisciplinary Journal of Study Abroad, 15,* 149–172.

Hovland, K. (2014). *Global learning: Defining, designing, demonstrating.* AAC&U & NAFSA: Association of International Educators. Retrieved from https://www.aacu.org/sites/default/files/files/Global/global_learning_2014.pdf

Institute for International Education. (2019). Fast facts. *Open Doors report on international education exchange.* Retrieved from https://www.iie.org/Research-and-Insights/Open-Doors/Fact-Sheets-and-Infographics/Fast-Facts

Sobania, N. W. (2015). The faraway nearby: Putting the local in global education. In N. W. Sobania (Ed.), *Putting the local in global education: Models for transformative learning through domestic off-campus programs* (pp. 16–35). Sterling, VA: Stylus Publishing.

Young, G. E. (2014). Reentry: Supporting students in the final stage of study abroad. *New Directions for Student Services, 2014*(146), 59–67.

CHAPTER 1

FACULTY AS GLOBAL LEARNERS

Joan Gillespie, Lisa Jasinski, and Dana Gross

> Over time, my teaching has evolved to tackle questions of *global learning* [emphasis added] more aggressively. In my early career, I was content to introduce knowledge of other societies with the expectation that students would make connections between their coursework and the practical skills of globally aware citizenship. As my understanding of the needs of *global learning* [emphasis added] has evolved, I have more actively engineered experiential and critical learning moments as a means to advance student awareness of the limitations of their existing perspectives and the pathways necessary to promote their own learning.

> As a teacher and scholar, I have broadened my research and course offerings, making them more interdisciplinary in nature . . . I believe this is in the best *liberal arts* [emphasis added] tradition; it is also the way many disciplines, including art history and musicology, are evolving.

> Study Abroad courses cause me to be more authentic as an educator. Because more of the course is in real-time on-the-spot, and involves physical, emotional, psychological stress, I find that I

am more willing to be flexible, vulnerable, and meet the students where they are. Study abroad makes me a *better teacher* [emphasis added].

These reflections were written by faculty members who participated in a recent survey, Faculty as Global Learners, in response to the question, "As a teacher and scholar, how have you developed or changed as a result of leading a Study Away–Study Abroad program?" Their responses represent the three narratives that are the starting points for this study: liberal arts education, faculty development, and global learning in the early decades of the 21st century. Any number of other faculty responses might have introduced this chapter and similarly represented the foci of this book. Taken together, they form a compelling body of evidence about the profound impact of teaching on a study abroad or study away program in the liberal arts.

This chapter details how global learning and faculty development in the environment of liberal arts colleges informed the Faculty as Global Learners survey. It begins with a review of the literature on liberal arts education and high-impact teaching practices. The chapter then connects the dimensions of global learning in the Association of American Colleges & Universities (AAC&U) Global Learning VALUE rubric with faculty responses regarding the relationship between their teaching and research and their own global learning.

LIBERAL ARTS COLLEGES AND OFF-CAMPUS STUDY PROGRAMS

Private liberal arts colleges occupy a niche in global higher education—U.S. American in origin, with characteristics that distinguish them from other types of higher education in the United States and from systems abroad. Their focus on undergraduate education combines a general curriculum with discipline-specific and interdisciplinary study, and a student's four-year program of coursework may be highly individualized. These institutions deliberately plan for a small student population with a concurrent low student-to-faculty ratio, a dynamic that encourages creative pedagogy and a high level of student-faculty interaction. Holistic student development holds a central place in this educational vision and is supported by the structured residential community and co-curriculum that guide students in their growing sense of self and purpose.

One tangible benefit to students who choose to live and learn at a liberal arts college is offered by faculty who embrace the educational ethos. Faculty at liberal arts colleges are known as dedicated teachers (Chopp, Frost, & Weiss, 2014; Koblik & Graubard, 2000). Compared to students at research universities and regional institutions, students at liberal arts colleges more frequently encounter empirically tested high-impact practices in undergraduate education (Pascarella, Cruce, Wolniak, & Blaich, 2004), specifically, pedagogies that are "invariably student-centered" and "require higher levels of academic rigor" (Hill, 2014, p. 86). These factors help explain why liberal arts colleges have consistently posted high graduation rates (Kiley, 2011).

Outstanding teaching figures among several other institutional practices at liberal arts colleges that contribute to student success, as measured by quantitative data such as graduation rates and qualitative results. Astin (1999) and Seifert et al. (2008) warn that one of the most significant challenges facing higher education researchers who study liberal arts colleges is the "black box" effect—identifying the specific environmental factors, conditions, and practices that lead to positive outcomes. In many cases, it is not a single treatment but the combination of factors—multiple, diverse, interdependent, and reinforcing experiences or conditions that influence change (Pascarella & Terenzini, 2005). These distinctions are especially difficult to delineate in residential liberal arts colleges that provide students a "comprehensive, seamless, and relevant environment" where "education takes place around the clock and in all venues" (McCardell, 2014, pp. 173, 178). Some of the distinctive environmental characteristics besides high-impact pedagogical practice that might explain the effectiveness of liberal arts colleges include on-campus residence (Jessup-Anger, 2012), institutional selectivity (Pascarella et al., 2004), and high per-pupil expenditures (Astin, 1999). An added challenge of studying elite liberal arts colleges is that a disproportionate number of students enrolled at these institutions enter college with the intersecting advantages of high socioeconomic status, strong pre-college educational experiences, and stable families and communities; they already possess forms of social and cultural capital that enable academic success in college.

Academic success and high graduation rates may stand as proxies for another goal of liberal arts institutions, less readily given to quantitative measures: building a foundation for students' lifelong learning. Recent qualitative studies have sought to more precisely define the benefits for students and to identify the underlying structures that enable such outcomes. In order to produce the transformative effects of education that are cumulative over a lifetime, including the commitment to lifelong learning, colleges must take the long view: "It is not about getting the 'A' in the quickest and most painless way. It is about allowing, even embracing, mistakes. It is about exploring and considering possibilities. It is about going deep, a task that is neither easily defined nor readily confined to a checklist" (Johansson & Felten, 2014, p. 58). This approach—"allowing, even embracing, mistakes"—would seem to contradict the emphasis on academic success in a high-energy, competitive academic environment. However, a forum that gives students the freedom to fail also fosters personal growth, as students learn from their mistakes, and nurtures the love of learning. A recent campus trend designates open, collaborative spaces apart from the classroom as "innovation labs" that sanction exploration and acknowledge the possibility of failure. Whether the "innovation lab" is a room in a basement corner with a sign over the door or every classroom on campus, whether it is overseen by students or by faculty, the emphasis is placed on the process, not product, and supports the ultimate goal of lifelong learning.

Another mark of many liberal arts colleges is the high percentage of students who participate in study abroad (IIE, 2019a; Twombly, Salisbury, Tumanut, & Klute, 2012). These institutions have been and continue to be the source of the highest participation rates in study abroad in U.S. higher education (Brewer, 2010, p. 86). Ten of the top 40 colleges conferring baccalaureate degrees that send students abroad reported a participation rate greater than 100% in 2017–2018 (IIE, 2019b), with students taking advantage of multiple opportunities during their undergraduate years. All of the top 40 colleges with the highest percentage of participation sent more than 60% of their students abroad in 2017–2018 (IIE, 2019b). By comparison, the 40 doctorate-granting institutions with the highest percentage of participation include 14 with greater than 60% participation, and nine institutions with percentage of participation between 50% and 59% (IIE, 2019b). In absolute numbers, doctorate-granting institutions contribute many times more students than liberal arts colleges to the total study abroad population of undergraduates who are pursuing a bachelor's degree (16%; IIE, 2019a). However, the notable percentage of participation at liberal arts colleges distinguishes them in this field.

The high participation rates at liberal arts colleges reflect the commitment to internationalization and global learning that are explicitly valued in mission statements and strategic plans and are operationalized by the successful collaboration across campus offices and academic departments. For example, an academic calendar that includes a three- or four-week January interim or May-mester encourages students to enroll in multiple programs over the course of their undergraduate years. The office of financial aid, in concert with the office of a provost or dean, calculates the cost, or partial cost, of institutional programs in aid packages to enable a broader population to study abroad. Across institutional types, the interest of undergraduate students and their parents in off-campus study opportunities has grown, along with the multiplicity of study abroad locations and academic options as the field has expanded beyond language immersion and area studies to new disciplines and cross-departmental studies in business, communications, and health, plus the STEM fields. Relevant to this study, these new possibilities concurrently have offered opportunities to faculty in many more disciplines to investigate place-based learning in study abroad and study away programs.

FACULTY DEVELOPMENT AND OFF-CAMPUS STUDY PROGRAMS

In the literature of international education, there is broad consensus that simply traveling to a new or unknown location does not ensure deep learning; rather, student transformation is dependent on the presence of certain pedagogical structures (Brewer & Cunningham, 2009; Feller, 2015; Young, 2014). A syllogism that gives faculty an essential role in student learning in off-campus study is as follows: "The purpose of study abroad is transformational learning and intercultural learning; faculty are central to students' transformational learning; faculty development must be part of an institution's internationalization strategy" (Brewer, 2010, pp. 86–89).

The premise of this syllogism—and of this book—is that an institution's goals for student learning outcomes in study abroad fit into a larger agenda of campus internationalization that must involve faculty. Childress (2018) and Hudzik (2015) provide comprehensive information on steps for creating and implementing this agenda through collaboration among administrative staff in a number of campus offices and faculty members representing multiple fields, tenure levels, and experiences. Dedicated time and energy are required to attend to logistical concerns, and those concerns may overshadow the central importance of faculty development in teaching strategies to support student learning in the context of internationalization.

Good practice in teaching requires the methodologies of experiential learning, cross-cultural learning, and transformational learning (Passarelli & Kolb, 2012). Student preparation and opportunities for guided reflection and debriefing are common to these methodologies (Anderson & Cunningham, 2009). Faculty members with training in these methodologies will be able to capitalize on the total off-campus environment as a learning opportunity. As discussed in chapter 3, a campus center for teaching and learning may offer workshops in pedagogies that are appropriate for study abroad–study away. Faculty need not teach off-campus to apply them, as the structure of select on-campus courses may be reconfigured to incorporate these methodologies. This practice not only gives faculty members the chance to practice them but also introduces students to new ways of learning that will prepare them for an off-campus program, should they enroll (Brewer, 2010; Gillespie, 2019).

Global Learning

The definition of "global learning" and its application to undergraduate education in the United States has evolved concurrent with progressive and intersecting strategies in campus internationalization, diversity and inclusion, and student engagement and research on intercultural competence. In tracking these pliable definitions since 1982, when the Global Learning Division of United Nations University aimed "to convey both the sense of learning as a global process that must include all levels of society, and the sense of learning to think globally, in the recognition that the world is a finite, closely interconnected, global system" (Doscher & Landorf, 2018, p. 4), one sees a shift in focus. The definition has been refined to address the development of students' awareness of their own and other cultures and to emphasize the quality of opportunities. A significant change in the formulation envisions global learning as an iterative process; this change acknowledges intercultural competence as a component of global learning. While personal attributes contribute to intercultural competence, the development of cognitive and communicative skills, among others, likewise are iterative (Deardorff, 2006, p. 248). These concepts apply equally to faculty, whose opportunities for hands-on practice and experience advances their own global learning and, consequently, an institutional commitment to the process of student learning and development in a global environment.

The Global Learning VALUE rubric of the AAC&U (n.d.), created by faculty from multiple disciplines and a variety of higher education institutions in the United States, begins with the premise of global learning as an iterative process to create categories of learning and introduce assessment strategies. The working definition is as follows:

> A critical analysis of and an engagement with complex, interdependent global systems and legacies (such as natural, physical, social, cultural, economic, and political) and their implications for people's lives and the earth's sustainability. Through global learning, students should (1) become informed, open-minded, and responsible people who are attentive to diversity across the spectrum of differences, (2) seek to understand how their actions affect both local and global communities, and (3) address the world's most pressing and enduring issues collaboratively and equitably. (Hovland, 2014b, p. 9)

The rubric focuses on "what global learners can do" across the curriculum and co-curriculum. It emphasizes the importance of learning how to solve problems in a global context and reflects "current shifts across higher education toward more problem-centered learning strategies that focus greater attention on competencies and proficiencies than on course content" (Hovland, 2014b, p. 9). As a single package, the definition and rubric offer higher education institutions an assessment framework and methodology for planning and operationalizing global learning in terms relevant to their own campuses and students. The format is not a formula but a reference point and another marker in the ongoing conversation about what constitutes global learning, for whom, and how it is measured. Because of its wide circulation and comprehensiveness, this definition and rubric served as part of the framework for the Faculty as Global Learners survey, which became part of our larger study.

Elon University's Center for Engaged Learning drew on the work of the seminar research groups, including the authors, who participated in Integrating Global Learning with the University Experience: Higher Impact Study Abroad and Off-Campus Domestic Study to define global learning "as a lifelong developmental process in which the learner engages with difference and similarity and develops capabilities to interact equitably in a complex world" (Center for Engaged Learning, 2017). The brief definition introduces two important points:

- It identifies faculty and staff with students as "learners," inviting them to participate in an iterative learning process, multiple opportunities for active and productive engagement and problem-solving, and a common goal of equity.
- It brings conversations of diversity and inclusion to the campus and community as part of the "complex world."

The institution that adopts this definition might refer to the AAC&U Global Learning VALUE rubric as a model to envision the steps required to work toward the aspirations set out by this definition and ways to measure their achievement.

The concept of "global citizenship" as a desired outcome of global learning has met with some opposition as a peculiarly Western construct, reserved for the select minority of undergraduates at

U.S. higher education institutions who can afford the expense of a term of off-campus study. Supporters of the term argue that global citizenship "connects global education to the larger civic mission of colleges and universities. . . . Reconciling and learning to live with the tensions between local, national, and global citizenship is an important dimension of global education" (Reimers, 2014, p. 5). This position echoes an early formulation of global learning as a reflection of one's self-awareness.

Expanding on this formulation, the argument in favor of global citizenship draws on the categories of the AAC&U rubric that apply to global learning:

> The knowledge, skills, and competencies needed for global citizen-ship require an understanding of topics related to public health, demographics, economics, and politics, and also those rooted in literature, art, and languages. Integrating learning across these disciplines and connecting it with opportunities for students to design and construct solutions to shared global challenges can only enhance the depth of understanding available through discrete fields of study. (Reimers, 2014, p. 7)

The relevance of this argument to faculty members as global learners lies in the evolving concept of global learning. It similarly applies to their self-awareness as well as to their approach to teaching and research as opportunities for engagement locally, nationally, and globally.

The next section describes the Faculty as Global Learners survey, detailing the sample of faculty who led off-campus programs at liberal arts colleges, the two surveys that researchers administered, and the statistical analyses of data. The demographics of faculty participants are reported, along with program locations and program term lengths. The discussion highlights the five major findings identified by the researchers that gave impetus to this book.

THE FACULTY AS GLOBAL LEARNERS SURVEY

It is within the context of liberal arts education, faculty develop-ment, and global learning that this book's authors set out with two other researchers, Sarah Glasco and Prudence Layne, to gather data about the impact of leading off-campus study programs on liberal arts college faculty members' teaching, research, service, and overall well-being. In many ways, findings from this two-part survey provided one point of departure for this book.

Research Methodology

The research team intentionally adopted an inclusive definition of off-campus study to incorporate domestic off-campus programs and international study (Sobania, 2015) and used the identifier "study abroad–study away (SA/SA)" in the survey. Program length was set at a minimum of one week, with no specified maximum length.

Criterion sampling (Creswell, 2013) was used to identify research subjects who were employed as faculty at a participating institu-tion and had led at least one off-campus study program. To iden-tify potential participants, researchers conducted web searches of participating colleges and worked with institutional gatekeepers (i.e., deans, directors of education abroad offices). In a few cases, members of administrative staff who had served as program co-leaders were included in the sample.

The 31 private liberal arts colleges whose faculty members were identified as potential survey participants were the 14 member institutions of the Associated Colleges of the Midwest (ACM) (Beloit College, Carleton College, Coe College, Colorado Col-lege, Cornell College, Grinnell College, Knox College, Lake Forest College, Lawrence University, Luther College, Macalester Col-lege, Monmouth College, Ripon College, and St. Olaf College); 16 member institutions of the Associated Colleges of the South (ACS)

(Birmingham-Southern College, Centenary College, Centre College, Davidson College, Furman University, Hendrix College, Millsaps College, Morehouse College, Rhodes College, Rollins College, Sewanee: the University of the South, Southwestern University, Spelman College, Trinity University, University of Richmond, and Washington and Lee University); and Elon University. Although these institutions differ in governance and history, they share educational values, notably, their commitment to the liberal arts, and the characteristics of private residential liberal arts colleges noted earlier in this chapter, with low student-to-faculty ratios, moderate to high selectivity, and relatively small enrollments (ranging from 1,000 to 5,000 students).

Survey Content

Researchers used an IRB-sanctioned mixed method, two-phase electronic survey to assess faculty experience and impressions of teaching in study abroad–study away. Survey instruments were delivered using SurveyMonkey Pro.

Phase 1. The first survey, Understanding Faculty & Student Transformation in Study Abroad/Study Away Programs at Liberal Arts Institutions, was conducted in 2015 (Gillespie, Glasco, Gross, Layne, & Jasinski, 2015). Researchers contacted 876 prospective participants and received 230 responses (26% response rate) from 27 institutions. Institutions that were not represented in the responses were Davidson, Morehouse, Richmond, and Southwestern. The survey included 59 items that solicited demographic data, including age, gender, race, academic rank, discipline, and years at current institution. Three factors were specific to program leadership:

1. *Program responsibilities.* Thirteen activities were listed, including instruction in-class and in the field, arrangements and oversight of student housing, planning and leading student orientation and cross-cultural training, enforcement

of the student disciplinary code, addressing student medical needs, creating and oversight of the budget, and leading a post-program debriefing.

2. *Pre-program training.* Thirteen topics were listed, including student health care, student safety, emergency guidelines, the student code of conduct, the Family Educational Rights and Privacy Act (FERPA), student housing, and cross-cultural adaptation.

3. *Forms of institutional support.* Seven factors were listed, including training through workshops or handbooks, support for planning and on-site program management and post-program services, compensation with a stipend or course release, and recognition for program leadership with merit pay or promotion.

Additional questions asked faculty to use a Likert scale to report any changes in attitudes and behavior related to their teaching, research agenda, and service that followed their experiences leading an off-campus program. The survey also asked faculty to what extent their experience had an impact on their personal life, relationships with colleagues, and relationship to their institution.

Three open-ended questions sought to probe more deeply the impact of the leadership experience on their behavior and attitudes:

1. What changes (if any) did you notice in your teaching, research, service, and/or personal life after leading a SA/SA program?

2. What advice would you give to a faculty colleague who was considering leading a SA/SA program at your institution for the first time? What should he/she consider before agreeing to lead the program?

3. What impact has leading a SA/SA program had on your students and your institution? How do you know?

Phase II. To build upon the preliminary analysis of Survey 1 responses, researchers developed a second survey entitled Follow-Up Questions for Faculty Members Who Lead Study Away and Study Abroad at Liberal Arts Institutions (Gillespie, Glasco, Gross, Layne, & Jasinski, 2016). The researchers contacted only the willing Phase 1 participants (150 invitations sent; 72 responses received; 48% response rate). The survey instrument included eight questions, three of which focused on teaching and learning, with drop-down menus that listed high-impact practices, assessment methods, and learning outcomes. Five open-ended questions solicited narrative responses about respondents' personal and professional experiences:

1. The Association of American Colleges and Universities identifies global learning in its VALUE rubric as an essential learning outcome for students. What is the relationship between your global learning and your teaching and research?
2. Please describe a single critical incident (positive or negative) that occurred while preparing to lead a Study Away/Study Abroad program, during a program, or upon return and how that incident contributed to your global learning as defined in Question 1.
3. Describe one thing your current institution has done to make the biggest (positive or negative) impact on your ability to lead Study Away/Study Abroad programs.
4. Describe one thing your current institution could do to enhance your ability to lead Study Away/Study Abroad programs.
5. As a teacher and a scholar, how have you developed or changed as a result of leading a Study Away/Study Abroad program?

Data Analysis and Results

All survey data was extracted from SurveyMonkey Pro. Narrative responses were coded using Dedoose, and researchers achieved inter-coder reliability by collaboratively coding the open-ended participant statements. Quantitative analyses were completed in SPSS. Independent-sample t tests and one-way ANOVAs were used to compare means and identify any differences in outcomes as a function of respondents' characteristics, which were measured as categorical variables.

Demographic characteristics. The demographic profile of faculty respondents (Table 6) shows a slightly higher percentage of women (53%) compared to men serving as program leaders. The overwhelming majority were tenured (76.2%), perhaps an artifact of college and departmental policies that do not factor international experience into tenure and promotion policies or that actively discourage untenured faculty from leading programs. Similarly, the overwhelming majority identified as White, perhaps also an artifact of both tenure status and the overall faculty demographics at the institutions included in the survey. Fifty-nine percent of faculty respondents were age 50 or older, and 78% reported having minor children. The academic disciplines represented by the respondents show 39% in arts and humanities, 18.8% in social sciences, 13% in interdisciplinary studies, 12.6% in STEM fields, and 9.4% in pre-professional fields. The remaining 7.1% identified as "other" or did not specify their discipline.

Program locations. The geographic locations of programs led by the respondents are notable for the differences with study abroad destinations for all U.S. students as reported in the annual Open Doors census in 2017–2018 (IIE, 2019a). Europe is at the top of both lists, but a markedly lower percentage of programs led by faculty participants in the study took place in Europe: 27.8% compared to 54.9% reported in Open Doors data. Furthermore, faculty-led programs operated in other regions of the world at a

Table 6. Demographic Characteristics of Faculty as Global Learners Survey Respondents

	Percentage of Respondents
Gender	
Female	53.0
Male	43.9
Other/no response	2.7
Marital status	
Married/partnered	77.1
Single	19.7
No response	3.5
Parental status	
Has minor children	78.0
Does not have children/minor children	22.0
Faculty rank	
Full Professor	43.9
Associate Professor	30.5
Assistant Professor	12.2
Emeritus	2.7
Non-tenure-track appointment	7.5
Tenure status	
Tenured	76.2
On tenure track, not tenured	9.9
Not on tenure track/others	13.9
Age	
39 or younger	11.2
40–49	26.5
50–59	25.6
60–69	25.1
70 or older	8.5
No response	3.1
Race/ethnicity	
White	84.8
Black or African American	3.6
Asian	3.1
Hispanic/Latinx	4.0
Other	7.0
Academic discipline	
Arts and humanities	39.0
Social sciences	18.8
Interdisciplinary	13.0
STEM	12.6
Pre-professional	9.4
Other/not specified	7.1

Table 7. Geographic Locations of Programs Led by Faculty Respondents and All Study Abroad Programs

Region	Faculty as Global Learners	Open Doors
Europe	27.8%	54.9%
Latin America	19.3%	14.9%
Asia	12.6%	11.2%
Sub-Sahara Africa	7.2%	4.2%
Middle East/North Africa	5.4%	2.1%
Oceania	1.8%	4.0%
More than one location	8.1%	7.9%
Did not indicate	11.2%	n/a

much higher rate, with Oceania being the only exception, a likely reflection of the appeal to the U.S. study abroad market of direct enrollment programs in Australia and New Zealand. Table 7 compares data from faculty participants in the Faculty as Global Learners survey with the national census reported in IIE's Open Doors annual report (2017–2018), according to regions identified by the latter.

In addition, 6.7% of the Faculty as Global Learners survey respondents led domestic programs, a category not included in the Open Doors report. Future studies could explore these differences further to determine how liberal arts faculty leaders' interest in non-Western regions is related to students' interests and the areas of disciplinary and cross-disciplinary study that are found at most liberal arts institutions.

Length of program. Of the survey participants who specified the length of the program that they led, more than half (94) were engaged in short-term programs of 15 to 30 days. The next most common length of program was more than 30 days (62 respondents), followed by programs lasting less than two weeks (20 respondents).

Study Limitations

Although the Faculty as Global Learners survey relied on a self-selected subset of faculty program leaders and used self-report measures, the findings provide a rich set of findings. Together, they suggest fruitful directions for future research and institutional policy and practice in support of internationalization and global learning.

FIVE MAJOR FINDINGS

The five major findings from the survey are as follows:

1. Faculty members at liberal arts colleges reported benefiting from consistent, strong institutional support across the entire off-campus study experience (from proposal to reentry).
2. Faculty who led off-campus study programs reported a variety of positive changes.
3. Faculty respondents perceive a gap between institutional support for global learning as a priority for students and institutional support for faculty who lead off-campus programs.
4. Demographic variables—such as tenure-status, discipline, and gender—did not make a difference in the impact on teaching, research, and service of off-campus study program leaders.
5. Faculty members integrated many AAC&U recognized high-impact practices into their off-campus study programs.

Finding #1: Institutional Support and Leadership Responsibilities

The survey asked faculty respondents to indicate the forms of institutional support they had received, including pre-departure training in a workshop and/or with a handbook, compensation with a stipend or course release, recognition such as consideration for merit pay or promotion, and post-program support and services. It also queried their responsibilities in program leadership, from pre-program planning to post-program follow-up, in two main categories: administration and academics. The level of responsibility was determined using several survey items. Fifty-two percent of respondents reported that they were responsible for carrying out eight or more of the following tasks:

- Pre-departure: arrange student housing, plan and lead student orientation, present cross-cultural training, create program budget.
- In-country, on-site: oversee student housing, plan and present student orientation, enforce student disciplinary code, address student medical needs, continue cross-cultural training, oversee program budget and payments to local vendors, mentor a co-instructor or program assistant.
- Post-program: plan and lead a debriefing session with students.

The survey also asked respondents to indicate their level of confidence on a number of topics (see Figure 5). Faculty felt most confident in designing effective teaching methods for off-campus programs, guiding students through cross-cultural adaptation, and managing administrative tasks.

Respondents' narrative responses about institutional support showed that faculty leaders valued opportunities for mentorship, co-leading a program with an experienced colleague, consulting

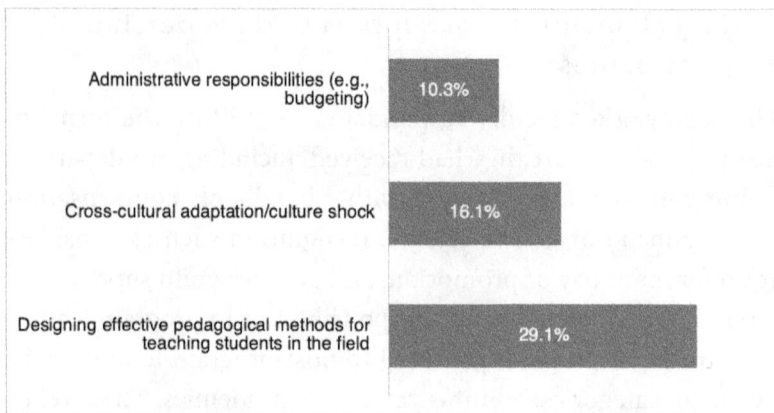

Figure 5. Self-Reported Areas of Greatest Confidence

on a course proposal to take advantage of on-site learning opportunities, and being introduced to local partners as positive contributions to their program design.

The topics about which faculty felt least confident were those that fall outside their purview when they are on campus (see Figure 6). These areas—student health care, adherence to FERPA, and assessment of student learning—are typically the responsibility of specialized staff members in the counseling center, office of the dean of students, or office of institutional research. These topics either received no attention or were covered in less than 30 minutes in pre-departure faculty training, according to survey responses (Gillespie et al., 2015).

Finding #2: Program Leadership and Outcome Variables

To explore the relationship between characteristics of program leaders and the impact of leading an off-campus program, 4-point Likert scale (*To A Great Extent, To Some Extent, To A Lesser Extent,* and *Not at All*) responses to several statistically linked survey items

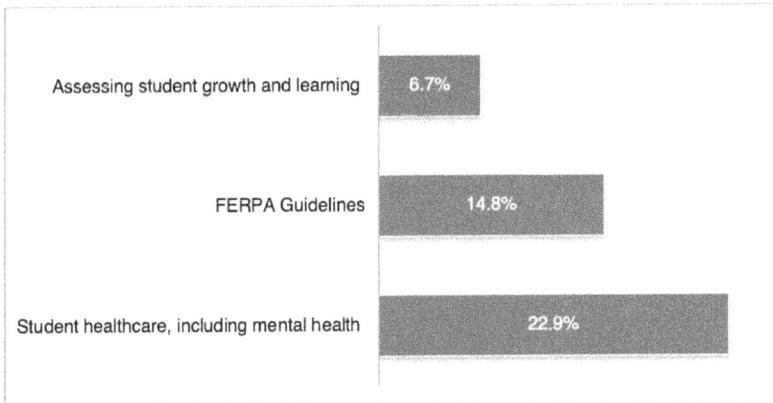

Figure 6. Self-Reported Areas of Least Confidence

were combined to produce composite variables for Teaching (5 items), Research (6 items), Service (6 items), Positive Feelings (6 items), and Negative Feelings (5 items). The items combined are shown in Tables 8 and 9.

To study the impact of the level of institutional support, based on the number of forms of support indicated, respondents were sorted into two categories, one above and the other below the mean. This resulted in two groups: (a) respondents with Low Institutional Support (n = 90) and (b) those with High Institutional Support (n = 101).

Composite scores for each of the outcome dependent variables were used in t tests (or ANOVAs, for independent variables with more than two categories) to explore mean differences. Analyses showed that survey participants' ratings of the impact of program leadership on their teaching, research, service, and negative feelings were unrelated to demographic factors, one of the study's major findings. Institutional support, by contrast, was related to faculty leaders' positive feelings. Participants who reported that their institutions offered a high amount of support for global learning (determined by the degree to which they were trained,

Table 8. Impact of Program Leadership on Teaching, Research, Service

TEACHING	RESEARCH	SERVICE
Referenced my program experiences in another course I teach (e.g., a case study, significant anecdote/ example in lecture)	Published or presented findings generated by leading a program (e.g., scholarship of teaching and learning, presentation of field research)	Increased the number of or the depth of my service obligations on campus or in the community
Attempted at least one new pedagogical strategy in another course I teach (e.g., experiential learning, team teaching)	Expanded my research agenda to include new topics/methods/ areas of interest (e.g., a new regional focus, a new interdisciplinary approach	Decreased the number of or the depth of my service obligations on campus or in the community (e.g., resigned from committees or a nonprofit board)
Developed a new course to incorporate content or pedagogy I developed while leading a study abroad/ study away program	Applied for or received research funding from my employer/institution (e.g., summer support, sabbatical assistance)	Accepted a new leadership role on campus (e.g., became a program administrator or department chair)
Revised an existing course to incorporate content or pedagogy I developed while leading a study abroad/ study away program	Applied for or received research funding from an external source (e.g., Fulbright, NEH, NSF)	Had at least one service commitment of an international nature (e.g., Fulbright proposal review committee, advisor to a student cultural group)
Taught a new course outside of my department (e.g., first year seminar, interdisciplinary programs)	Seen an increase in my overall research productivity	Agreed to mentor a colleague leading a study abroad/study away program (e.g., shared course materials, offered advice)
	Seen a decline in my overall research productivity	Encouraged a student to study abroad

Table 9. Post-Program Positive and Negative Feelings

POSITIVE FEELINGS	NEGATIVE FEELINGS
Eager to lead the same study abroad/ study away program again	Convinced that I would not lead a study abroad/study away program again
Eager to lead a different study abroad/ study away program (e.g., a different location)	Felt "burned out"
Renewed/energized	An increase in stress at work
More connected to my colleagues; improved relationships with peers	An increase in stress at home/personal life
More connected to the mission of my institution	Concern about my research productivity
Leading a study abroad/study away program was a worthwhile use of my time and energy	

supported, compensated, recognized, and offered post-program support) were significantly ($p < .01$) more likely than faculty with low levels of support to experience the positive feelings shown in Table 9.

Narrative responses provided further detail for the statistical data. Among the changed behaviors that faculty participants reported were becoming more multidisciplinary, developing a language or secondary expertise, and improving their problem-solving skills. They also described changed attitudes such as a renewed interest in their work, intentionally teaching to transform, a deeper reflection on their own identity, and tackling global learning more aggressively.

Many narrative responses reflected faculty members' positive feeling of a stronger connection to their institution. They described service commitments focused on campus internationalization and study abroad–study away initiatives, for example, through continuing program leadership and committee work. In some cases, narrative responses also cited service related to campus diversity and international students, key points in a global learning agenda.

Finding #3: Institutional Support for Global Learning

Faculty perceive a gap between institutional support for global learning for students and institutional support for faculty who lead off-campus programs. While 59% of faculty agreed that "Global Learning is a priority for my institution," only 22% agreed that "Supporting faculty members who lead global programs is a priority for my institution." These two findings provide the context for chapter 2, with details of pre-program, on-site, and post-program support to increase the immediate effectiveness of faculty leaders of off-campus programs and to support their long-term career and job satisfaction.

Finding #4: Impact on Teaching, Research, and Service Apply to All Faculty

As noted in relation to Finding #2, statistical analysis showed no significant relationships between faculty leader characteristics— Tenure Status, Academic Rank, Sex, Marital Status, Parental Status, Program Destination, Academic Discipline, Amount of Leadership Responsibilities for Study Abroad/Study Away Program—and the behavioral and attitudinal outcome measures. This finding implies that all faculty members can realize the positive impacts on their teaching, research, and service through the experience of leading an off-campus program.

Finding #5: High-Impact Teaching Practices

The positive changes that faculty reported (Finding #2) are linked to their choice to use one or more high-impact practice (Finding #5), as defined by AAC&U, in their teaching. Chapter 3 focuses on these findings, describing the teaching practices and benefits that faculty articulated in terms of their changed behaviors and attitudes.

The AAC&U Global Learning VALUE rubric sets up six domains of knowledge, including self-knowledge, each with four stair-step measures of learning outcomes, from benchmark to capstone. The rubric is designed to assess a student's progress across the under-graduate years, through curricular and co-curricular experiences. Survey 11 asked faculty respondents to define the relationship between their own global learning and their teaching and research. Many faculty responses aligned with one or more of the rubric domains and reflect global learning at the capstone level. One pur-pose of the VALUE rubric was to create "lifelong global learners" (Hovland, 2014b, p. 9), an aspiration that is realized in many faculty program leaders. The sample of responses in Table 10 demonstrate how faculty members' self-awareness as global learners and their pedagogical practice support the characteristics of global learning as defined by the AAC&U rubric.

Throughout this book, we utilize the term *global learning*, and in doing so, we implicitly reference these multiple, complex levels. Rather than define global learning as being one thing or another, we advance the idea that the term carries several meanings and invokes patterns of thought, areas of knowledge, and potential action. Recognizing global learning as a dynamic concept that sig-nifies different things, we take advantage of its plurality of mean-ings and their application to faculty members.

CONCLUSION

Major findings from the Faculty as Global Learners survey point to the many benefits that faculty draw from the experience of leading off-campus study programs. These benefits are not linked to demographic characteristics of faculty leaders, an analysis that suggests that all faculty can realize positive changes in behavior and attitudes and in their teaching, research, and service to the campus community. However, faculty members perceive a gap between institutional support for global learning as a priority for

Table 10. Relationship Between Global Learning, Teaching, and Research

AAC&U Global Learning VALUE Rubric: Capstone Level	Faculty as Global Learners Survey Response
Global self-awareness: "articulating one's identity in a global context"	"As a writing teacher, I feel that global learning is an excellent environment in which students can use writing as a tool to further their own self-awareness, as well as their understanding about cultural assumptions and contexts." (Female tenured faculty, arts & humanities)
Perspective-taking: "multiple perspectives" in students' thinking about "complex subjects within natural and human systems"	"My own global learning never stops; it is continually challenged by local, regional, national and international events. I strive constantly to understand the perspectives of people who think differently than I do, the perspectives of people whose opinions, beliefs, values are different than my own. In whatever course I each, I strive to initiate my students into this life-long quest and to help them develop the habits of heart and mind to move forward." (Female tenured faculty, arts & humanities)
Cultural diversity: "deep understanding of multiple world views, experiences, and power structures"	"To recognize that peoples of the world look at ideas, issues, institutions (family, religion, government) in many different ways and further that those ways of knowing are embedded in culture and history. I always teach with global learning in mind, even U.S. courses" (Female tenured faculty, social sciences)
Personal and social responsibility: "informed and responsible action to address ethical, social, and environmental challenges in global systems"	"I emphasize cultural diversity and our role as global citizens in the world. In this sense, the course I taught presented food insecurity in many parts of the world as a human rights problem to be addressed on a global scale." (Female tenured faculty, arts & humanities)
Understanding global systems: "deep knowledge . . . to develop and advocate for informed, appropriate action to solve complex problems in the human and natural worlds"	"Work on any parts or the whole of environmental systems require an appreciation for scales of space and time. As a consequence of that core, one cannot think about teaching and research in environmental studies without considering scales at the local, regional, and global levels." (Male tenured faculty, STEM)
Applying knowledge to contemporary global contexts: "address complex global problems using interdisciplinary perspectives"	"I teach educational psychology and Middle East human geography. . . . It is vital that (students) develop critical analysis and synthesis skills as they engage topics like diversity in classrooms, conflict, religious differences, etc." (Male tenured faculty, arts & humanities)

Note: Adapted from Global Learning VALUE rubric, by Association of American Colleges & Universities, n.d., retrieved from https://www.aacu.org/resources/global-learning; *Understanding faculty and student transformation in study abroad/study away programs*, by J. Gillespie, S. Glasco, D. Gross, P. Layne, & L. Jasinski, 2015, unpublished survey.

students and institutional support for faculty who lead these programs. Liberal arts colleges are presented with the opportunity to offer these benefits to all faculty and to increase the likelihood of faculty success through training, workshops, and administrative support. The following chapters expand on these opportunities.

REFERENCES

American Council on Education. (2012). *Mapping internationalization on U.S. campuses*. Retrieved from https://www.acenet.edu/news-rom/Documents/ Mapping-Internationalization-UScampuses-2012-full.pdf

Anderson, C. S., & Cunningham, K. (2009). Culture, religion, and nationality: Developing ethnographic skills and reflective practices connected to study abroad. In E. Brewer & K. Cunningham (Eds.), *Integrating study abroad into the curriculum: Theory and practice across the disciplines* (pp. 63–84). Sterling, VA: Stylus Publishing.

Association of American Colleges & Universities. (n.d.). Global Learning VALUE rubric. Retrieved from https://www.aacu.org/resources/global-learning

Astin, A. W. (1999). Student involvement: A developmental theory for higher education. *Journal of College Student Development, 40*(5), 518–529.

Brewer, E. (2010). Leveraging partnerships to internationalize the liberal arts college: Campus internationalization and the faculty. In P. L. Eddy (Ed.), *International collaborations: Opportunities, strategies, challenges* (pp. 83–96). San Francisco, CA: Jossey-Bass.

Brewer, E., & Cunningham, K. (Eds.). (2009). *Integrating study abroad into the curriculum: Theory and practice across the disciplines*. Sterling, VA: Stylus Publishing.

Center for Engaged Learning. (2017). *Elon statement on integrating global learning with the university experience: Higher-impact study abroad and off-campus domestic study*. Retrieved from http://www.centerforengagedlearning.org/ doing-engage-learning/elon-statement-on-integrating-global-learning

Childress, L. K. (2018). *The twenty-first century university: Developing faculty engagement in internationalization* (2nd ed.). New York, NY: Peter Lang.

Chopp, R., Frost, S., & Weiss, D. H. (Eds.). (2014). *Remaking college: Innovation and the liberal arts*. Baltimore, MD: Johns Hopkins University Press.

Creswell, J. W. (2013). *Qualitative inquiry and research design: Choosing among five approaches* (3rd ed.). Thousand Oaks, CA: Sage.

Deardorff, D. (2006). The identification and assessment of intercultural competence. *Journal of Studies in International Education, 10*, 241–266.

Doscher, S., & Landorf, H. (2018). Universal global learning, inclusive excellence, and higher education's greater purposes. *Peer Review, 20*(1), 4–7. Retrieved from https://www.aacu.org/peerreview/2018/Winter/FIU

Feller, A. E. (2015). Where experience meets transformation: Pedagogy and study away. In N. W. Sobania (Ed.), *Putting the local in global education: Models for transformative learning through domestic off-campus programs* (pp. 52–72). Sterling, VA: Stylus Publishing.

Gillespie, J. (2019). Faculty roles in advancing student learning abroad. In E. Brewer & A. C. Ogden (Eds.), *Education abroad and the undergraduate experience: Critical perspectives and approaches to integration with student learning and development* (pp. 213–228). Sterling, VA: Stylus Publishing.

Gillespie, J., Glasco, S., Gross, D., Layne, P., & Jasinski, L. (2015). *Understanding faculty and student transformation in study abroad/study away programs.* Unpublished survey.

Gillespie, J., Glasco, S., Gross, D., Layne, P., & Jasinski, L. (2016). *Follow-up questions for faculty members who lead study away and study abroad programs at liberal arts institutions.* Unpublished survey.

Helms, R. M., Brajkovic, L., & Struthers, B. (2017). *Mapping internationalization on U.S. campuses: 2017 edition.* Washington, DC: American Council on Education. Retrieved from https://www.acenet.edu/Documents/Mapping-Internationalization-2017.pdf

Hill, W. L. (2014). Interdisciplinary perspectives and the liberal arts. In R. Chopp, S. Frost, & D. H. Weiss (Eds.), *Remaking college: Innovation and the liberal arts* (pp. 85–95). Baltimore, MD: Johns Hopkins University Press.

Hovland, K. (2014a). *Global learning: Defining, designing, demonstrating.* AAC&U & NAFSA: Association of International Educators. Retrieved from https://www.aacu.org/sites/default/files/files/Global/global_learning_2014.pdf

Hovland, K. (2014b). What can global learners do? *Diversity & Democracy, 17*(2), 8–11.

Hudzik, J. K. (2015). *Comprehensive internationalization: Institutional pathways to success.* Abingdon, UK: Routledge.

Institute of International Education. (2019a). Fast facts. *Open Doors report on international education exchange.* Retrieved from https://www.iie.org/Research-and-Insights/Open-Doors/Fact-Sheets-and-Infographics/Fast-Facts

Institute of International Education. (2019b). Leading institutions. *Open Doors report on international education exchange.* Retrieved from https://www.iie.org/Research-and-Insights/Open-Doors/Data/US-Study-Abroad/Leading-Institutions

Jessup-Anger, J. E. (2012). Examining how residential college environments inspire the life of the mind. *The Review of Higher Education, 35*(3), 431–462.

Johansson, C., & Felten, P. (2014). *Transforming students: Fulfilling the promise of higher education.* Baltimore, MD: Johns Hopkins University Press.

Kiley, K. (2011, November 16). Better than yours. *Inside Higher Ed.* Retrieved from https://www.insidehighered.com/news/2011/11/16/annapolis-group-survey-finds-high-satisfaction-among-liberal-arts-college-graduates

Koblik, S., & Graubard, S. R. (Eds.). (2000). *Distinctively American: The residential liberal arts colleges.* New Brunswick, NJ: Transaction Publishers.

McCardell, J. M. (2014). "Glowing against the gray, sober against the fire": Residential academic communities in the twenty-first century. In R. Chopp, S. Frost, & D. H. Weiss (Eds.), *Remaking college: Innovation and the liberal arts* (pp. 169–179). Baltimore, MD: Johns Hopkins University Press.

Pascarella, E. T., Cruce, T. M., Wolniak, G. C., & Blaich, C. F. (2004). Do liberal arts colleges really foster good practices in undergraduate education? *Journal of College Student Development, 45*(1), 57–74.

Pascarella, E. T., & Terenzini, P. T. (2005). *How college affects students: A third decade of research* (Vol. 2). San Francisco, CA: Jossey-Bass.

Passarelli, A. M., & Kolb, D. A. (2012). Using experiential learning theory to promote student learning and development in programs of education abroad. In M. Vande Berg, R. M. Paige, & K. Hemming Lou (Eds.), *Student learning abroad: What our students are learning, what they're not, and what we can do about it* (pp. 137–161). Sterling, VA: Stylus Publishing.

Reimers, F. M. (2014). Bringing global education to the core of undergraduate curriculum. *Diversity & Democracy, 17*(2), 4–7.

Seifert, T. A., Goodman, K. M., Lindsay, N., Jorgensen, J. D., Wolniak, G. C., Pascarella, E. T., & Blaich, C. (2008). The effects of liberal arts experiences on liberal arts outcomes. *Research in Higher Education, 49*(2), 107–125. doi:10.1007/s11162-007-9070-7

Sobania, N. W. (2015). The faraway nearby: Putting the local in global education. In N. W. Sobania (Ed.), *Putting the local in global education: Models for transformative learning through domestic off-campus programs* (pp. 16–35). Sterling, VA: Stylus Publishing.

Twombly, S. B., Salisbury, M. H., Tumanut, S. D., & Klute, P. (2012). Study abroad in a new global century: Renewing the promise, refining the purpose. *ASHE Higher Education Report, 38*(4).

Young, G. E. (2014). Reentry: Supporting students in the final stage of study abroad. *New Directions for Student Services, 2014*(146), 59–67. doi:10.1002/ss.20091

IN OTHER WORDS

Susan Jaret McKinstry

I was scheduled to teach a semester of theatre in London—
something I had done before—when enrollment shifts made it
necessary for me to teach the first half semester in Florence, Italy,
followed by a half semester in London. I fretted, then embraced the
opportunity, and it was transformative. Like our students, I experi-

enced the unknown every day. That is something we as faculty do not regularly do: we are authorities in our fields, we teach courses we plan because they intersect with our research or interests, and we display and convey knowledge. What happens when we set off into unknown territory?

I teach visual literacy, and I ask my students to practice observation, then description, then interpretation—to slow the process of locating answers, to see everything, to find the unexpected even in the familiar. My photograph of a Florence street scene captures the layers of familiarity and strangeness we encounter daily on an off-campus study program. The narrow stone street, the parked bicycle and *motorino*, the arched doorway and tall windows all signal Florence, while the antique gold leaf armoire, shield, and bizarre manikin with necklace and skull seem less certain, and the reflections make the distinction between inside and outside ambiguous. What better image for seeing strangeness in the intersecting processes of self-discovery, intellectual growth, and global understanding that are the heart of an off-campus program?

In Florence, I decided to teach a writing/travel course that used 19th-century writers experiencing Florence and Italy—including Henry James, Charles Dickens, Robert and Elizabeth Browning, and E. M. Forster—to spark the students' own writings about their cultural and personal discoveries. Jhumpa Lahiri's 2015 memoir *In Other Words*, explaining her decision to write in Italian rather than English, framed the course and became a symbol of our shared exploration of place and language. Lahiri's Italian was translated into English by Ann Goldstein on facing pages, so the book literally juxtaposed the two languages. The students studied Italian, and I took intensive Italian every morning, and we could see Lahiri's developing facility with Italian when we read her final chapters: we were all, together, writers working in unfamiliar territory, in other words.

I want students to see and explore that unfamiliarity. Reflection, a cornerstone of off-campus studies programs, starts with the self and considers how it has altered, but creative writing can start outside the self, outside the known. In Italy, in short weekly writings, I asked the students to map their commute to school by describing surprising objects along the way, to experience and explain the different culture of Italian cafés, to describe Venice using all their senses, to write a dramatic monologue in the voice of a figure in an Italian Renaissance painting or sculpture that they saw in a Florence museum. Each assignment asked them to observe without immediately naming or knowing, instead to wonder freely, even as it developed their precision with language and form. ("Verbs matter," one student announced. "Who knew?") That final assignment, the dramatic monologue, beautifully connected every aspect of the program, as the students demonstrated their art history and Italian knowledge, the detailed observation and genre experimentation of the writing workshops, and the empathy they developed by thinking and living cross-culturally and trans-historically.

In London, the best assignments, like the dramatic monologue in Florence, highlighted the delights of the unfamiliar while linking it to what students were learning. For the theatre course, they each proposed a Romeo and a Juliet for Shakespeare's *Romeo and Juliet* from portraits in London's National Gallery, creating actors' bios that the class debated to select our cast—before we saw the Royal Shakespeare Company (RSC) production in Stratford-upon-Avon and then debated the RSC casting decisions and implications. In teams, students wrote and performed the opening scene for a play set in a precise London site, using local speech and gestures. For their final project, they worked alone or in teams to create a digital essay examining a British spectacle in words and images (and, in several cases, song). Students were invited to challenge themselves, alone or in teams, to articulate their intellectual and cultural experiences through the forms—writing, art, theatre, history—they were studying.

What about my own unfamiliar territory? I am a Pre-Raphaelite scholar, but until I lived in Florence, went on the art history excursions, and explored the streets and museums every day, I could not grasp the complex allusions of the name "Pre-Raphaelite," how the Italian Renaissance reshaped art and daily life, or the similar stakes for art and public life during the Renaissance and in my familiar 19th-century context. I myself was in strange territory, no longer a scholar but a learner—deeply engaged, curious about what I did not know, full of questions. I participated fully in the program, collaborated with the exceptional local faculty, learned all I could as I designed assignments and deepened my knowledge. In short, I did precisely what we ask students to do.

When I returned to the United States, I was invited to give a talk on the extraordinary exhibit *Truth and Beauty* at the Fine Arts Museums of San Francisco, which for the first time displayed Pre-Raphaelite art with the Italian and Northern European Renaissance art that inspired it. I could not have given that talk had I not spent two months studying the Italian Renaissance in Italy, walking the streets of Florence, asking questions, living Italian culture (in Italian whenever I could). I asked my students to see strangeness differently and to write in other words; I returned to my research and teaching with deeper knowledge of my specialty as well as conviction that we should highlight the unknown for ourselves as well as our students. Liberal arts work best across disciplines, at the border of our understanding, where what we see is not yet understood. Off-campus programs provide an opportunity for us all to delight in the daily unfamiliar as we try to translate it into a new known.

"LET ME INTRODUCE YOU TO THE CHIEF"

Today's College Students Encounter Traditional Rulers in West Africa

Claudena Skran

One of the most difficult aspects of taking college students to West Africa is helping them to understand the role of traditional chiefs in both politics and society. The challenge starts with an obvious

problem: How do you introduce a U.S. American college student to a paramount chief? Over the past 10 years, in which I have brought 150 students to Sierra Leone, I have had multiple chances to do just that. The experience is one full of contradictions. On the one hand, typical liberal arts students are often committed to ending patriarchy, decolonizing Africa, and promoting global human rights. On the other, traditional rulers, usually male, represent continuity with the past, harmony within society, and deep connections to the land. While they may not share the same values or perspectives, students traveling in rural West Africa must both meet and interact with traditional rulers on the rulers' terms. This is especially true in rural areas where acknowledging the local chief is a matter of respect, and seeking his permission for any group activities is required.

My starting point for preparing students to encounter traditional rulers is an extended pre-departure orientation. Students at my home institution, Lawrence University, are required to take a twice-weekly course that combines the history, culture, and society of the place they are visiting. There they have the opportunity to learn not only about the role that "ruling families" played in the colonial period but also about the reconstitution of hereditary rulers after a decade of civil war and state failure. While on their familiar home campus, it's not unusual for students to be critical of the role of chiefs, as they represent non-democratic, authoritarian traditions continuing in modern Africa.

The next stage takes place during actual travel to West Africa as part of a "traveling classroom" during the college's long break. Our groups vary in size from 15 to 30 faculty and students and are composed of students with diverse majors and backgrounds. Once in country, the students quickly encounter the realities facing a country recovering from war in which many institutions in society are unable to effectively exercise authority. It doesn't take long for most students to realize that chiefs, especially paramount chiefs, exercise both authority and power at the local level and sometimes at the national as well. When a group travels to rural villages and small towns, our first stop must be to announce our visit with the local chief and, if appropriate, to ask permission for our activities.

In preparing for these encounters, I've learned from experience to be explicit about what students should do—and not do. Just relying on manners common on a U.S. American college campus is not sufficient for an encounter with a traditional ruler; typically, chiefs expect to be treated with a level of respect that students generally don't show to their faculty members, administrators, parents, or even coaches. Before our meeting, we brainstorm some of the key dos and don'ts, such as "do sit down when bid" or "do accept the soda offered you, even if it is a Coke and you prefer Fanta." Similarly, understanding rules of prohibition is key, such as "don't interrupt when the chief is speaking" or "don't pull out your phone and start texting."

Generally, students are pleasantly surprised by these meetings, which usually take place in the chief's compound, and quickly adapt to their role as foreign guests. In the chiefs, they often find articulate, educated rulers who have the capacity to think about the long-term future of the community. One of our most memorable visits was to Koidu, in the heart of the diamond-mining region of Sierra Leone. The local chief slaughtered a goat in honor of our group and additionally brought the meat to us for a special dinner.

Of course, on some occasions, students are critical of the corrupt practices associated with particular chiefs and often of their family living arrangements, which may include plural marriage or young wives. In this case, a debriefing conversation is essential. I try to talk to the students about what they object to and why and also ask how the situation might be different. We further discuss who is responsible for change, considering the role of individuals in the local community and also that of organizations that form part of the "international community."

Perhaps the most challenging encounter that my students have ever had with a traditional ruler took place in a village that had been badly impacted by Ebola. Our meeting with the local chief was warm and enthusiastic, but some of the students were uncomfortable with the degree of emotion shown by the chief. Afterward, when we had returned to our guest house, I dropped our planned activities and called a special debriefing for the students to discuss the visit. At the meeting, students shared their feelings about visiting the community, including their feelings about the role of the chief. This gave me, as the faculty leader, an opportunity to ask the students to think about how Ebola had impacted the community and its leaders. I shared some of the things the village had experienced, including days of quarantine, seeming abandonment by the outside world, and the loss of many lives. The chief, an Ebola survivor himself, had lost many close family members but had come to embody the voice of the community in its struggle both to survive during the outbreak and then to care for orphans afterward. One of my students later described the chief as an "icon of hope" who used his exuberance for the betterment of his people.

Upon return to the United States, further consideration in our post-departure discussions has shown me that students are divided about the continued viability of traditional rulers in modern Africa. Some adopt a republican position that such leaders are outdated in a democratic age; others see in the chiefs an equivalent of the constitutional monarchs of Great Britain and other countries. Few of them, however, forget their experiences with traditional rulers nor underestimate their importance for contemporary Africa.

NOT TEACHING HIROSHIMA

Michael A. Schneider

Hiroshima. Few place-names evoke such a profound and transcendent sense of historical moment. As the site of a local tragedy with global implications, few places carry such potential for ready-made critical incidents in a study abroad context. Hiroshima looms over nearly every discussion in the training of Japan specialists, and no instructor of Japanese studies can teach without having some basic competence in handling student questions about this daunting topic. As a pedagogical matter, Hiroshima is an endless resource for teaching historiography, compelling students to grapple with ethics and decision-making, historical context, human error, strategic planning, war responsibility, guilt, and shame—you name it, the topic gives and gives.

All of this would suggest that Hiroshima's allure as a site for critical education is self-evident and irresistible. Indeed, it all feels too easy. Hiroshima is quickly and easily accessible from Kyoto and Osaka, so there is no excuse not to get there. The Hiroshima Peace

Park is a major destination and uncomplicated tourist site by any usual measures. The park's museum is graphic in detail and depiction of suffering, the city is disarmingly charming and welcoming, and the surrounding area strikingly beautiful. Moments of deep and personal engagement and reflection are, with this extraordinary combination, quite easily achieved. Students feel angry and sad, all the more acutely if they are U.S. Americans. Stunned by the ferocity of the violence inflicted on a mostly non-combatant population and sobered by the looming menace of the nuclear age the event subsequently unleashed, students cannot evade the weight of their own moral agency. For a faculty leader, this all comes out of the box, no assembly required. There is little art in processing these raw emotions and inviting continued reflection. It happens. Assisted by multiple blows to student psyches, an instructor easily claims victory in the battle against U.S. American myopia.

This formulaic episode, replayed by countless visitors and groups, had rendered Hiroshima unwanted territory to me. I could tell students of the dangers they would encounter there. Figuring that any serious students would find their way there anyway, I deferred for most of my career any serious engagement myself. Instead, it took a student group visit to a very different place, a German concentration camp, to cause me to revise my thinking. Due to a convoluted string of events, I ended up in charge of 25 students visiting the Sachsenhausen camp outside Berlin one early December. Even though I was not a faculty leader of the group, I was thrust into the role I did not relish. As late afternoon darkness enveloped our train back to Berlin center, I sensed a wide despair passing through the group. One student, no doubt speaking for most, lashed out, "Why did you make us see that?!" In that moment of pained incompetence, I understood why I had to include Hiroshima in my teaching.

Rather than seeing human tragedies as the raw material for critical moments in cross-cultural learning or critical moments in learning about Japan—which they surely are—in that moment I understood the transcendence of the Hiroshima experience. After all, the transcendence of Hiroshima manifestly unfolds in many layers: historic, strategic, technological, ethical, symbolic, met-onymic. One further level that is easily forgotten from a histo-rian's gaze is the relevance of the present moment. Students live powerfully in the present and need tools to unpack a host of simi-larly complex moments. Avoiding the mistakes of the Sachsenhau-sen visit has, thus, shaped my preparations for Hiroshima. These preparations have drawn on institutional supports and perspec-tives that a historian rarely calls on. Historians can call on the mat-ters of historical memory and how they inform our understanding today, what historians refer to as two sets of historical amnesia by the victims and perpetrators of this tragedy. But how should one teach tragedy? What emotional allowances do we make for those around us? What are the psychological effects on those who suffered the trauma? What is their effect on us? What does one make of the spiritual lives of students, when those perspectives lay dormant in the usual history class?

It is now broadly accepted that the emotional lives of our stu-dents should inform our teaching, or the topic is at least discussed widely enough to be scorned by some. While 1 still insist on my historian's goals for the Hiroshima visit, 1 invite and expect reac-tions far beyond my narrow ambitions for the visit. Of the many student reactions to Hiroshima in the intervening years, one epi-sode stands out as a constant reminder of my fundamental conver-sion on this matter. One group of three students had distinguished themselves largely by a lackadaisical and half-hearted embrace of cultural learning during a three-week trip to Japan. 1 did not ques-tion their sincerity, but their approach to their first two weeks in Japan was marked by superficial encounters and mostly platitudi-nous reactions. 1 expected Hiroshima to be more of the same for them. After a perfunctory perusal of the museum, they quickly exited to wander the peace garden without the scrutinizing glare of their instructors. There they met an elderly gentleman, gliding along the rainy streets in a bright green jacket, a signal of his status as a volunteer interlocutor. As darkness fell on the park, he exhorted them to see the Hiroshima experience in a positive light, arguing that it is an obligation of those who remember Hiroshima to make something positive out of it. Not allowing them to glower behind a curtain of shame and self-pity, he gave them a lesson in the importance of encountering Japanese on their own terms and engaging in real conversation. Whatever the students understood about Hiroshima that day, they left the city with their first deep cross-cultural encounter. They left uplifted and eager for more opportunities to engage with Japanese. I cannot take credit for their step forward—but that has been perhaps always the case.

CHAPTER 2

SYNERGISTIC APPROACHES TO GLOBAL LEARNING

Effective Institutional Support for Faculty Leaders of Off-Campus Study Programs

Dana Gross

> *The earth has become a place of global cultures . . . and increasingly a global commons. An appropriate university education for everyone . . . must prepare women and men for participation in these cultures and this commons. (Bennett, Cornwell, Al-Lail, & Schenck, 2012)*

Over the past decade, global learning has become increasingly strategically important, at least in part due to the high value that employers and accreditors place on global activities and outcomes, such as intercultural skills and knowledge (AAC&U, 2018; Helms, Brajkovic, & Struthers, 2017). Across many different types of institutions, including liberal arts colleges, more resources are being allocated to promote study abroad and enable faculty and students to "function effectively in global knowledge networks and to thrive in global electronic communities" (Plater, 2015, p. 7). At the same time, "institutions have gone from counting participants to focusing on quality and on what students are learning, doing, and applying across the disciplines" (Whitehead, 2017, p. v). Investing institutional resources to help students maximize their learning is now an essential component of a comprehensive and strategic approach to global engagement, just as important as articulating measurable intended learning outcomes for that engagement (Calahan, 2018; Doscher & Landorf, 2018; Helms et al., 2017). One of the most effective ways to maximize students' global learning is by investing in faculty (Anderson, Lorenz, & White, 2016; Hulstrand, 2013, 2015; Vande Berg, Paige, & Lou, 2012).

Small liberal arts colleges surpass other types of institutions in the proportion of students for whom global learning and engagement—preparation for the "global commons"—includes immersive, face-to-face interactions, often in another part of the world. Increasingly, these interactions occur during short-term programs led by a faculty member from students' home campuses (Chieffo & Griffiths, 2009; IIE, n.d.). While faculty leaders of off-campus study programs at liberal arts colleges play a unique and critical role in facilitating students' understanding of the world and of themselves as global citizens (Niehaus, Reading, Nelson, Wegener, & Arthur, 2018), liberal arts faculty do not always feel supported or valued when they engage in this kind of high-impact experiential pedagogy (Dewey & Duff, 2009). Faculty as Global Learners, a recent survey of more than 200 faculty members at private liberal arts colleges across the country who had led off-campus study programs, found that, while 59% agreed "to a great extent" that global learning is a priority at their institution, only 22% agreed "to a great extent" that supporting faculty members who lead off-campus programs is an institutional priority (Gillespie, Glasco, Gross, Jasinski, & Layne, 2017).

One example of this disconnect is that, although an increasing number of colleges place a high value on internationalization, global partnerships, and study abroad opportunities for students, the 2016 Mapping Internationalization on U.S. Campuses survey (described in more detail later in this chapter) found that 93% of baccalaureate institutions do not specify international work or experience as considerations in faculty promotion and tenure decisions. Another example of a missed opportunity for increasing global learning across the curriculum is that only 6% of baccalaureate institutions report that they "frequently" hire faculty with international background, experience, or interests in fields that are not explicitly international/global; 47% report that they "occasionally" prioritize these characteristics; and 47% report that they "rarely" or "never" give preference to such candidates (Helms et al., 2017). These examples show that although many liberal arts colleges have articulated clear goals related to internationalization and global learning, this has not translated into criteria for hiring or reviewing faculty (Helms, 2015).

This chapter addresses the perceived gap between the high priority that baccalaureate institutions place on global learning and the limited support that many faculty members report receiving for their direct contributions to that strategic goal. It offers ideas that provosts and academic deans, as well as directors of off-campus study offices and teaching-and-learning centers at liberal arts colleges, can use to provide effective, continuous support for faculty leaders of off-campus study programs. In the best case, that support begins with program development and includes reentry and post-program activities that are beneficial for faculty as well as students. The chapter emphasizes the value of providing synergistic support—investing resources that both enhance the immediate effectiveness of program leaders and contribute to their long-term job satisfaction and career success. Doing this requires that leaders of liberal arts colleges recognize and respond to differences that exist among faculty in their career trajectories, disciplinary contexts, expectations for scholarship or creative work, and teaching and travel experience as well as their personal and cultural roles and identities.

FACULTY JOB SATISFACTION AND INSTITUTIONAL SUPPORT

Most college faculty in the United States are positively engaged and satisfied with their jobs. In many national surveys, such as those conducted since 1989 by the Higher Education Research Institute (HERI) and by the Collaborative on Academic Careers in Higher Education (COACHE, n.d.), the majority of faculty consistently report that if they had it to do over again, they would still want to be a college professor (approximately 85%) and work at their current institution (approximately 70%); the majority (approximately 75%) also state that they are satisfied with their job overall (Eagan et al., 2014; Finkelstein & Cummings, 2012; Helms, 2010). Even in the context of increased budgetary pressures and public scrutiny mixed with skepticism about the value of the liberal arts, a 2018 survey with nearly 1,000 respondents from different types of institutions found that faculty "report having particularly high levels of satisfaction from teaching and mentoring students, say they find their jobs challenging and exciting, and state that, if they had to do it all over again, they would still work in higher education" (*The Chronicle of Higher Education*, 2018, p. 10). Consistent with other studies (Helms, 2010; Mathews, 2014; Trower, 2008, 2010), this survey found that senior faculty tended to express higher levels of job satisfaction than associate and assistant professors, and tenured and tenure-track faculty were more satisfied than faculty who were not tenure-eligible. Nearly all respondents, however, agreed or strongly agreed with the statement "By doing my job, I make a difference in the world" and believed that their teaching benefits students and their lives.

Other, less positive findings from the 2018 survey were also in keeping with previous studies. Whereas teaching, mentoring, and interacting with students were significant sources of job satisfaction, 53% of survey respondents disagreed or strongly disagreed that "The relationship between the faculty and administrators at my college is favorable and strong," and 51% disagreed or strongly disagreed with the statement "Administrators at my college understand the needs of the faculty" (*The Chronicle of Higher Education*, 2018). One reason for this disconnect may be that when strategic planning and institutional branding takes place—on average, once every five years—faculty often do not see their roles highlighted (Goldman & Salem, 2015). Instead, strategic plans typically focus on facilities, infrastructure, and the student experience without explicitly aligning those goals with faculty development programming (Baker, Lunsford, & Pifer, 2017) or recognizing the impact of those goals on faculty members' professional and personal well-being (Berg & Seeber, 2016; Felten, Bauman, Kheriaty, & Taylor, 2013).

These issues were explored in a multi-year study that surveyed nearly 550 faculty members from 13 liberal arts colleges in the Great Lakes Colleges Association (Baker et al., 2017). The researchers also conducted follow-up interviews with 77 of the respondents to identify opportunities and challenges facing faculty at liberal arts colleges and examine the effectiveness of a range of faculty development strategies. The study found that although strategic plans for teaching and learning at liberal arts colleges increasingly depend on faculty being able to incorporate active learning pedagogies in their courses, mentor undergraduates in research, and support institutional goals for diversity, equity, and inclusion, faculty development programming does not consistently, effectively, and synergistically support those goals.

In particular, the researchers found that faculty development efforts aimed at promoting institutional goals often are not designed to help advance individual faculty members' interests and address their unique career-stage needs within the institutional context. As one example, liberal arts colleges typically direct mentoring programs toward the teaching and research needs of early-career faculty, for whom the greatest reported source of job stress tends to be "disconnects between their academic preparation and the realities of the liberal arts context"—the challenge of meeting expectations for teaching, research, and service (Baker et al., 2017, p. 7). For mid-career and senior faculty, by contrast, the primary stressors are often related to taking on leadership and mentoring roles with little training or support, yet colleges often overlook the need for mentoring for those roles and other tasks that tend to be taken on in mid- and later career stages (Austin, 2010; Baker et al., 2017; Mathews, 2014; Ponjuan, Conley, & Trower, 2011).

However, considering the influence of career stage is just the first step in understanding "the faculty experience." Studies employing survey and interview methods and an intersectionality framework have documented that faculty members' needs, job satisfaction, and productivity are also related to their identities—notably, gender, race, and ethnicity—and life circumstances outside of the academy, including family roles and cultural obligations (Bozeman & Gaughan, 2011; Campbell & O'Meara, 2014; Denson, Szelényi, & Bresonis, 2018; O'Meara & Stromquist, 2015; Pifer, 2011; Trower, 2009; Webber & Rogers, 2018). "Personal characteristics, previous professional and academic experiences, and personal responsibilities (for example, as caregiver or parent) influence one's willingness to engage in and need a variety of faculty development supports" (cited in Baker et al., 2017, p. 189).

Responses to the Tenure-Track Faculty Job Satisfaction Survey (COACHE, 2014b) illustrate this point for gender and generational cohorts. Trower (2010) found that although pre-tenure faculty overall rated informal mentoring as more valuable than formal mentoring through an official program, women gave higher ratings than did men of the value of both forms of mentoring, and women valued informal mentoring significantly more than formal arrangements. The COACHE survey also revealed that while today's

tenure-track faculty may want the same things as their predecessors, younger Boomers (born 1956–1963) and Gen X faculty (born 1964–1980) live and work in a very different world than older Boomers (born 1946–1955) and Traditionalists (born before 1946). . . . Gen Xers, in particular, have been vocal about wanting increased flexibility, greater integration of their work and home lives, more transparency of tenure and promotion processes, a more welcoming, diverse, and supportive workplace/department, and more frequent and helpful feedback about progress. (Trower, 2010, p. 27)

Gen X faculty tend to express low levels of satisfaction with their "balance between professional time and personal or family time" and often disagree that the institution does what it can to make having and raising children and the tenure-track compatible (Trower, 2010, p. 29).

Most studies of college faculty, including the COACHE and HERI surveys and the Great Lakes Colleges Association study, have not explicitly addressed the experience of faculty leaders of off-campus study programs. Nevertheless, the findings are relevant to and inform the recommendations in this chapter for supporting institutional strategic goals for global learning. Many liberal arts colleges can do more to align their institutional missions with policies and programming to ensure that faculty have the skills, knowledge, and support they need to succeed, and grow, as leaders of off-campus study programs.

INSTITUTIONAL INTERNATIONALIZATION AND GLOBAL LEARNING: FACULTY POLICIES AND PRACTICES

One valuable resource for aligning policies and practices with strategic plans for global learning and engagement is a comprehensive internationalization model developed by the American Council on Education's (ACE) Center for Internationalization and Global Engagement (CIGE). Comprehensive internationalization is defined as "a strategic, coordinated process that seeks to align and integrate policies, programs, and initiatives to position colleges and universities as more globally oriented and internationally connected institutions" (ACE, n.d.-a). As shown in Table 11, faculty policies and practices are one of six key areas addressed in the CIGE model.

Examples of policies, programs, documents, and assessment tools and evidence for all six areas are available in an online Internationalization Toolkit maintained by the CIGE (ACE, n.d.-b). The section on faculty policies and practices includes examples of programs to promote faculty mobility; faculty awards and grants for international engagement, teaching, and research; and guidelines for internationalized tenure and promotion.

Table 11. CIGE Model for Comprehensive Internationalization (American Council on Education)

Target Areas	Opportunities for Implementation
Articulated institutional commitment	Mission statements and strategic plans that prioritize internationalization, allocate funding, and develop formal assessment procedures
Administrative leadership, structure, and staffing	Internationalization committees, full-time administrator and staff overseeing internationalization activities and programs, professional development opportunities for staff across campus
Curriculum, co-curriculum, and learning outcomes	General education and language requirements, co-curricular activities and programs, specified student learning outcomes
Faculty policies and practices	Hiring guidelines, tenure and promotion policies, and faculty development programming
Student mobility	Education abroad programs, international student recruitment and support
Collaboration and partnerships	Institutional partnerships, joint degree programs, and branch campuses

The CIGE periodically assesses the state of internationalization through a national survey, Mapping Internationalization on U.S. Campuses. The mapping survey is first sent to provosts, then senior international officers and institutional research directors; for nonresponding institutions, presidents of the institutions are invited to participate. The most recent mapping study, in 2016, gathered survey responses from 1,164 accredited, degree-granting colleges and universities, out of 2,945 invited to participate (a 39.5% response rate).

The 2016 mapping survey found that more institutions had articulated an institutional commitment to internationalization than in the previous mapping study in 2011 (Helms et al., 2017). A higher percentage of baccalaureate institutions in 2016 compared with 2011 reported that international or global education is specifically referred to in their mission statement (61% versus 42%) and is one of the top five priorities in their current strategic plan (56% versus 48%).

Table 12 shows that among baccalaureate institutions, internationalization efforts are typically focused on external elements, including student mobility and international partnerships, while comparatively less attention is devoted to internationalizing the curriculum or faculty professional development.

Summarizing the findings of the 2016 mapping study, Brajkovic and Helms (2018) conclude that,

When it comes to faculty policies and support, progress over time has been markedly slower than in many other areas, and recognition of faculty contributions to internationalization is a concern going forward. . . . As the primary drivers of teaching and research, faculty are the lynchpins of student learning; in order for students to achieve global learning goals, faculty must be globally competent themselves, able to convey their international experience and expertise in the classroom, well prepared to engage effectively with international students, and actively committed to the internation-

Table 12. Mapping Internationalization Survey Responses From Baccalaureate Institutions: The Highest Priority Internationalization Activities, 2012–2013 to 2014–2015

Internationalization Activity	Respondents Including This Activity Among the Top Three Internationalization Activities
Recruiting international students	63%
Increasing study abroad for U.S. students	63%
Partnerships with institutions/organizations abroad	45%
Internationalizing the curriculum/co-curriculum	43%
Faculty development	22%

Note: Adapted from *Mapping internationalization on U.S. campuses: 2017 edition*, by R. M. Helms, L. Brajkovic, & B. Struthers, 2017, Washington, DC: American Council on Education.

alization endeavor. . . . Attention to these areas is critical in order for internationalization to fully take hold throughout colleges and universities, rather than remaining a peripheral activity. (pp. 11–12)

Given that nearly half of baccalaureate institutions report that they rarely or never give preference to hiring faculty with international background, experience, or interests in fields that are not explicitly international/global (Helms et al., 2017), many institutions need to provide additional resources to help faculty develop global networks and acquire relevant knowledge and skills to lead off-campus study programs. The next section summarizes the most common forms of support that institutions provide to enable faculty to contribute to these strategic goals.

INSTITUTIONAL SUPPORT FOR FACULTY DEVELOPMENT: FUNDS AND ACTIVITIES FOR INTERNATIONALIZATION

Broadly considered, institutional support for faculty development typically consists of professional development funds, awards of time, and access to educational enrichment activities (Baker et al., 2017). All three categories of support are evident in Tables 13 and 14, which are based on baccalaureate institutions' responses to the 2016 mapping survey (Helms et al., 2017). Table 13 shows that the majority of institutions reported that faculty received monetary support to lead students on study abroad programs, travel to international meetings and conferences, and study or conduct research abroad. Only slightly more than 40% of institutions, however, reported providing funds to faculty to internationalize courses or programs. Table 14 shows that even fewer institutions (27%) reported offering faculty workshops on internationalizing the curriculum; other faculty workshop topics offered by a small number of institutions included foreign language skills, using technology, and assessing global learning. Only 9% of institutions reported that faculty were recognized through awards for international activity.

Table 13. Mapping Internationalization Survey Responses From Baccalaureate Institutions: Percentage of Respondents Including Specific Funding for Faculty Activities in the Last Year, 2011 and 2016

Activities	2011	2016
Leading students on study abroad programs	75%	75%
Travel to meetings or conferences abroad	64%	75%
Studying or conducting research abroad	50%	58%
Internationalization of courses or programs	35%	42%
Hosting visiting international faculty	42%	39%
Faculty development seminars abroad	19%	33%
Teaching at institutions abroad	27%	29%

Note: Adapted from *Mapping internationalization on U.S. campuses: 2017 edition*, by R. M. Helms, L. Brajkovic, & B. Struthers, 2017, Washington, DC: American Council on Education.

Table 14. Mapping Internationalization Survey Responses From Baccalaureate Institutions: Percentage of Respondents Offering Opportunities to Faculty in the Last Three Years, 2011 and 2016

Opportunities	2011	2016
Workshops on internationalizing the curriculum	30%	27%
Workshops that include a focus on how to use technology to enhance the international dimension of their courses	14%	14%
Workshops on global learning assessments	14%	12%
Workshops on teaching and integrating international students	n/a	28%
Opportunities to improve their foreign language skills	15%	16%
Recognition awards specifically for international activity	8%	9%

Note: Adapted from *Mapping internationalization on U.S. campuses: 2017 edition,* by R. M. Helms, L. Brajkovic, & B. Struthers, 2017, Washington, DC: American Council on Education.

While the mapping study is informative about the funding and programming that institutions reported offering, it does not reveal how many faculty overall and at different career-stages received funding, how much they received, or what the eligible expenditures were. Just as importantly, given the focus of this chapter, the mapping survey results do not shed light on faculty perceptions of that support—the extent to which faculty felt that it advanced their global learning goals and contributed to their long-term career success and personal well-being.

The study of Great Lakes Colleges Association institutions described earlier, by contrast, asked faculty directly about their perception of institutional supports for professional development. The researchers found that,

> To best engage in their work and have sustainable and rewarding careers, they need financial resources; supports that are a good use

of their time and meet their needs; recognition and acknowledgment of their work; and opportunities to connect with colleagues. (Baker et al., 2017, p. 185)

The researchers learned, for example, that many faculty development programs take place through on-campus workshops, but Great Lakes Colleges Association faculty reported that they valued other kinds of experiences even more, specifically, peer discussions and off-campus professional development. Faculty in this study explained that exchanging ideas with colleagues in off-campus settings was particularly valuable, given that they have few colleagues with the same disciplinary or interdisciplinary interests and expertise on their small liberal arts college campuses.

The Great Lakes Colleges Association researchers concluded that

administrators and faculty developers . . . might take away a seemingly simple but powerful lesson. Engage in frequent conversations with faculty members. Ask them what they need and want and be transparent in working to provide it. If finances or some other obstacle prevent you from acting on what you learn from those conversations, then consider offering a short and long-term plan of how and when you will be able to provide the needed support. . . . The only behavior worse than not asking your employees for feedback is to ask for it and [do] nothing with it. . . . Faculty members are more likely to be engaged and empowered to participate in faculty development when they have had an active role in designing it. Such an environment creates buy-in, respect, and trust. (Baker et al., 2017, pp. 194–195)

The next section considers the implications of these findings for supporting faculty who lead off-campus programs and offers recommendations, drawn from studies of faculty perspectives on internationalization and global learning, for investing resources to both enhance the immediate effectiveness of program leaders and contribute to their long-term job satisfaction and career success. It also highlights responses to the Faculty as Global Learners survey that more than 200 liberal arts college faculty leaders of off-campus study programs gave to two survey prompts: "Describe one thing your current institution has done to make the biggest (positive or negative) impact on your ability to lead Study Away/ Study Abroad programs" and "Describe one thing your current institution could do to enhance your ability to lead Study Away/ Study Abroad programs."

SUPPORTING THE IMMEDIATE EFFECTIVENESS OF OFF-CAMPUS STUDY FACULTY LEADERS

Faculty perceive both opportunities and obstacles when they consider their institution's strategic goals for internationalization and global learning. They consider the availability of off-campus study offices and funding as well as factors such as their own career stage, disciplinary context, expectations for scholarship or creative work, teaching and travel experience, and personal and cultural roles and identities (Bikos, Chism, Forman, & King, 2013; Dewey & Duff, 2009; Moseley, 2009; Niehaus et al., 2018). Table 15 summarizes recommendations to support the immediate effectiveness of off-campus study faculty leaders.

Recommendation 1: Establish and Provide Resources for an Off-Campus Study Office

The 2016 mapping study found that 61% of baccalaureate institutions had a single office on campus leading internationalization activities and programs, and 56% had a full-time administrator overseeing or coordinating multiple internationalization activities or programs. The majority of internationalization administrators (62%) report to their institution's chief academic officer.

Table 15. Recommendations to Support Faculty Leaders, Before, During, and After Off-Campus Study Programs

Administrative leadership, structure, and staffing	Establish and provide resources for an off-campus study office
Program development	Provide faculty resources for program development and scouting trips
Pre-departure	Assist faculty leaders with recruitment and applications, selection of students, orientations, logistical assistance, and resources for intercultural learning and off-campus study pedagogy
During the program	Provide on-call assistance, a co-leader or program assistant, and implement family-friendly policies
Post-program	Assist faculty with record-keeping, program evaluation, and reentry activities and resources

At a minimum, professional staff in off-campus study offices can assist faculty leaders of off-campus study programs with budget development, travel logistics, publicity, and student applications.

Directors and professional staff in off-campus study offices can also elevate the quality of an institution's off-campus programs (Hulstrand, 2013, 2015). Staff who are knowledgeable about *The Standards of Good Practice for Education Abroad* (The Forum on Education Abroad, 2015), for example, and U.S. State Department travel advisories can work with provosts and academic deans to put in place policies regarding student health and safety, crisis and risk management, and U.S. federal mandates. Well-informed directors and professional staff can also guide and support faculty off-campus study leaders as they make plans and decisions and help them understand and navigate changing protocols.

Although faculty are responsible for the academic content and rigor of off-campus study programs, international education professionals can help faculty create well-organized programs, contribute to pre-departure orientation activities, and assist with reentry and post-program reflection. Professional staff at liberal arts institutions with highly regarded off-campus study programs regard their role as "nurturing faculty" and share responsibility with them for "developing, nurturing, and maintaining academically sound programs . . . and ensuring that they are recognized" (Hulstrand, 2015, p. 58). A clear communication plan is essential, however, since faculty may not be aware of the variety of ways in which off-campus study offices can support program development activities and enhance the skills and knowledge of off-campus study faculty program leaders.

Recommendation 2: Provide Faculty Resources for Program Development

Faculty development programming at liberal arts colleges is often governed by elected faculty committees, enabling academic administrators to collaborate with faculty to implement policies and provide funds for professional development activities related to off-campus study. Faculty who are developing new off-campus programs need institutional support to make professional contacts and select host institutions, partners, and locations for those programs. At some institutions, faculty receive a stipend for participating in an on-campus workshop and then qualify for travel funds for a scouting trip to implement the new off-campus program. Faculty can use these funds to travel to a proposed destination to gather information and meet with potential hosts and partners to discuss guest lecturers, excursion sites, classroom space, housing, and local transportation. Ideally, scouting trips should take place one to two years in advance of a new off-campus program (Abrams, 2016). Even when an existing off-campus program has been offered multiple times over many years, using the same sites, hosts, and other partners, travel grants play an important role in orienting and preparing faculty who will be leading that program for the first time.

Scouting trips and program development support may be particularly important in disciplines that have limited experience offering off-campus options, since faculty teaching in those fields may not have had opportunities to incorporate off-campus study into their own undergraduate education (Bikos et al., 2013; Green & Shoenberg, 2006; Gross, Abrams, & Enns, 2016; Lutsky, 2016; Niehaus et al., 2018). This point was made in the Faculty as Global Learners survey by a faculty leader who wrote, "Even though I and others from disciplines [are] not associated traditionally with study abroad, [the off-campus study staff] have repeatedly encouraged and supported persons such as myself to do so and provide salary and other support." (Gillespie et al., 2017).

Studies of Gen X faculty members described earlier in this chapter found that they "are likely to enjoy collaboration and many have extensive networks of colleagues around the world, something technology has enabled" (Trower, 2010, p. 29). Although many younger cohorts of faculty have existing global connections and interests, providing program development funding that enables them to build on this foundation is an important long-term investment. "Fostering a global focus among faculty in the early stages of their careers sets the stage for continued interest and activity in the international realm, and helps institutions build a globally engaged professoriate from the ground up" (Helms, 2015, p. 5).

The impact of investing in a single faculty member's efforts may extend well beyond that individual. In the Faculty as Global Learners survey (Gillespie et al., 2017), one off-campus study faculty leader noted that,

> Opportunities to develop courses (funding and time off) . . . made it possible for someone before me to develop the course that I am teaching. The fact that the university is truly prioritizing and privileging study abroad programs makes it so that it is an expectation that our department has this course and that someone is always teaching it.

Another reported that, "My department supported me in developing a new Interim abroad in a country where I had numerous institutional contacts so that the program could be taught in the future by many colleagues in the department."

Recommendation 3: Provide Pre-departure Support

Whether an off-campus program is new or well-established, pre-departure support enhances the experience for faculty leaders as well as students. In addition to logistical and clerical support, a key factor in off-campus study program success is educating leaders about strategies and activities to maximize students' global learning and personal growth.

Recruitment and applications. Provide staff time to assist faculty with publicizing off-campus programs by organizing events such as off-campus open houses. One satisfied off-campus study faculty leader observed that

> the institution does an excellent job of promoting study abroad programs which draw interested students to the college as well as promoting students taking multiple study abroad trips. Having students who have explored multiple cultures helps to create a diverse enrollment and makes for a richer travel experience.

Professional staff in off-campus study offices can also help faculty leaders develop program-specific application questions. An online system makes it easy for students to submit applications and for faculty and staff to review those files.

Selection of students. At some institutions, a campus committee reviews all applications and matches students to specific programs according to predetermined criteria such as class year, gender, major, and grade point average. Where it is possible for faculty leaders to be involved in those decisions, they value the opportunity:

> I appreciate that the policy at my college allows faculty leaders of off-campus programs with more applicants than spots available

to select students for those programs and to shape the application process by creating our own short-essay questions and interview prompts. Although there are general institutional guidelines and suggestions . . . the flexibility that I have enables me to identify students with relevant academic preparation and to create as diverse a group of students as possible.

Regardless of the selection process, it is essential to facilitate partnerships between faculty off-campus study leaders, off-campus study offices, and offices that work with students in other capacities, such as Student/Residence Life, the Wellness/Counseling Center, and Academic Support. Professional staff and administrators in these offices are knowledgeable about a range of student needs and can advise faculty leaders about concerns or accommodations that might be relevant for specific off-campus programs.

Orientations. It is helpful if personnel from the off-campus study office take the lead in organizing group orientations and online resources about intercultural learning and topics of general interest, such as risk management and physical and mental health. They can also distribute a self-report form to gather information about students' medical issues, allergies, or other concerns that the faculty member should be aware of. Faculty leaders can then focus on developing orientation activities and resources that provide students with destination- and course-specific information.

Assistance with budgets and logistics. Faculty can be involved in the development of program budgets and consulted about travel and housing options, but professional staff should usually have primary responsibility for negotiating and finalizing contracts, ticketing, and other logistics. Providing faculty leaders with a toolkit that includes a customized Excel spreadsheet template can help them keep track of expenditures and remaining funds during the program. For off-campus programs that require visas, professional staff can help faculty and students complete the necessary forms and track the status of those applications. Off-campus study offices can also assist faculty by providing scanned copies of passports and visas for all participants and by archiving electronic copies on campus.

Resources for intercultural learning and off-campus study pedagogy. Whereas disciplinary content is unequivocally the faculty leader's area of expertise, an off-campus study toolkit and guidance from knowledgeable professional staff can help faculty incorporate opportunities for reflection and effective site-based learning assignments that promote intercultural competence (Vande Berg et al., 2012). Chapter 3 provides more detail about evidence-based activities and approaches that can be delivered through "brown bag" lunches, on-campus workshops, and off-campus retreats (COACHE, 2014c).

Other best practices include interdisciplinary faculty learning communities (also known as mentoring communities and communities of practice), which "provide faculty the opportunity for sustained reflection on a substantial and timely teaching question" (COACHE, 2014c, p. 4; Felten et al., 2013; Hara, 2009; Seaman, 2008; Wenger, McDermott, & Snyder, 2002). In communities of practice, faculty from different disciplines can learn together, and more experienced faculty off-campus study leaders can mentor their less experienced colleagues (Calahan, 2018; Hall et al., 2018). One off-campus study faculty leader's involvement progressed from participating in to leading communities of practice that

> aimed to support the development of research projects focused on mentoring UR [undergraduate research] in global contexts over the course of an academic year via monthly meetings during which members presented on in-progress projects and discussed selected articles that the group read in advance. . . . Participants with varied levels of experience shared successful research strategies and approaches; brainstormed about research and logistical challenges; discussed project design, measures, and assessment; and offered insights, advice, and ideas to one another. (Allocco & Fredsell, 2018, p. 2)

Recommendation 4:
Provide Support During the Program

While pre-program support is integral to launching new programs and preparing faculty to lead a program for the first time, colleges must continue to provide support during the program.

On-call assistance. Whether an off-campus study program takes place in an international setting or within the United States, faculty leaders need to be supported 24/7 until the conclusion of the program. Knowing that professional staff and administrators at their institution will be available to answer questions and manage unforeseen events helps alleviate the stress that faculty leaders experience if they must deal with missed flights, health emergencies, natural disasters, or individual student crises. In addition to communicating with airlines, embassies, and health care providers on behalf of the faculty leader, staff in off-campus study offices can also support faculty by informing students' families about the situation and plans for addressing the group's needs.

Co-leader or program assistant. Faculty leaders whose institutions allow them to be accompanied by a co-leader, sometimes the leader's spouse/partner, are more likely to feel that their college understands and supports them. This view is reflected in the survey response of a faculty leader who wrote that their institution

> provides funds to support a co-leader for [a] semester-length program. Without such an opportunity, I would never be able to do long programs, as my family is a high priority and my spouse, while not a college educator by training, significantly contributed to the educational and personal development of every person on the program.

Family-friendly policies. Allowing faculty leaders' family members to accompany them is another important form of support and may be a particularly salient issue for Gen X faculty (Trower, 2010).

The absence of this support leads some faculty to choose not to participate in off-campus study programs.

> My institution has a policy that for . . . 3-week programs, faculty can bring a spouse (at their own expense), but cannot bring children. Since I have two young children, this policy impacts my ability to lead a program. I did it once, but I don't see myself doing it again, because of the difficulty/cost of childcare and the simple fact of being away from them for so long.

Recommendation 5: Post-Program Support

Record-keeping and program evaluation. Upon returning, faculty leaders of off-campus study are responsible for reviewing students' coursework during the program, reading final exams and essays, and assigning a final grade. Whether they are simultaneously preparing to teach courses on campus in just a few days or weeks, faculty leaders also need post-program time to address their own emotional and physical needs and perhaps the needs of family members. Professional staff in off-campus study offices can lighten faculty leaders' workload by providing them with templates that they can use to prepare written reports about the budget and program activities. It is also helpful if off-campus study offices, rather than faculty leaders, take responsibility for gathering information and feedback from students about the quality of accommodations and the academic program overall.

Facilitating reentry. The research literature makes clear the value of providing training, time, and resources to enable faculty leaders of off-campus study to engage students in meaningful reflection about their off-campus experience. Chapter 3 addresses strategies that faculty leaders can use, post-program, to help students maximize their learning and minimize the discomfort or disorientation of reentry (Vande Berg et al., 2012).

SUPPORTING THE LONG-TERM JOB SATISFACTION AND CAREER SUCCESS OF FACULTY LEADERS OF OFF-CAMPUS STUDY

In addition to simply establishing and staffing offices for internationalization and global learning and supporting off-campus study leaders in the short term, provosts and academic deans can synergistically advance their institution's goals by supporting the long-term job satisfaction and career success of faculty leaders of off-campus study and the professional staff who work with them, as shown in Table 16.

Table 16. Recommendations to Support Long-Term Job Satisfaction and Career Success of Faculty Program Leaders

Administrative leadership, structure, and staffing	Support the professional development and continuing education of off-campus study staff through conferences, workshops, and international seminars
Program development	Support the professional development and continuing education of off-campus study faculty leaders through conferences, workshops, international seminars, and funding for international summer research projects
Pre-departure	Recognize faculty work through stipends, course releases, and reduced expectations for committee service
During the program	Recognize faculty work through stipends, program assistants or co-leaders, and family-friendly policies
Post-program	Publicly celebrate faculty work and recognize its value through awards, tenure and promotion criteria, support for SoTL, and reduced expectations for committee service

Recommendation 6: Support the Professional Development and Continuing Education of Off-Campus Study Staff

Providing funds for international education staff to participate regularly in a range of professional development programs should be part of liberal arts colleges' strategies for supporting individual faculty leaders of off-campus study programs. Opportunities are available each year through conferences and workshops, such as those organized by the Forum on Education Abroad, the Association of International Education Administrators, or NAFSA: Association of International Educators. The value of this investment is reflected in this comment from a faculty leader:

> The study abroad office at [my liberal arts institution] is amazing! They handled all the travel insurance requirements, made sure we, as faculty, were prepared to address group dynamics, nightly reflections, writing assignments, and how to get the most from cultural visits. They also had a 4-hour training session covering emergencies, transportation, behavioral expectations, etc. . . . This was my first time leading a class abroad; because of the efforts of our study abroad office, I felt very prepared.

Another way to support the continuing education and development of professional staff is through one- to two-week international seminars. Fulbright's International Education Administrators (IEA) seminars "help U.S. international education professionals and senior higher education officials create empowering connections with the societal, cultural and higher education systems of other countries" and enhance their "ability to serve and encourage international students and prospective study-abroad students" (Council for International Exchange of Scholars, n.d.). Seminar participants visit a cross-section of universities and colleges; meet with faculty and administrators, government officials, and education experts; and tour significant historical and cultural sites. Other organizations, such as the Council on International Educational Exchange (CIEE) and the Institute for the International Education of Students (IES Abroad), offer similar international opportunities.

Recommendation 7: Support the Professional Development and Continuing Education of Faculty Leaders of Off-Campus Study Programs

Just as staff members benefit from regular forms of professional development, faculty members also benefit from supplemental workshops to expand their knowledge and skills.

Conferences of disciplinary associations. Provide faculty with travel funds to attend national and international conferences of their disciplinary associations and encourage them to seek out international scholars in their field. In addition to offering possibilities for future off-campus study programs, networking with international colleagues affords opportunities for faculty to incorporate international scholarship and global perspectives in their on-campus courses and may lead to collaborative research or artistic projects (Green & Shoenberg, 2006; Lutsky, 2016).

Conferences about international education and global learning. Organizations such as the Association of American Colleges & Universities, the American Council on Education, the Forum on Education Abroad, and NAFSA: Association of International Educators hold annual conferences and workshops in the United States that attract international participants and presenters as well as representatives of study abroad vendors. As noted earlier, directors of off-campus study offices and their staff also benefit from networking and enhancing their knowledge about guidelines and standards for best practice in the dynamic field of international education. The value of enabling both faculty and staff to attend these conferences can be multiplied back on campus, when they collaborate to apply what they have learned about helping students maximize their off-campus study experience (The Forum on Education Abroad, 2018).

Travel funds can also be used to enable faculty to participate in international study/travel opportunities organized by institutional partners. CIEE (2018), for example, offers 10- or 11-day international faculty development seminars, in which faculty attend lectures by faculty and experts and engage in discussions with international colleagues on topics of broad global interest. IES Abroad (n.d.) offers faculty development seminars that "are designed to bring together U.S. faculty, international faculty, and local experts for an intellectual exchange of ideas."

Fulbright programs for faculty. Provide grant-writing assistance to help faculty develop proposals for one of several types of Fulbright U.S. Scholar Programs (Lutsky, 2016). The Core Fulbright U.S. Scholar Program makes awards to distinguished scholars as well as early- and mid-career faculty for three- to 12-month programs focused on teaching, research, or both teaching and research in one of 125 countries. Faculty who are unable to spend extended periods of time abroad can engage in multiple short-term stays in a host country over a period of one to two years through the Fulbright Flex Award, while the Fulbright Global Scholar Award supports faculty who propose research or combined teaching/research activity in two to three countries within a single academic year or over two consecutive years (Fulbright Scholar Program, 2018).

Recognize off-campus study faculty leaders. The COACHE survey described earlier found that "while many tenured faculty members feel valued by undergraduate and graduate students . . . they do not receive much recognition from other faculty and upper-level administrators" (COACHE, 2014a, p. 1). Tenured faculty (especially at smaller institutions)

> felt that extramural service that increases the reputation of their colleges . . . is not recognized and goes unrewarded . . . [and] yields

neither recognition from senior colleagues nor appreciation from others at their home institutions. This gap between expectations and appreciation discouraged many faculty from serving their institutions in this way. (p. 1)

Given that only 9% of baccalaureate institutions in the 2016 mapping survey reported offering recognition awards specifically for faculty members' international activity (Helms et al., 2017), one synergistic, vastly underutilized way for provosts and academic deans to advance strategic goals for internationalization and global learning is to get to know off-campus study leaders at their institution and find ways to "take note of what faculty are doing and celebrate that work . . . at some point every year; such occasions do not have to be costly to be meaningful" (COACHE, 2014a, p. 2). Directors of off-campus study offices can facilitate this recognition by providing detailed reports and letters of support that help provosts and academic deans understand off-campus study faculty leaders' contributions.

Other forms of recognition for faculty include offering teaching credit or a stipend or reducing expectations for committee work during the year a faculty member is leading an off-campus program. Faculty who receive funding or release time feel supported, whereas faculty who receive neither form of compensation often perceive these activities as an insufficiently acknowledged overload. Some off-campus study faculty leaders in the Faculty as Global Learners survey noted that "an outmoded notion of chaperoning still dominates the thinking of administrators and beginning faculty" (Gillespie et al., 2017).

Support faculty research and scholarship. Directors of off-campus study programs and teaching-and-learning centers can help off-campus study faculty leaders identify relevant academic conferences and journals to disseminate their program experiences through the scholarship of teaching and learning (SoTL). One Faculty Voices contributor to this book, William Moseley, incorporated off-campus study program leadership into his professional activities as a pre-tenure assistant professor and reflected on his experience of study abroad as a "win-win opportunity" in a 2009 article in *Frontiers: The Interdisciplinary Journal of Study Abroad*. He called on study abroad administrators and faculty deans

> to consider the potential synergies that exist for faculty and study abroad. In the face of little to no action, most junior faculty will likely continue to steer clear of study abroad. However, administrative recognition of the particular circumstances faced by junior faculty will help bring these faculty to study abroad. Furthermore, deans and study abroad administrators should consider adopting policies and programs that would encourage junior faculty involvement. (p. 237)

These policies, discussed in more detail in chapter 5, include

> providing small amounts of funding for faculty and student research done within the context of study abroad programs; consideration of involvement with study abroad programs as a positive contribution when reviewing a fa[c]ulty member's tenure portfolio; support of publications based on faculty-student collaborative research which evolves out of study abroad programming; and greater recognition that junior faculty who become involved with study abroad programs may have different needs than more senior faculty (such as time for research and writing, responsibilities related to young children, etc.). (Moseley, 2009, p. 237)

The powerful long-term impact of supporting early-career faculty involvement in off-campus study is evident in reflections from another liberal arts faculty leader, who wrote that senior faculty

> began mentoring me into related practices by the end of my first year.... While the benefits of UR for students are well-established

and attested, and I recognized mentoring excellence as beneficial for and indeed essential to my development as a teacher, I did not anticipate the impact that the mentoring relationship I developed with one student . . . would ultimately have on my own research and scholarship. . . . [The student's] participation in my ethnography in South India catalyzed new questions, generated fresh insights, and shaped my thinking about collaboration and reciprocity in fieldwork. (Allocco & Fredsell, 2018, p. 1)

It is clear that the institution's practices and policies supported the career goals of this off-campus study leader, now a tenured faculty member, contributed to her feelings of job satisfaction, and advanced strategic goals for internationalization and high-impact global learning:

lunchtime programs and other informal discussions about mentoring with more experienced faculty members . . . deepened my own mentoring skills and helped me cultivate several valuable new habits and strategies. These experiences, coupled with the opportunity to co-lead two communities of practice on mentoring UR in global contexts, . . . challenged me to reflect on and interrogate my mentoring practices, to be even more intentional in framing mentoring relationships, and to focus on aligning my mentoring process with desired research outcomes. . . . In addition, my role as a co-leader . . . has encouraged me to extend my skillset to blend instrumental guidance with psychosocial support in order to effectively mentor—and encourage peer mentoring in—a multidisciplinary research community. (Allocco & Fredsell, 2018, p. 2)

CONCLUSION

The concept of "horizontal alignment"—clear, consistent, and mutually reinforcing policies between faculty work and faculty lives (Baker et al., 2017)—offers a useful strategy for synergistically supporting faculty leaders of off-campus study programs. As outlined in this chapter, there are many opportunities for provosts and academic deans, working with individuals and committees charged with guiding faculty development programming, to utilize the full range of institutional supports. Funds for professional travel, summer work, and start-up activities and materials—as well as sabbatical leaves, communities for mentoring and co-learning, and workshops—can all be used intentionally to meet institutional goals for global learning and priorities for long-term faculty success.

REFERENCES

Abrams, K. (2016). Teaching cross-cultural psychopathology in Prague. In D. Gross, K. Abrams, & C. Z. Enns (Eds.), *Internationalizing the undergraduate psychology curriculum: Practical lessons learned at home and abroad* (pp. 37–55). Washington, DC: American Psychological Association.

Allocco, A., & Fredsell, A. (2018). Mentoring in global contexts: Embodying feminist ethnography in South India. *Perspectives on Undergraduate Research and Mentoring, 7*(1). Retrieved from https://blogs.elon.edu/purm/2018/10/25/mentoring-in-global-contexts-embodying-feminist-ethnography-in-south-india-purm-7-1/

American Council on Education. (n.d.-a). *Comprehensive internationalization.* Washington, DC: American Council on Education. Retrieved from https://www.acenet.edu/Research-Insights/Pages/Internationalization/Comprehensive-Internationalization.aspx

American Council on Education. (n.d.-b). *Internationalization toolkit.* Retrieved from https://www.acenet.edu/research-insights/Pages/Internationalization/Internationalization-Toolkit.aspx

Anderson, C. L., Lorenz, K., & White, M. (2016). Instructor influence on student intercultural gains and learning during instructor-led, short-term study abroad. *Frontiers: The Interdisciplinary Journal of Study Abroad, 28,* 1–23.

Association of American Colleges & Universities. (n.d.). *Shared futures: Global learning and social responsibility.* Retrieved from https://www.aacu.org/shared-futures

Association of American Colleges & Universities. (2018). *Fulfilling the American* dream: Liberal education and the future of work. Retrieved from https://www.aacu.org/research/2018-future-of-work

Austin, A. E. (2010). Supporting faculty members across their careers. In K. J. Gillespie & D. L. Robertson (Eds.), *A guide to faculty development* (pp. 363–378). San Francisco, CA: Jossey-Bass.

Baker, V. L., Lunsford, L. G., & Pifer, M. J. (2017). *Developing faculty in liberal arts colleges: Aligning individual needs and organizational goals.* New Brunswick, NJ: Rutgers University Press.

Bennett, D. C., Cornwell, G. H., Al-Lail, H. J., & Schenck, C. (2012). An education for the twenty-first century: Stewardship of the global commons. *Liberal Education, 98*(4). Retrieved from https://www.aacu.org/publications-research/periodicals/education-twenty-first-century-stewardship-global-commons

Berg, M., & Seeber, B. K. (2016). *The slow professor: Challenging the culture of speed in the academy.* Toronto, Canada: University of Toronto Press.

Bikos, L. H., Chism, N. F. D., Forman, R. L., & King, D. R. (2013). Internationalizing the U.S. undergraduate psychology curriculum: A qualitative investigation of faculty perspectives. *International Perspectives in Psychology: Research, Practice, Consultation, 2*(2), 116–131.

Bozeman, B., & Gaughan, M. (2011). Job satisfaction among university faculty: Individual, work, and institutional determinants. *The Journal of Higher Education, 82*(2), 154–186.

Brajkovic, L., & Helms, R. M. (2018). Mapping internationalization on US campuses. *International Higher Education, 92,* 11–12.

Calahan, C. (2018). A six-year journey of global learning faculty and student development. *Peer Review, 20*(1). Retrieved from https://www.aacu.org/peerreview/2018/Winter/Calahan

Campbell, C. M., & O'Meara, K. (2014). Faculty agency: Departmental contexts that matter in faculty careers. *Research in Higher Education, 55,* 49–74.

Chieffo, L., & Griffiths, L. (2009). Here to stay: Increasing acceptance of short-term study abroad programs. In R. Lewin (Ed.), *The handbook of practice and research in study abroad: Higher education and the quest for global citizenship* (pp. 365–380). New York, NY: Routledge.

The Chronicle of Higher Education. (2018). *Committed but concerned: How faculty view their work, their profession, and the leadership of colleges.* Washington, DC: The Chronicle of Higher Education.

Collaborative on Academic Careers in Higher Education. (n.d.). *Faculty job satisfaction survey.* Cambridge, MA: Harvard Graduate School of Education. Retrieved from https://coache.gse.harvard.edu/faculty-job-satisfaction-survey

Collaborative on Academic Careers in Higher Education. (2014a). *Benchmark best practices: Appreciation & recognition.* Cambridge, MA: Harvard Graduate School of Education. Retrieved from https://coache.gse.harvard.edu/research/researchers-and-practitioners/benchmark-best-practices

Collaborative on Academic Careers in Higher Education. (2014b). *Benchmark best practices: Mentoring.* Cambridge, MA: Harvard Graduate School of Education. Retrieved from https://coache.gse.harvard.edu/files/gse-coache/files/coache-mentoring.pdf

Collaborative on Academic Careers in Higher Education. (2014c). *Benchmark best practices: Nature of work: teaching.* Cambridge, MA: Harvard Graduate School of Education. Retrieved from https://coache.gse.harvard.edu/files/gse-coache/files/coache-nature-of-teaching.pdf

Council for International Exchange of Scholars. (n.d.). *IEA seminars.* Retrieved from https://www.cies.org/program/fulbright-international-education-administrators-seminars

Council on International Educational Exchange (2018). *International faculty development seminars.* Retrieved from https://www.ciee.org/go-abroad/educators/international-faculty-development-seminars

Denson, N., Szelényi, K., & Bresonis, K. (2018). Correlates of work-life balance for faculty across racial/ethnic groups. *Research in Higher Education, 59,* 226–247.

Dewey, P., & Duff, S. (2009). Reason before passion: Faculty views on internationalization in higher education. *Higher Education, 58,* 491–504.

Doscher, S., & Landorf, H. (2018). Universal global learning, inclusive excellence, and higher education's greater purpose. *Peer Review, 20*(1), 4–7. Retrieved from https://www.aacu.org/peerreview/2018/Winter/FIU

Eagan, K., Stolzenberg, E. B., Berdan Lozano, J., Aragon, M. C., Suchard, M. R., & Hurtado, S. (2014). *Undergraduate teaching faculty: The 2013–2014 HERI Faculty Survey.* Los Angeles, CA: Higher Education Research Institute. Retrieved from https://www.heri.ucla.edu/monographs/HERI-FAC2014-monograph.pdf

Felten, P., Bauman, H.-D., L., Kheriaty, A., & Taylor, E. (2013). *Transformative conversations: A guide to mentoring communities among colleagues in higher education.* San Francisco, CA: Jossey-Bass.

Finkelstein, M., & Cummings, W. (2012). American faculty and their institutions: The global view. *Change: The Magazine of Higher Learning, 44*(3), 48–59.

The Forum on Education Abroad. (2015). *Standards of good practice for education abroad* (5th ed.). Carlisle, PA: The Forum on Education Abroad. Retrieved from https://forumea.org/wp-content/uploads/2014/08/Standards-2015.pdf

The Forum on Education Abroad. (2018). *State of the field 2017.* Carlisle, PA: The Forum on Education Abroad.

Fulbright Scholar Program. (2018). *Fulbright Scholar program.* Retrieved from https://www.cies.org/programs

Gillespie, J. G., Glasco, S., Gross, D., Jasinski, L., & Layne, P. (2017). *Faculty as global learners: The transformative impact of leading study away and study abroad program*. Paper presented at the Association for the Study of Higher Education, Houston, TX.

Goldman, C. A., & Salem, H. (2015). *Getting the most out of university strategic planning: Essential guidance for success and obstacles to avoid*. Retrieved from https://www.rand.org/pubs/perspectives/PE157.html

Green, M. F., & Shoenberg, R. (2006). *Where faculty live: Internationalizing the disciplines*. Washington, DC: American Council on Education.

Gross, D., Abrams, K., & Enns, C. Z. (Eds.). (2016). *Internationalizing the undergraduate psychology curriculum: Practical lessons learned at home and abroad*. Washington, DC: American Psychological Association.

Hall, E. E., Walkington, H., Vandermaas-Peeler, M., Shanahan, J. O., Gudiksen, R. K., & Zimmer, M. M. (2018). Enhancing short-term undergraduate research experiences in study abroad: Curriculum design and mentor development. *Perspectives on Undergraduate Research and Mentoring, 7*(1). Retrieved from https://blogs.elon.edu/purm/2018/10/22/enhancing-short-term-undergraduate-research-experiences-in-study-abroad-curriculum-design-and-mentor-development-purm-7-1/

Hara, N. (Ed.). (2009). *Communities of practice: Fostering peer-to-peer learning and informal knowledge sharing in the work place*. Information science and knowledge management (Vol. 13). Berlin: Springer-Verlag.

Helms, R. M. (2010). *New challenges, new priorities: The experience of Generation X faculty*. Collaborative on Academic Careers in Higher Education. Cambridge, MA: Harvard Graduate School of Education. Retrieved from http://coache.gse.harvard.edu/files/gse-coache/files/coache_genx-newchallengesnewpriorities_2010.pdf?m=1456518493

Helms, R. M. (2015). *Internationalizing the tenure code: Policies to promote a globally focused faculty*. Washington, DC: American Council on Education.

Helms, R. M., Brajkovic, L., & Struthers, B. (2017). *Mapping internationalization on U.S. campuses: 2017 edition*. Washington, DC: American Council on Education. Retrieved from https://www.acenet.edu/Documents/Mapping-Internationalization-2017.pdf

Hulstrand, J. (2013, September/October). Preparing faculty to teach abroad: Best practices and lessons learned. *International Educator, 40–43*.

Hulstrand, J. (2015, May/June). Best practices for short-term, faculty-led programs abroad. *International Educator, 58–64*.

IES Abroad. (n.d.). *Faculty development seminars*. Retrieved from https://www.iesabroad.org/advisors-faculty/professional-development/faculty-development-seminars

Institute of International Education. (n.d.). Fact sheets and infographics. Retrieved from https://www.iie.org/en/Research-and-Insights/Open-Doors/Fact-Sheets-and-Infographics

Lutsky, N. (2016). Beyond borders: Faculty development to enhance internationalization of the psychology curriculum. In D. Gross, K. Abrams, & C. Z. Enns (Eds.), *Internationalizing the undergraduate psychology curriculum: Practical lessons learned at home and abroad* (pp. 19–34). Washington, DC: American Psychological Association.

Mathews, K. R. (2014). *Perspectives on midcareer faculty and advice for supporting them.* Cambridge, MA: Collaborative on Academic Careers in Higher Education. Retrieved from http://coache.gse.harvard.edu/files/gse-coache/files/coache-perspectives-on.pdf?m=1447625224

Moseley, W. G. (2009). Making study abroad a win-win opportunity for pre-tenure faculty. *Frontiers: The Interdisciplinary Journal of Study Abroad, 18,* 231–240.

Niehaus, E., Reading, J., Nelson, M. J., Wegener, A., & Arthur, A. (2018). Faculty engagement in cultural mentoring as instructors of short-term study abroad courses. *Frontiers: The Interdisciplinary Journal of Study Abroad, 30*(2), 77–91.

O'Meara, K., & Stromquist, N. P. (2015). Faculty peer networks: Role and relevance in advancing agency and gender equity. *Gender and Education, 27*(3), 338–358.

Pifer, M. J. (2011). Intersectionality in context: A mixed-methods approach to researching the faculty experience. *New Directions for Institutional Research, 2011*(151), 27–44.

Plater, W. M. (2015). *Globalization and faculty work in the United States.* New York, NY: TIAA Institute. Retrieved from https://www.tiaainstitute.org/publication/globalization-and-faculty-work-united-states

Ponjuan, L., Conley, V. M., & Trower, C. (2011). Career stage differences in pre-tenure track faculty perceptions of professional and personal relationships with colleagues. *The Journal of Higher Education, 82*(3), 319–346.

Seaman, M. (2008). Birds of a feather? Communities of practice and knowledge communities. *Curriculum and Teaching Dialogue, 10*(1–2), 269–279.

Trower, C. A. (2008). Young faculty and their impact on academe. In D. E. Heller & M. B. D'Ambrosio (Eds.), *Generational shockwaves and the implications for higher education.* Northampton, MA: Edward Elgar.

Trower, C. A. (2009). Toward a greater understanding of the tenure track for minorities. *Change: The Magazine of Higher Learning, 41*(5), 38–45.

Trower, C. A. (2010). A new generation of faculty: Similar core values in a different world. *Peer Review, 12*(3), 27–30. Retrieved from https://www.aacu.org/publications-research/periodicals/new-generation-faculty-similar-core-values-different-world

Vande Berg, M., Paige, R. M., & Lou, K. H. (Eds.). (2012). *Student learning abroad: What our students are learning, what they're not, and what we can do about it.* Sterling, VA: Stylus Publishing.

Webber, K. L., & Rogers, S. M. (2018). Gender differences in faculty member job satisfaction: Equity forestalled? *Research in Higher Education, 59,* 1105–1132.

Wenger, E., McDermott, R. A., & Snyder, W. (2002). *Cultivating communities of practice: A guide to managing knowledge.* Boston, MA: Harvard Business Press.

Whitehead, D. M. (2017). Foreword: Global learning: Shifting from an option to a priority. In I. Nair & M. Henning, *Models of global learning* (pp. v–vi). Washington, DC: Association of American Colleges & Universities.

AN EDUCATIONAL RIOT IN BOTSWANA

Stephen Volz

I first realized the seriousness of the situation when I heard loud chanting coming from elsewhere in the classroom building. A group of protestors was moving from floor to floor, enforcing a boycott of classes by chasing out any students and faculty who

dared to remain. The students in my research seminar, Development in Botswana, had respected my intention to hold class that afternoon despite rumors of a student strike, but our resolve faded as the shouts of the protestors grew louder, and we quickly exited the building to continue our discussion outside in a shady spot elsewhere on campus.

I was serving as the faculty director of a semester-long study program based at the University of Botswana (UB) that was administered by the Associated Colleges of the Midwest (ACM). I had been involved with the program in various ways since its inception in 2006, and it had long been a dream of mine to be the director of such a program. As a scholar of African history whose interest in the continent has been propelled by personal experiences in Botswana and other African countries, I regard residence in Africa as essential to African studies. Students in my courses at Kenyon College who have spent time in Africa are consistently more engaged, motivated, and nuanced in their understanding of African affairs than other students, and I expected the same results from the students who were with me in Botswana.

Those expectations were challenged by the sudden need to reconcile my carefully designed curriculum with the realities of a campus in upheaval. When the protestors' demands were ignored by university administrators, some students resorted to violence, looting the school bookstore and cafeterias and then vandalizing some public art while marching toward parliament. The university responded by suspending classes and closing campus, and although international students were allowed to stay, those on the ACM program were shaken by the sight of riot police beating other students and the forced removal of their Botswana roommates. Having witnessed student protests at the university before, as well as more serious strife elsewhere, I expected a quick restoration of order, but my plans for the semester were now in disarray, compelling me to seek the assistance of colleagues in Botswana and to make some uncomfortably sudden decisions.

After ensuring the safety of the ACM students, I urgently consulted with the International Studies office at the university, the ACM office in Chicago, and other knowledgeable people to consider various options for continuing the program. Fortunately, the ACM students were already scheduled to do a four-day village home-stay just as the campus closed, removing them from a stressful situation (albeit while putting them in another one) and giving us an opportunity to gather information and set up contingency plans. When UB announced that the campus would re-open after three weeks, we were able to adapt accordingly by changing the timing of some of our excursions, arranging off-campus classrooms for the ACM-run classes, helping the students find food in the absence of a cafeteria, and altering the schedule of topics, assignments, and guest speakers in my classes. It was a very stressful time, but I felt pretty good about all the adjustments that we managed to make in only a few days, confirming the value of my connections with numerous people in Botswana and my knowledge of its culture and history.

Although the students were understandably quite anxious at first about the changes, they demonstrated an admirable resilience and willingness to put in the extra effort required to make things work. Once it was clear that their basic needs would continue to be met and that the program's various components would mostly be salvaged, they soon regarded the closure of the campus as a temporary inconvenience that was part of the challenge of studying in Africa. At the same time, after beginning the semester with several readings and discussions critiquing stereotypes of Africa as "uncivilized," it was good to see them wrestle with the question of what constitutes a "normal" campus and the frequent role of college students around the world as instigators of social change.

Only one student, however, chose to focus their research project on UB student political activism, and there still seemed to be less synthesis of their experiences and academic interests than I had hoped for. Most of them ultimately managed to incorporate some aspect of their internship positions or other activities in their studies, but interest and ability to do so varied significantly from one student to another. Some of that variation was the natural consequence of different backgrounds and personalities, but I also could not help feeling that the campus closure had disrupted more than enhanced the development of the skills, attitudes, and confidence needed for the students to engage effectively with Botswana and its people. In retrospect, I wish that I had altered my syllabus to include some study of civil disobedience and student activism. Most of the students were already committed to other research goals as part of their academic programs back in the United States, but we all undoubtedly could have learned more from the events at UB if we had included some discussion of relevant readings.

The UB student protests were certainly among the more memorable experiences of the semester, demonstrating the power dynamics of confrontation between young people and institutions in a democratic African country, but they were also rather intimidating and perplexing to the American students, provoking a certain amount of caution and withdrawal from campus life. The closure of the university also compelled me to modify the curriculum and accept limitations on my ability to manage connections between the academic and experiential dimensions of the program and to allow for different levels of immersion in Botswana society by the students. More generally, it also illustrated the strengths and weaknesses of reliance on a host institution for an off-campus study program, which could provide useful support and structure but also frustrate plans. Fortunately, ACM and I were able to utilize other connections and resources in Botswana during the closure of UB, demonstrating the value of flexibility and familiarity with the wider local community. Despite limits on how well we could incorporate them, those chanting protestors became an important part of the semester.

MENTAL HEALTH CRISES AND THE FALTERING STUDENT

Assessment and Response

Nancy K. Barry

It's a hectic emergency room in the middle of London on a Friday night. The waiting period to be seen by a member of staff is more than four hours. I am accompanying a student in the midst of a mental health crisis. The decision to come to urgent care has taken most of the evening. I have been in contact with the "home office" of the program, the student's mother, and a "911" dedicated help line for mental health emergencies that has made a recommendation that we seek medical care.

By the time we left the hospital, the sun was coming up. The student had requested that I not be part of the consultations, and with so many questions, I could only offer a bland gesture. I asked meekly, "It has been a long night. How are you feeling now?" When the student answered "Fine," I was bewildered, so I responded with another question: "Really?"

It's often assumed that liberal arts faculty members will form strong bonds with students—it's one of the hallmarks of teaching in residential colleges. Faculty at small colleges play an active role in mentorship, engagement with students, and an implicit concern for their welfare. A study abroad environment complicates this assumption, particularly one in which students from different campuses are enrolled under the supervision of one faculty member who may or may not know the individual students and thus has a more tenuous and fragile sense of any particular student's well-being. When mental health issues emerge, directors must diagnose problems quickly. How can we best help faculty leaders to be "on the lookout" for issues of mental health and stability among students while studying abroad?

To be a faculty leader in a global city is to take on the role of teacher, docent, travel agent, and supervising adult. These differing roles shift by the minute, but day-to-day classroom teaching is the best indicator of when a student is veering off course. Through a scheduling quirk, there was one student whom I didn't cross paths with in the classroom, so she was, from the start, outside the scope of my consistent assessment. This was a crucial error in the organizational web and a strong argument for faculty leaders to be an active instructor to all students they supervise. Faculty leaders need consistent access to students about content that is related to the scene of global learning. Of course, they also need to afford students sufficient freedom to feel they are capable of negotiating the environment on their own. But the best indicator of a struggling student is a student who cannot cope with the behaviors that the student should be prepared to do: reading texts, writing papers, participating in class discussions. The student's performance in an academic context is the very best measure of how well he or she is coping mentally with the stress of a new environment.

Unfortunately, by the time we do sense something is amiss regarding a student's mental health, it may be too late to make any meaningful intervention, if by meaningful intervention we mean being able to adjust or reconfigure the material conditions of the student's life in the global environment.

Given these complexities, here are a few suggestions:

1. Before embarking on the trip, have at the ready the names of one or two vetted mental health professionals in the places where traveling.

2. When the slightest warning sign appears, respond more directly than we are inclined to when discussing mental health. At the very least, of course, talk with the student and try to find the cause of the anxiety or disruption. Pay close attention in these meetings to what is said and not said. Make a concrete plan with the student and make clear the scope and limits of what you can do as the faculty leader.

3. Treat FERPA and HIPAA guidelines with seriousness but also with a grain of salt, measured against what you need to understand to make the situation more manageable. Ask the student if there is a faculty member at his/her home institution to consult. Ask the sponsoring organization if they have enlisted the help of a mental health professional that you can speak with, to be sure that you are handling the situation with the help of professional expertise.

4. When the situation requires it, lobby hard for the student to return home. This is an extreme action, and one that anyone in this situation is very reticent to do. But it can sometimes be a healthy solution because our reticence to send a student home can have the counterproductive effect of helping the impacted student avoid the genuine implications of mental health disorders.

When that student turned to me after saying "Fine," and I asked her, "Really?" her answer was, "Well, I guess I didn't find that very helpful." Of course the student hadn't found her "treatment" that night very helpful. She was looking for a kind of support that the city of London could not provide her on a moment's notice.

Whether we can provide mental health support in a timely fashion is one of the trickier situations to navigate in our work as global teachers. We probably do not prepare ourselves sufficiently for the deeply nuanced work that such a crisis requires. Whenever we ask students, "How is it going?" we should be focused more on behaviors rather than on what is said or not said. A student who has "fallen away" from the most rudimentary of assignments is a student who may not be coping with the entire enterprise; we should not assume that faltering academic work is symptomatic of a "distracted student" but rather a student whose equilibrium is seriously threatened, and our intervention needs to be more than providing an extension on a paper. The sooner we intervene, the better, and the questions we need to ask can be difficult ones, but that doesn't relieve us the burden of having to ask them.

A MIDNIGHT HIKE

Emily Margaretten

Ol Doinyo Lengai, or "The Mountain of God," is a fitting name for a volcano that rises more than 10,000 feet in the East African Rift range of Tanzania. It's a fitting name for a volcano that nearly wiped out a group of 21 students who were participating in the ACM Tanzania: Ecology and Human Origins study abroad

program. I was the director of the program, an assistant professor of anthropology at Ripon College where I had two years of teaching under my belt and an immense desire to bring students "to the field" to realize the full potential of experiential learning. *Ol Doinyo Lengai* was our last stop before returning to the University of Dar es Salaam, an excursion that was meant to cap off six weeks of camping, collecting field data, and visiting world heritage sites.

Previous ACM directors—notably the geologists and archaeologists—excitedly told me about *Ol Doinyo Lengai*. The volcano, which is the only active volcano in Tanzania, produces a unique composition of black lava (natrocarbonatite) that erupts at a low temperature and quickly hardens to grey. Given that an academic component of the program was geared toward environmental studies, it seemed reasonable to me that the group should see *Ol Doinyo Lengai*. My students also were eager to explore its lunar-like topography, and when it appeared on our itinerary as a midnight hike, I did not question whether we should climb it or not. As our three guides explained, it's cooler to climb a volcano at night with the added benefit of watching the sunrise from the summit. So, at midnight we convened at the base of the mountain with our headlamps, bottles of water, and some apple slices in our pockets. We were, to put it mildly, unprepared.

The start to the hike was unremarkable, the trail rocky and studded with prickly bush. As it became steeper, students started to drop off one-by-one from fatigue and aggravated injuries; two of the guides left to help students find their way back to the base. Onward the rest of the group ascended, with one remaining guide to navigate a pathway that became more treacherous the higher we climbed. The beam of our headlamps, which were low on battery power, did not illuminate the trail much, let alone the steep ravines that had been carved out by previous lava flow. One misplaced foot could lead to a fall with no end in sight. As headlamps fizzled out, more students sat down. Alone, they called out to one another in the dark for moral support, their voices becoming less audible as we climbed higher and higher. The remaining guide was far out in front, his radio ineffective since the other two guides were at the base. Thirteen of us pressed on, and the sun eventually rose (see photo). We had not reached the summit, but we could see it enticingly close, or so it seemed. Two hours later we crested the summit and then turned around for the descent. One ingenious student realized that we could use the unmoored gravel to our advantage to slide down the mountain, which we did by the seat of our pants.

It was only after the hike ended and we were back at the campsite well rested, fed, and hydrated that I realized *Ol Doinyo Lengai* was written up in my travel guidebook. It described the volcano as a "delight" but also as a "distinctly masochistic" hike with an almost 45-degree slope, loose terrain, spitting cobras, occasional leopards, lava bombs, and an intense sun that was best avoided by setting out before sunrise (note, not midnight). It also said the hike would take seven hours. It took us 12.

After reading the guidebook, my initial reaction was disbelief, which quickly turned into immense relief that we survived *Ol Doinyo Lengai* with injuries no more serious than scrapes and sunburns. The students on the trip often joked that I had an emergency or contingency plan for every occasion, an insight that was close to the truth. I am, in general, a well-organized and prepared person. Yet *Ol Doinyo Lengai* blindsided me in large part because I had been complacent. As a junior scholar new to study abroad ventures, I did not press my senior colleagues—all full professors—to explain the importance of the hike as a group excursion. Since it was the end of our field stay, we already had plenty of opportunities to congeal as a group. We also could have marveled at the geological composition of *Ol Doinyo Lengai* from the base of the mountain during the day. I was complacent with the guides too. It is important to recognize and utilize local knowledge and expertise in study abroad programs. In this case, however, I relied on the suggestions of the guides without following up with my own independent research. We could have been better informed—and forsaken the idea of everyone hiking *Ol Doinyo Lengai*—if I had merely looked at my travel guidebook.

After my report of the hike, the ACM did not put it on the group itinerary again. Still, I often think about what I gained from *Ol Doinyo Lengai*, an excursion that, like many study abroad experiences, is not about the place itself but rather about the people who are part of the experience. Just like I made assumptions about the suitability of the hike, I also made assumptions about the students who participated in the program. I could not have accurately predicted which students would be wise enough to turn back or those who would sit down in the dark calling out to one another in solidarity or those who would persevere, climb to the top, and slide back down. In our debriefing afterward, the students marveled at their varied responses to the challenges of the hike. I expected the ones who reached the summit to boast of their accomplishment, yet instead they praised their peers for making their own choices based on their own abilities. The pathways to experiential learning, I have come to realize, are as varied as students themselves, motivated by different reasons and rationales yet all equally valid and meaningful. And so, while I would advocate for shorter, safer study abroad group activities, I also am appreciative of what *Ol Doinyo Lengai* offered us. From many different vantage points, we all saw the sunrise that morning.

CHAPTER 3

THE WORLD IS MY CLASSROOM

The Distinctive Pedagogies of Off-Campus Study Programs at Liberal Arts Colleges[1]

Lisa Jasinski

Many faculty members who have traveled alongside undergraduates while facilitating an off-campus study program describe the experience as markedly different from teaching on campus, in so-called traditional classrooms. Some have gone a step further and credited their involvement with inspiring subsequent changes in their teaching (Sandgren, Ellig, Hovde, Krejci, & Rice, 1999). Case in point, teaching Elon University students during a semester-abroad course in Costa Rica, Nina Namaste, associate professor of Spanish, experienced lasting and dramatic effects:

> The intensity of learning was what I would call, "teacher crack."
> I don't know how to describe it other than that. The intensity of

---

[1]. This title acknowledges a book by the same name by Benham Rennick and Desjardins (2013).

how much the students learned in one semester and how much I could help them with the whole learning experience. It was more like mentoring. It was very intense. . . . When I came back to campus, I thought: I need to try and recreate this. [Since then I've been] trying to recreate this really transformative pedagogy.

Off-campus study programs have long been shown to impart positive benefits for students (Finley & McNair, 2013; Malmgren & Galvin, 2008; Salisbury, 2011; Vande Berg, Paige, & Lou, 2012; Wang, Peyvandi, & Coffey, 2014). Namaste's comments and a growing body of research reveal that they may be equally transformative for faculty members (Davis, 2014; Goode, 2008; Rasch, 2001). Consistent with the goals of this collection, this chapter seeks to reposition faculty program leaders—and their learning—in the center of a broader scholarly discussion of the value and role of study abroad within liberal arts colleges. By listening to and learning from faculty members, and the ways in which they approach and teach off-campus study programs, there are far-reaching benefits for college leaders, policymakers, faculty developers, and campus structures and policies. This chapter seeks to restore the long imbalance within study abroad research by privileging the voices of faculty program leaders.

Consensus exists that simply traveling to a new or unknown location does not ensure students' deep learning; rather, it is dependent on the presence of effective pedagogical structures and timely interventions by supervising faculty (Anderson, Lorenz, & White, 2016; Feller, 2015). To make the claim that off-campus study programs constitute a characteristically different form of teaching and learning from traditional on-campus courses, we must categorize the distinctive pedagogical structures, course elements, and instructor choices that make this form of learning unique. By analyzing why these experiences can be so profound for faculty members like Namaste, this chapter seeks to identify the unique pedagogical structures of faculty-led off-campus study programs.

This chapter begins by examining faculty-led off-campus study programs using the foundational principles of the scholarship of teaching and learning (SoTL) as well as research-based effective pedagogical practices. This framework was used to identify five elements of off-campus study pedagogy, identified from a sample of program syllabi and interviews with 11 faculty members representing a variety of academic disciplines. The findings demonstrate that faculty members have used the unique schedule of an off-campus study program to their advantage: to interact more frequently and in meaningful ways with their students; to use site-based learning opportunities; to expand the expectations of academic rigor; and to experiment with creative, flexible, and interdisciplinary approaches to teaching. This chapter provides specific examples of how faculty members have used off-campus study programs to promote active learning and engender student engagement.

MAKING TEACHING "APPROPRIATELY PUBLIC"

Twenty-five years ago, Shulman (1993) lamented the "pedagogical solitude" of a college professor. While academic disciplines have long fostered vigorous scholarly debates around core issues of a field, the question of how best to teach was frequently met with silence. In response, Shulman issued a call for a paradigm shift to "change the status of teaching from private to community property," not only "making teaching more visible" but creating mechanisms to ensure that "teaching gets treated seriously, systematically, and as central to the lives of individual faculty and institutions" (pp. 6–7). If Shulman issued an initial call to change the way the professoriate approached teaching, Boyer's (1997) seminal book *Scholarship Reconsidered* provided a shared vocabulary and guidelines to enact the change.

Across the contemporary academy, the legacy of Shulman and Boyer has taken many forms; it has led to widespread adoption of faculty development (O'Meara & Terosky, 2010), an increased use of evidence-based teaching practices, the growth of SoTL as an academic field, and the creation of professional societies like the Professional and Organizational Development Network devoted to the advancement of student learning. SoTL is built on the premise that teaching methods and their application in instructional contexts are worthy topics for rigorous evaluation, as the field "concerns the thoughtfulness with which [instructors] construct the learning environments they offer students, the attention they pay to students and their learning, and the engagement they seek with colleagues" (Hutchings, Huber, & Ciccone, 2011, p. 11). Another core tenet of SoTL, argued Felten (2013), is that its practitioners go "appropriately public" by sharing insights about teaching and learning, for example, by engaging in informal discussions with faculty peers or publishing in peer-reviewed journals devoted to pedagogy. Many faculty program leaders have begun the work of going appropriately public by documenting their successes and challenges teaching in off-campus study programs.

Existing Studies About Off-Campus Study Programs

In the spirit of making teaching public and exploring the impact of pedagogical choices, many off-campus program leaders have described course elements, celebrated their successes, and identified areas for continued improvement. To date, much of this research has been directed at disciplinary readerships. Published case studies have examined off-campus program structures and student outcomes within specific academic disciplines, including business (Fitzsimmons, Flanagan, & Wang, 2013; Le, Raven, & Chen, 2013), education (Dunn, Dotson, Cross, Kesner, & Lundahl, 2014), the humanities and arts (Gonsalvez, 2013; Namaste, 2017; Schenker, 2018), the social sciences (Ellis, 2014; France & Rogers, 2012; Jokisch, 2009), and STEM fields (Alexis, Casco, Martin, & Zhang, 2017; Gross, Abrams, & Enns, 2016; Malloy & Davis, 2012). Other scholars have considered the effects of off-campus program participation on specific student populations, including graduate students (Anderson Sathe & Geisler, 2016; Jasinski & Davis, 2018), men and women (Squire et al., 2015), and first-generation college students (Andriano, 2010). Another strand of research has identified pedagogical, logistical, and legal advice for practitioners (Andrade, Dittloff, & Nath, 2019; Benham Rennick & Desjardins, 2013; France & Rogers, 2012; Young, 2014). In a recent study, academics at Australian universities reflected upon how leading off-campus study programs later inspired them to alter how they taught their traditional courses, citing a willingness to forge personal connections with students, adopt a more conversational and less formal tone while lecturing, and incorporate historical objects and visual arts into teaching a variety of subjects (Ellinghaus, Spinks, Moore, Hetherington, & Atherton, 2019). This international case study published in *Frontiers* speaks to a growing interest to better understand the ways that leading an off-campus study program can support transformative learning for faculty.

Rather than examine the implications for off-campus study programs within a particular discipline or a student group, this chapter adopts an integrative approach by examining instructors' pedagogical choices within a single institution type, the small private liberal arts college. This is not to suggest that all teaching practices are universal; rather, a more holistic analysis of practices across disciplines is proposed to encourage greater cross-pollination of ideas.

Consistent with the goals of this co-authored collection, it is necessary to consider the perceived, and often privileged, value of off-campus study within small private liberal arts colleges. These colleges often market study abroad opportunities as "eye-opening experiences" (Johansson & Felten, 2014, p. 25), and given that upward of half of students at many selective private liberal arts colleges study abroad before graduation, it can be said that such messaging has been effective. Liberal arts colleges frame study abroad as a holistic experience that will prompt independent living, maturation, and worldview expansion:

> For many undergraduates, immersion in an unfamiliar culture and location prompts questions about both the larger world and the particulars of home. Some students begin to consider questions of poverty and privilege only when they witness the dynamics of a foreign context. In recognizing and beginning to critique the social, economic, cultural, and political structures that shape our world and our individual experiences in the world, students begin to see themselves as part of a larger system rather than simply isolated individuals. (Johansson & Felten, p. 51)

Rather than a specific set of educational or personal outcomes, this more expansive understanding of study abroad is embedded into the fabric and culture of the liberal arts college. These pervasive norms shape how students (and likely faculty members and advisors) think about off-campus learning and its educative value.

The variety and novelty that off-campus programs offer, with or without their marketing tagline as once-in-a-lifetime experiences, provide great appeal for students. Having interviewed more than 200 students at seven elite liberal arts colleges in New England, Cuba, Jennings, Lovett, and Swingle (2016) found that students see

> Spending a semester or year in an entirely different place as an opportunity to restart, to break out of academic and social routines that have become, for some students, stultifying and boring. . . . [Students see] study abroad as a college restart that creatively disrupts routines, social ties, and, on a deeper psychological level, a sense of order and continuity in one's life. (p. 77)

This is not to say that students' expectations should drive programmatic offerings, but colleges (and faculty program leaders) should keep in mind that many students are motivated to study abroad because they seek something new and different. Aiming to replicate the routines, relationships, and forms of learning that students regularly encounter on their campuses may be counterproductive; students see study abroad as a break from the norm. Although these norms, preferences, and attitudes may also exist at other types of postsecondary institutions—large public universities, regional state campuses, and community colleges—we maintain that the lore is particularly strong at small, private liberal arts colleges. Given that our investigation of faculty members' experiences leading off-campus programs is focused on a single type of postsecondary institution, it is prudent to keep these attitudes in the front of mind when considering faculty perspectives.

Findings from the Faculty as Global Learners Survey

Our Phase 1 survey of 230 faculty members found that off-campus study programs had lasting positive effects for faculty leaders at private liberal arts colleges. One indication of the appeal was the high rate at which instructors sought to repeat teaching in an off-campus program; 87% of respondents indicated that they were "eager to teach the same program again" to a "great extent" or to "some extent," and 74% responded that they were "eager to lead a different program" in the future. The high percentage of survey respondents who reported that they were "renewed or energized after leading a program" (76.9%) far surpassed those who reported feeling "burned-out" (16.3%) or "experienced an increase in stress at work" (30.9%) upon returning. By and large, faculty leaders' satisfaction can be inferred from a reported willingness to lead off-campus programs again and positive feelings about the experience.

Survey respondents also reported changes in their attitudes and behaviors, further evidence that leading off-campus study programs can have significant consequences on faculty members'

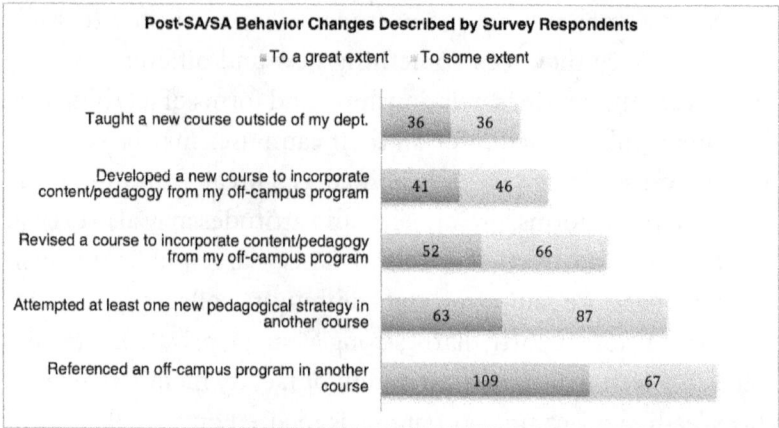

Post-SA/SA Behavior Changes Described by Survey Respondents

■ To a great extent   ■ To some extent

Behavior	To a great extent	To some extent
Taught a new course outside of my dept.	36	36
Developed a new course to incorporate content/pedagogy from my off-campus program	41	46
Revised a course to incorporate content/pedagogy from my off-campus program	52	66
Attempted at least one new pedagogical strategy in another course	63	87
Referenced an off-campus program in another course	109	67

Figure 7. Number of Faculty Respondents Who Reported Behavior Changes After Leading an Off-Campus Study Program

careers. As noted in Figure 7, 98% of respondents made at least one change in *what* they taught or *how* they taught after leading a study away or study abroad program.

The most commonly reported behavioral changes included referencing their program in another class (94%) and attempting at least one new pedagogical strategy in another course (76.5%). These findings are encouraging for several reasons. First, they show that faculty members who have led off-campus study programs are contributing to broader efforts to globalize curricular offerings. By creating new classes that incorporate content from an international program—or including more international examples or illustrating theory with concrete examples from their travels—more students at the institution benefit from the instructor's global repertoire of knowledge. Leading an off-campus study program appears to result in an instructor's interest and willingness to engage in pedagogical exploration. More than 70 survey respondents reported that they taught a new class outside of their department after leading an off-campus study program, revealing participants' willingness to strengthen interdisciplinary program offerings at their institution.

Taken together, these responses reveal that leading an off-campus program can have ripple effects that benefit students beyond those who participated in the program itself—faculty members reported changes in their teaching that occurred long after returning to their campuses.

In the follow-up Faculty as Global Learners survey administered a year later (Phase II), 72 respondents shared additional information about their pedagogical practices during off-campus study programs. Participants reported incorporating several high-impact practices (HIPs) as designated by the Association of American Colleges & Universities (AAC&U) into their off-campus study program. Kuh (2008) championed HIPs for providing students with opportunities to try out their learning, to incorporate feedback, and to interact with diverse others. Many HIPs foreground active learning and demand that students spend additional time on task often working on consultation with other students, faculty mentors, and community members—the combination results in learning gains, enhanced practical competencies, and improved social development (Finley & McNair, 2013). HIPs impart considerable benefits to students from all backgrounds, producing more substantive gains for students from historically underrepresented groups.

Global learning/study abroad is considered a HIP; 94% of respondents to this survey reported incorporating at least one additional HIP into their off-campus study program (Kuh, 2008). Survey respondents most often reported the following pairings: collaborative projects (74.7%), writing-intensive assignments or courses (50.7%), and undergraduate research (46.5%). Further analysis of survey results revealed that 86% of respondents reported combining two or more HIPs into their off-campus study program; common combinations included collaborative projects and writing-intensive courses or collaborative projects and undergraduate research. All participant responses are charted in Figure 8. Combined responses reported as "another HIP" included capstone projects (22%), internships (21%), and first-year courses (7%). These

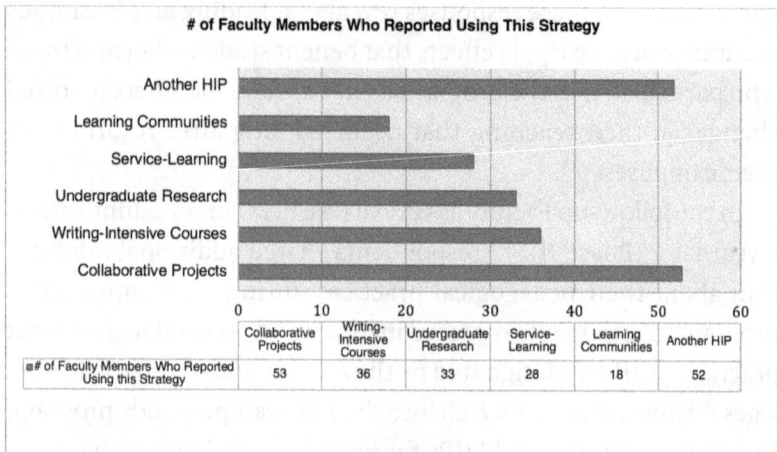

# of Faculty Members Who Reported Using This Strategy

	Collaborative Projects	Writing-Intensive Courses	Undergraduate Research	Service-Learning	Learning Communities	Another HIP
■# of Faculty Members Who Reported Using this Strategy	53	36	33	28	18	52

Figure 8. Number of Faculty Respondents Who Incorporated High-Impact Practices Into Their Off-Campus Study Program

findings indicated that the vast majority of respondents structured their off-campus study programs as sites wherein students encountered multiple and intersecting beneficial forms of learning.

FURTHER UNDERSTANDING FACULTY MEMBERS' APPROACHES TO TEACHING

Using the aforementioned surveys and extant research as a point of departure, I extended this line of inquiry to explore the firsthand experiences of faculty members who led an off-campus program at a private liberal arts college in recent years. Two research questions structured my continued data collection and analysis:

1. What pedagogical structures and functions make faculty-led off-campus study programs distinctive?
2. How do instructors compare teaching in off-campus study programs and traditional on-campus courses?

Effective Teaching Defined

For the purposes of this study, effective teaching was defined using two taxonomies: the 11 high-impact educational practices (HIPs) endorsed by the Association of American Colleges & Universities (AAC&U; Kuh, 2008) and Chickering and Gamson's (1987) "Seven Principles for Good Practice in Undergraduate Education." The scales are defined in Table 17.

Without overgeneralizing, the documented use of Chickering and Gamson's principles and AAC&U's HIPs are good proxies for student engagement and deep learning. These measures are widely accepted within the higher education community and form the basis of some of the most commonly used campus surveys, including the National Survey of Student Engagement (NSSE) and the Wabash Study. These inventories are not meant to be seen as mutually exclusive or exhaustive, nor are they intended as measures of actual, demonstrable gains in student learning.

Table 17. Indicators of Effective Teaching

AAC&U: High-Impact Education Practices	Chickering and Gamson: Seven Principles for Good Practice in Undergraduate Education
High-impact educational practices:	Good practice in undergraduate education:
1. First-year seminars and experiences	1. Encourages student-faculty contact
2. Common intellectual experiences	2. Encourages cooperation among students
3. Learning communities	3. Encourages active learning
4. Writing-intensive courses	4. Gives prompt feedback
5. Collaborative assignments and projects	5. Emphasizes time on task
6. Undergraduate research	6. Communicates high expectations
7. Diversity/global learning	7. Respects diverse talents and ways of learning
8. ePortfolios	
9. Service learning, community-based learning	
10. Internships	
11. Capstone courses and projects	

Keep in mind that a HIP does not guarantee achievement; learning gains are only achieved when such practices are "done well" according to Kuh (2007, p. 9). Recognizing how these taxonomies might overlap and intersect, a savvy instructor could maximize the potential benefits of a writing-intensive course (HIP #4) by giving students prompt feedback on draft papers (Principle #4) and meeting frequently with students outside of class to discuss their progress (Principle #1). Teaching might be said to be most "effective" when it exhibits many of these research-based characteristics.

Research Methodology

Initial findings from the exploratory Faculty as Global Learners survey prompted the development of this qualitative case study (Merriam, 2001). This research design is suitably "employed to gain an in-depth understanding of the situation and the meaning for those involved" (p. 19). The first methodological consideration was to define the case under study: the case included faculty members from liberal arts colleges and concerned their pedagogical choices before, during, and after leading an off-campus study program. *Off-campus study programs* was used as an umbrella term to reference faculty-designed and supervised, credit-bearing academic experiences—both international and domestic. Short-term programs spanned at least one week, whereas longer-term programs lasted a semester or longer. This broad definition was flexible enough to include a diverse range of programs while still offering coherent parameters. Qualifying examples might include domestic travel to the Navajo nation to engage in a credit-bearing, week-long service-learning project; a month-long field-based course that incorporated collecting and analyzing data about geological formations in China; or a semester abroad program in Paris wherein students live with a host family, taking classes taught by a faculty member from their home institution as well as a local university. Given these parameters, a one-time, day-long field trip to a nearby art museum (too short) or the members of a college soccer team traveling with their coach to participate in an overseas tournament (not academic) were delimited from the study.

Participant selection criteria. Purposeful sampling was used to identify faculty for my continued investigation of this subject; participants were selected based on their ability to represent a variety of academic disciplines and for having the ability to speak knowledgably from their firsthand experiences as faculty members leading off-campus programs (Merriam, 2001). As there exists no national directory of off-campus program leaders, prospective participants were identified from the pool of survey respondents and using the co-authors' professional networks. No effort was made to select a random or representative sample, though care was taken to ensure that the sample included a mix of men and women, multiple disciplines, multiple institutional settings, and individuals with a varied amount of experience leading international programs (some were relatively new to the practice, others more seasoned). Although it was not a criterion for inclusion, some of the faculty members consulted have published research articles, presented at professional conferences, or led workshops at their home institution about their experiences leading off-campus programs. Participant characteristics for this case study are summarized in Table 18.

Roughly an equal number of men and women were interviewed. A majority held faculty appointments within the arts and humanities (55%), but perspectives from STEM (27%) and other fields (18%) were also included. In addition to their primary disciplinary appointment, several participants were also affiliated with interdisciplinary programs at their colleges (e.g., gender studies, environmental studies), either through a formal dual appointment or an informal affiliation. Participants led an average of 5.5 off-campus programs (often representing a mix of "repeated" programs and unique one-time offerings), though the number of programs led, per participant, ranged from one to more than 20. More

Table 18. Case Study Participant Characteristics

Characteristics	Total ($n = 11$)	Percentage
Gender		
Men	6	55
Women	5	45
Primary disciplinary appointment		
Arts & humanities	6	55
Professional programs	1	9
Social sciences	1	9
STEM	3	27
Number of off-campus programs led		
1 to 5	6	55
6 to 10	4	36
11 or more	1	9
Types of programs led*		
Short-term programs (1–6 weeks)	10	91
Long-term programs (7 weeks or more)	6	55

* Participants who led both short- and long-term programs were counted in both categories.

than half (55%) of participants were relatively new to the practice, having led between one and five off-campus study programs.

During the interview, participants were encouraged to base their responses on program leadership and teaching experiences from across their careers. While nearly all participants (91%) led at least one short-term off-campus program (one–six weeks), more than half (55%) had also led a longer-term summer or semester-abroad program (seven weeks or more), and one had only led a longer-term program (seven weeks or more). One participant also led international "faculty study tours" for his college for which he traveled abroad with professional faculty and staff colleagues (no students). To clarify, Table 18 does not reflect participants' past experiences serving in a secondary or support capacity during an off-campus program—while the experience of "shadowing" a colleague was often described as being useful, interviewees acknowledged playing a limited role in the design of the course in this capacity.

Participants led programs where the primary language of instruction was English, German, or Spanish. Within the sample, participants led programs to all continents except South America and Antarctica, including a mix of urban, rural, developed, and developing locations. Finally, for context, it should be noted the sample included faculty members who led off-campus programs both before and after earning tenure. Colleges represented in the study had different policies and practices regarding the participation of pre-tenure faculty in leading off-campus study programs.

All participants agreed to have their names and institutional affiliations included in this chapter. Consistent with the other chapters in this volume, this journalistic approach enabled claims to be supported with real examples and to grant deserved attention to the faculty members pioneering new pedagogical practices. The 11 participants who were part of this continued analysis are listed in Table 19.

Data collection and analysis. Consistent with the terms of the IRB protocol, each faculty member participated in one semi-structured, private interview during the summer of 2018; the interview protocol is included as Appendix A. Hour-long interviews were conducted by the chapter author via phone or Skype, recorded, and later transcribed for analysis. Nine participants also submitted at least one program syllabus or assignment description for document analysis. Following Merriam's case study research design, all data were analyzed using the defined measures of teaching effectiveness.

Transcripts and syllabi underwent two rounds of coding by the chapter author using the software program NVivo. In the first round, references to any of Chickering and Gamson's named principles or an AAC&U HIP were identified. Upon reviewing these

Table 19. Case Study Participant Names and Affiliations

Name	Institution	# of Off-Campus Programs Led	Countries/Regions Visited
Gundolf Graml	Agnes Scott College	8	Germany, Austria, Slovakia, Hungary, Jamaica
Georgia Duerst-Lahti	Beloit College	1	Botswana
Christian Haskett	Centre College	2	India
Aaron Godlaski	Centre College	1	Japan, Borneo
Nina Namaste	Elon University	2	Costa Rica
Sasha Pfau	Hendrix College	3	London, Costa Rica
Liz Carlin Metz	Knox College	20+	United Kingdom, Ireland, France, Cuba
Sarah Boyle	Rhodes College	1	Namibia
Paul Jackson	St. Olaf College	6	Australia, New Zealand, Japan
Bladimir Ruiz	Trinity University	9	Spain, Mexico
Roger Dean	Washington and Lee University	8	Ireland

patterns, the data were analyzed again and emic concept codes were applied. These second-round codes consisted of "a word or short phrase" used to "symbolically represent a suggested meaning broader than a single item or action," thus implying a "bigger picture beyond the tangible and apparent" (Saldaña, 2016, p. 119). Examples of assigned concept codes were "mentorship," "supporting students through moments of cognitive dissonance," and "interdisciplinarity." Often used in grounded theory approaches (Charmaz, 2014; Glaser & Strauss, 1967), concept coding is inductive and requires the researcher to adopt a "highly interpretive stance" to identify broader themes and to further investigate the ideas contained within the data. The rounds of coding were meant to be mutually informing—comparing pedagogical practice across established standards as well as preserving participants' ways of framing their goals and teaching experiences. Drawing on the patterns that emerged across the two rounds of coding, five findings were developed in response to the research questions. Findings are explored in the next section.

FINDINGS

The analysis of interviews and a review of off-campus study program syllabi resulted in the identification of five characteristics of teaching in off-campus study programs by faculty members at liberal arts colleges (see Table 20). In identifying the elements throughout the remainder of the chapter, direct participant quotations are used whenever possible to allow faculty to speak in their own voices. For the purposes of readability, minor corrections to the grammar and syntax have been made without changing the meaning of any direct quotations. The first three findings were identified in response to the first research question: "What pedagogical structures and functions make faculty-led off-campus study programs distinctive?"

Finding 1: Calendars and Schedules Enable Good Practice

Faculty members described how calendars and schedules—what we might consider the structure of an off-campus study program—readily lend themselves to forms of effective teaching. While program structure alone does not dictate how a faculty member must teach, study participants explained that off-campus study programs present the ideal conditions for active and engaged learning. Two features of off-campus study programs proved particularly helpful to instructors: (a) concentrated blocks of time during the academic calendar to hold such programs and (b) allotting time

Table 20. Case Study Research Findings

RQ1: What pedagogical structures and functions make faculty-led off-campus study programs distinctive?

    Finding 1: Calendars and schedules enable good practice
    Finding 2: Strategic use of time before, during, and after a program
    Finding 3: Student-faculty contact is central to the success of faculty-led
        study abroad

RQ2: How do instructors compare teaching in off-campus study programs and traditional on-campus courses?

    Finding 4: Academic rigor redefined
    Finding 5: Off-campus study programs encourage instructors to be more
        flexible, creative, and interdisciplinary

on a day-to-day basis to pursue forms of time-intensive teaching and learning that are difficult to achieve during a "normal" weekly academic schedule.

First, a college's academic calendar can set the stage for pedagogically rich off-campus study programs. Several institutions represented in this study have an abbreviated mini-semester that is tailor-made for month-long off-campus courses: this includes a January CentreTerm at Centre College, Interim at St. Olaf, or winter term at Elon, whereas Knox, Rhodes, and Washington and Lee have a similarly concentrated "May-mester" following the spring term. A required component of Agnes Scott's new general education curriculum called "Global Journeys" requires all first-year students to enroll in a semester-long spring course that incorporates a two- to four-week-long, faculty-led study tour. The faculty members who worked at a college without an abbreviated semester—such as Trinity, Beloit, and Hendrix—were more likely to have led a semester-long or lengthy summer program. At these institutions, some committed instructors created short-term off-campus courses, often occurring over spring break or during the summer, but it took greater planning, ingenuity, and financial resources to realize such programs that did not occur as part of the standard annual calendar. Proving the adage "if you build it, they will come," when colleges designate moments during the year to hold off-campus study courses, faculty members have responded by populating offerings.

Interviewees explained that daily schedule of an off-campus study program is particularly conducive to incorporating AAC&U's HIPs, because these off-site programs provide greater fluidity and the ability to meet with students for several consecutive hours. According to study participants, it can be challenging to structure time-intensive blocks during a typical school day on campus; many described liberal arts college campuses as hectic places where students divide their attention among four or more classes, significant co-curricular engagements, part-time jobs, and planning for life after graduation. As a result, in Namaste's words, "students are literally bouncing all over the place" rather than concentrating deeply on the one task at hand. For students, time on campus is now experienced in fractured, harried parcels, and, by comparison, off-campus programs enable learning to occur at a more natural, less rushed pace. Gundolf Graml of Agnes Scott College explained how he used the daily structure to support students' continuous learning:

> You have more time in the sense that you can pursue a topic in increments of 10 or 15 minutes throughout the day at various places and pick it up again, which makes for a different kind of learning rather than trying to pack everything into 75 minutes. Then [students] go on and have another class that might have nothing to do with [the previous class period].

Not only do off-campus study programs allow students to return to a topic throughout the day—giving them the chance to reflect and think more deeply in the interval—the longer stretches of time also provide instructors with the freedom and flexibility to incorporate new kinds of class arrangements and learning activities. Other study participants stated that the standard 50- and 75-minute class periods of a campus course schedule are not suited to accommodate many HIPs, such as internships, collaborative projects, or service-learning. For instance, Trinity University students on a summer or semester abroad program spend 20 hours (or more) per week in a professional internship in Madrid, gaining a depth of experience that would be otherwise challenging to replicate during a typical week on campus. Off-campus study programs, structured according to a more conducive daily schedule, do not burden faculty members and students with carving out blocks of time for groups to meet or for students to work with community partners.

Multiple study participants explained that the flexible daily schedule of an off-campus study program encouraged students to spend more "time on task" (Principle #5). Paul Jackson of St. Olaf College was responsible for teaching his students in multiple distinct courses during off-campus study programs in New Zealand and Australia. While time was allocated to what were technically separate courses, he often repurposed the scheduled time to accommodate what he called "intense field experiences." The ability to combine multiple classes together presented longer blocks of time in which he would instruct students to "design, in small groups, short-term [scientific field] studies. Like, a day or two where they're going to design an experiment, execute it, collect data, analyze it, and present it." When teaching students on campus, Jackson explained that he could not make such demands on students' time, which would already be committed to other courses and instructors. As these examples show, the daily schedule of an off-campus program, in the hands of a creative instructor, can enable the forms of ambitious and time-intensive projects that promote students' learning about academic principles and transferable skills.

Finding 2: Strategic Use of Time Before, During, and After a Program

Study participants conceived of off-campus programs in three phases: pre-departure, on-site, and post-program. Faculty members employed different types of assignments and structured interactions during each phase to achieve overall program goals.

Pre-departure assignments and interactions. Several program leaders sought to bookend a short-term off-campus experience with strategic meetings and assignments. Pre-departure meetings allowed the group to bond and provided a chance to review travel logistics, campus policies, and health and safety resources. These meetings also introduced relevant content, such as an overview of local cultures or a crash course in local languages. Associated pre-departure assignments can "prime students for the ideas of the course," described Aaron Godlaski of Centre College. In preparation for a month-long course on mindfulness in Japan, he assigned a "book and four or five scientific articles" for students to read during the December break, requiring them to submit their first paper before departing. At Beloit College, Georgia Duerst-Lahti interviewed students pre-program about their nascent ideas for the independent study research projects that she would mentor in Botswana. In sum, pre-departure sessions helped set the stage for learning and provided an optimal chance to address logistical matters; in this phase, faculty drew on conventional means of delivering content to students, including reading assignments, film screenings, mini-lectures, in-class discussions, and required meetings outside of class.

On-site program assignments and interactions. When structuring their off-campus study courses, participants took advantage of the opportunities afforded by the local context and culture to assign place-based experiential projects. For instance, Christian Haskett of Centre College had students create short documentaries and interview people in India. To offer an extended example of how faculty members used their destinations to inform course assignments, Sarah Boyle of Rhodes College expected her field biology students in Namibia to

> Keep a daily journal that they turned into me at the end of the trip. They also had to come up with a proposal for a research project and run it by me for approval. Then they collected the data, analyzed the data, and later submitted a paper. The deadline was three or four weeks after the course ended because we didn't have time—or even computer access—while we were on the course. Then they had a written exam that . . . we did at a field site. It was all paper-based. They had more of a practical exam where they had to go into the field and identify 20 species of plants.

Boyle's approach maximized experiential learning in the field and reserved the more contemplative and technology-intensive course components for students' return to the States. Moreover, she designed a low-tech, practical exam to take full advantage of the proximity of the natural environment.

In addition to site-specific assignments, faculty leaders set different expectations for their interactions with students. Boyle required several individual meetings with students to discuss their research projects and to check in on their broader learning. In Madrid, Trinity University's Bladimir Ruiz deliberately held his office hours in a coffee shop, both to encourage a more open exchange with students and to create another opportunity for cultural engagement and linguistic development.

Post-program assignments and interactions. Finally, off-campus programs, particularly those less than a month in length, often included additional components after students returned to campus. In Boyle's case, required course meetings provided time to discuss academic assignments (e.g., final papers, in-class presentations). These interactions were used to help students process and articulate what they learned abroad (e.g., debriefing discussions, reflections). Practical scheduling obstacles often made it less feasible for summer and semester-long programs to require post-program components; not all students returned to campus at the same time. Apart from a formal class meeting, many faculty members described hosting social gatherings—such as a communal meal or a group reunion—to solidify relationships and support students' cultural reentry. Students and faculty members described maintaining ties in other ways, such as by partnering as research collaborators in a future study or the student enrolling in another course taught by the instructor.

These examples demonstrate that faculty leaders often approach off-campus study programs as modular. They seek to use the time before, during, and after the on-site experience in distinct ways to both forge lasting relationships and use pedagogies and assignments tailored to the phase.

Finding 3: Student-Faculty Contact Is Central to the Success of Faculty-Led Study Abroad

Chickering and Gamson identified "student-faculty contact" as a principle of effective teaching and learning. All of the participants described their contact with students on off-campus programs as looking and feeling different from their contact with on-campus students. This characterization was a function of having classroom interactions as well as what Sasha Pfau of Hendrix College called the "informal spaces" of group travel excursions, including shared meals or incidental conversations (e.g., sitting together on a bus). Not only do students and faculty spend considerable time together during off-campus programs, but also being immersed in another culture or being far from home significantly altered the nature of their interactions. For Liz Carlin Metz of Knox College, the exchanges were "more intimate," wherein students might open up to talk about their families, fears, or hopes for the future. To sum up the difference, Ruiz said, "programs like these give us an opportunity to talk more, to do therapy. Without *doing therapy*." That is not to say that boundaries are not respected; Ruiz made clear to students, "I'm not your buddy. I am not going out dancing with you." Still, he recounted talking about a greater breadth of topics with students and being more aware of their challenges both inside and outside of the classroom.

These interactions often led study participants to understand their students better and to have a fuller picture of their lives. For instance, Namaste of Elon University described many benefits of regular contact with students: closely monitoring the pace at which each student was learning; using differentiated instructional strategies; and exploring more customized approaches to best serve individual needs. While other participants reported gaining insights into their students, off-campus study programs also humanized faculty members in the eyes of students. When traveling with his Agnes Scott students, Graml perceived,

> Students are initially always surprised that their professor also fights against jet lag when we are in an overheated room in a workshop and it's hot. We can use that moment to address, "Yes, these are the challenges, and we're all affected by them, and so we try to make the best of it. The fact that I have an academic degree does not equip me to deal with this any better."

As a result of traveling together, students and faculty often gained mutual understanding and empathy for each other's perspectives. Hearing participants describe the "intensity" and "intimacy" of their exchanges with students during off-campus study programs, it is easy to see how they exemplify many of the core promises made by residential liberal arts colleges. Perhaps ironically, according to faculty program leaders, these close relationships seem to blossom more readily thousands of miles away from the home campus.

These three findings have identified three distinctive characteristics of off-campus programs: (a) schedules that enable students to spend significant time engaged in experiential learning, (b) the modular nature of programs that support learning both on and off campus, and (c) structures that foreground student-faculty contact. The fourth and fifth findings that follow were identified in response to the second research question: "How do instructors compare teaching in off-campus study programs and traditional on-campus courses?"

Finding 4: Academic Rigor Redefined

Selective liberal arts colleges maintain their reputations by adhering to high standards of academic rigor. Since many faculty members feel beholden to maintaining a high standard, the matter of how much and the kind of work to assign students during an off-campus program remains a sensitive topic. On the one hand, no faculty leader wanted their travel-embedded course to be mistaken for an exotic vacation. On the other, faculty members recognized that to best achieve their multi-layered learning outcomes—to promote students' academic, cultural, linguistic, and personal development—a more expansive and nuanced concept of rigor was required. It is also important to remember that for many students, the decision to study abroad is often motivated by their desire to escape the "growing predictability and regularity of college life" (Cuba et al., 2016, p. 76). Part of the change that students seek is to learn in different ways about different things with new people; although students are not necessarily seeking a less rigorous experience, they welcome the variety of learning in different ways.

More than half of study participants sounded apologetic when explaining their decision to assign what might be judged as "less" academic work—the quantity of reading or writing—during an off-campus study program. In discussing the reason that he limited the amount of reading that students did during his CentreTerm course on mindfulness and meditation, Godlaski stated,

I feel like it's a little bit cheating them to say, "Somebody's spending thousands of dollars to get you to Asia. And you're going to go there, we're going to have a limited amount of time, and I don't necessarily want you to spend three hours of the afternoon sitting in the hostel reading something." There are people that would probably disagree with me about that, but for me, travel is for *experiencing*. So, once we're on the ground, students usually do a daily or every other day reading that dovetails with something that we're seeing. . . . So they do have some reading while we are there, usually something they can access digitally, so they don't have to take it with them.

Perceiving that an off-campus study program affords students the ability to learn in many ways, Godlaski justified assigning a lighter reading load to provide students with the ability to focus on experiencing their limited time in the country.

Graml, of Agnes Scott College, agreed that when discussing off-campus study programs, "workload" is not equivalent to "rigor" in the way that it is for traditional on-campus courses. In addition to leading programs for students, Graml had the unique experience of leading study tours for his faculty and staff peers. Faculty participation often resulted in individuals' reassessing their own attitudes about the kinds of work to assign during an off-campus program. Participating in the same guided reflective exercises that Graml used with students, faculty

came to see that this really profound article that they wanted to assign during the trip was completely lost. Because the faculty experienced for themselves being jet-lagged, being tired, feeling a bit uncomfortable due to the different food. The overstimulation by the environment can really interfere with any kind of typical academic scholarly engagement. Faculty study tour participants came to see that a different skill set, a different learning style, was important in that environment.

Prior to this intervention, many of Graml's colleagues planned to structure their off-campus study programs using the same norms, principles, and practices that they used in their traditional courses. Upon experiencing the conditions of being abroad, many began to see for themselves the pitfalls of replicating an on-campus course in an off-campus setting and came to value guided reflective exercises, activities requiring students to explore their many identities, and critical discussions informed by cultural immersion.

When constructing a program itinerary, Haskett (Centre College) came to the "counter-intuitive conclusion" that "more seems to be less," finding that he had the best results when he scheduled "one decent activity a day" and used the remaining time to allow students to "sit and think and process." Adopting a quality over quantity mindset, Haskett balanced the group's excursions with ample time for shared meals and debriefing conversations. To a colleague reviewing the syllabus—especially one who might not have realized the importance of what might appear as intervals of "downtime"—the inclusion of meals and discussions might be dismissed as a non-academic (and therefore frivolous) use of time. Even though a faculty member might have a sound pedagogical reason for including site excursions to local attractions, debriefing discussions, and shared meals on the syllabus, the value of these course activities might not be readily known to colleagues who review new course proposals, either on the curriculum review committee or during the tenure and promotion process. Given the unique needs of teaching and learning during an on-site program, it would not be appropriate to review the syllabus through the conventional expectations of academic rigor—allotting a preponderance of time to lecture-based instruction, giving in-class exams, or other mainstays of traditional on-campus courses. It is important that instructors with limited experience teaching in off-campus study programs have a working knowledge of the unique demands of these programs to achieve a broader, more inclusive type of academic rigor.

Just as faculty program leaders during an off-campus study course apportioned time differently and included course elements that might appear more social than intellectual, Namaste of Elon University endeavored to help students expand their conceptions of academic challenge. Objecting to the premise that critical self-reflection is less rigorous than other forms of writing, Namaste regularly assigned projects that challenged students to probe their values and assumptions about culture. She described her efforts to seek out strategies to convey her expectations to students:

> And I'm struggling with it because of the mere fact that even some students resist it and say that my courses are not as rigorous. And I'm still trying to formulate or frame it best for students to understand that the self-awareness piece in many ways is so critical.

Whereas Godlaski and Graml framed rigor as a matter in response to their peers' standards of an appropriate workload (e.g., pages of reading assigned), Namaste found that replacing academic papers with project-based learning challenged students' conceptions about rigor and learning. Given the distinctive characteristics of off-campus study programs, instructors should be transparent in explaining why and how they adopted alternate, and yet appropriate, conceptions of academic rigor. To recognize that off-campus programs provide distinct and valuable learning experiences, it can be useful to avoid binary definitions (e.g., better/worse, more rigorous/less rigorous) when comparing off-campus study with traditional on-campus courses. Each form of teaching and learning should be seen as complementary, mutually informing, and valuable. Expecting off-campus study programs to use the same instructional strategies and assign the same workload as on-campus courses provides no benefit to students or instructors, rather, by embracing the difference, everyone benefits.

Finding 5: Off-Campus Study Programs Encourage Instructors to be More Flexible, Creative, and Interdisciplinary

To hear faculty leaders talk about teaching during an off-campus study program, it was hard not to be swept up in their excitement. Study participants were motivated to teach in off-campus study programs, and many agreed to teach in them again, because they provided the desirable combination of freedom, flexibility, challenge, and reward. Teaching an off-campus study program often requires instructors to adapt to changing needs, react spontaneously, and explore the full potential of teachable moments as they arise.

Several participants characterized teaching in off-campus programs as an exercise in relinquishing control. Graml described hosting an impromptu discussion at a cultural site as "messier, not as carefully staged as a classroom setting." Having led dozens of off-campus programs, Graml has gradually come to adopt forms of what he calls "interactive teaching" and other strategies to equalize the power dynamic between him and his students. He now organizes his course syllabus to include opportunities for students to take the instructional lead at designated cultural sites—believing that he has become "less that sage on the stage" and now regularly "learns *with*" students. Ruiz at Trinity University described the appeal of leading programs in Spain and Mexico as taking him "out of his comfort zone" by being immersed in a new culture, teaching unfamiliar content, supervising internships for the first time, and having "personal and emotional" conversations with students. As a result of these experiences, Ruiz changed his approach to teaching on a greater level; upon returning to his campus, he revised assignments and, more generally, loosened the reins and "opened up more, relaxed more" with students. By adopting a less formal teaching persona and building relationships with his students, Ruiz believed that he has grown as a person and become a better teacher.

Faculty members conveyed that off-campus study programs enabled forms of interdisciplinary inquiry that were often not readily available to them on their campus. Recall that Jackson of St. Olaf College served as the instructor for multiple courses within the same off-campus study program. Not only did this structure allow him to apportion time in blocks to enable intensive field-based projects, but also teaching the same cohort of students in multiple courses allowed him to draw new connections. This approach appealed to him:

> As an environmental studies person and an interdisciplinarian, I thought, "Oh, this is ideal. This is immersive learning without the disciplinary boundaries. I love this." One of the best parts of the experience—this crossing barriers and taking down barriers—is having students come to me and say, "Which class does this project count for?" And I would typically ask them what class they *thought* it counted for. They would say, "I think it has elements of this terrestrial ecology class, but we're also talking about how policy is interfacing with that, so it could be the policy class. But also, it's embedded in this cultural context, so it has some anthropological theses." I replied, "Excellent!"
>
> The student just kind of looked at me as if to say, "Okay, you didn't really answer my question, but I guess it's part of all of these." And I said, "This is the heavy lifting. You're trying to build connections between all these things, around this experience, and the work is to integrate all of this."

This example shows how Jackson relished the moment when students saw their assignments as the culmination of themes across many different courses. For him, the fact that students were making sense of how ideas overlapped between classes achieved the larger aims of interdisciplinary thinking and inquiry in which they "crossed boundaries and took down boundaries." Jackson contrasted this rich "border crossing" experience with the traditional chemistry classes he often taught on campus. Whereas stand-alone courses might be better suited to helping students examine a topic through the lens of a single discipline, the ability to "intertwine courses" while abroad challenged students to adopt and synthesize multiple perspectives in a way that Jackson perceived to be advantageous.

When the unexpected happens during an off-campus study program—be it a travel delay, a health crisis, an unforeseen reaction, or other disappointing news—faculty members described being called upon to respond spontaneously to a teachable moment. Carlin Metz of Knox College described the choices she made after one of her theatre students was mugged outside the British Museum. She immediately paused the day's scheduled topic for discussion and gently reminded students about situational awareness and safety protocols. Then Carlin Metz asked her students, "Why does anybody mug anybody? What's that about? Is it about kicks? Is it about thrills?" She proceeded to facilitate an on-the-spot conversation that uncovered students' assumptions about the homeless, addiction, global migration, and poverty. By reframing the narrative—allowing students to process their reactions to this event as well as its larger implications—she accomplished a much larger goal:

> I don't want the lesson they took away [from the incident] to be paranoid. I don't want them to walk around frightened. I also don't want them to walk around with their purses open. But if they're only seeing this from a risk management point of view, then they're not actually having an experience that is transformational.

While such a conversation would be unlikely to arise in the theatre courses Carlin Metz taught on the Knox campus, the discussion was timely and necessary in this context. And while she remained committed to ensuring students' health and safety, this impromptu conversation starter allowed her to deviate from the day's lesson plan without abandoning her larger goals of helping students to think about their privileges and responsibilities as global citizens. For Carlin Metz, responding spontaneously to unexpected moments, often to bolster their educative potential, was one of her favorite parts of teaching in the field.

Although there are potentially an infinite number of these latent teachable moments during an off-campus study program, knowing how and when to respond is truly an art. As faculty members proceed developmentally and gain greater facility teaching in off-campus study programs, many eventually master the "constructive reframing" technique that Carlin Metz displayed in London. Centre College's Godlaski identified a potential teachable moment that he wished he had handled differently during one of his first experiences leading an off-campus program. While his group was hiking in Borneo through "the oldest forest on earth" and he was trying to "soak things in," a group of

> students were talking about whatever film they watched on the plane ride over. And in my sense of frustration, I turned around and said, "Really? Seriously? Look at where you are, and this is what you're choosing to talk about?"

Upon reflection, Godlaski considered how he might have responded differently. Aided with the wisdom of hindsight and his previous professional experience as a licensed psychologist, he has since come to interpret students' behavior in the forest that day as manifestations of their internal states:

> How students are engaging with a space, or how they're behaving, is indicative of their engagement in the course. But it's also indicative of how they're managing their personal experience. Some of them may be homesick, some of them may be really nervous, or maybe they haven't been in a crowded city before. We all deal with

anxiety, those sorts of anxieties consciously or unconsciously, in very different ways.

Rather than admonish students for talking about superficial things in what he perceived to be a sacred place, Godlaski wished that he had named the behaviors he observed and provided an opportunity for students to think about them or invited them to comment upon their reactions. This example demonstrates how faculty members come to recognize the potential teachable moments that occur during an off-campus study program and also that it takes tact and wisdom to do such moments their justice.

When the unexpected happens on an off-campus study program, faculty program leaders must make instantaneous decisions about whether and how to intervene, including whether to say something in the moment or hold their observation for a later time. As Carlin Metz's and Godlaski's experiences illustrate, a well-timed question can prompt students to check their assumptions, give voice to their emotional states, and reengage with what they can be learning from their immediate surroundings. An instructor's question can help students come to an insight that they might have otherwise ignored. These examples illustrate, moreover, that such moments can broaden the awareness, skills, and insights of faculty program leaders. Faculty program leaders described how they developed over time a nuanced repertoire of teaching strategies and the ability to ask the right question, thus enabling them to constructively reframe an unexpected setback into a moment of deeper recognition. It is easy to imagine how this transferable skill would enable an instructor to take advantage of a teachable moment that presents itself during a traditional on-campus course, be it a student's errant comment or a significant national event that students feel compelled to discuss. Off-campus study programs stretch program instructors to practice new postures and approaches to teaching. These often include shedding some formality, sharing responsibility for instruction with the learners themselves, and asking a powerful question to refocus the group during a moment of distraction or danger. The faculty members interviewed for this chapter all saw these changes as evidence of becoming better equipped, more insightful, and more effective teachers.

Participants developed new terms of academic rigor for off-campus programs to take full advantage of students' time in the field and to support the concentrated periods of self-reflection that make global learning so impactful. The final finding of the study contended that interviewed faculty members were drawn to off-campus programs because they provided interesting and worthy challenges for instructors. Teaching in off-campus study programs prompted instructors to reimagine how to structure assignments to highlight interdisciplinary connections and how to transform a setback or obstacle into a teachable moment.

RECOMMENDATIONS FOR PRACTICE

This chapter described many of the salient teaching strategies, attitudes toward pedagogy, and university structures that faculty members reported as having a beneficial effect on off-campus study programs. Insights from conversations with 11 faculty members present several implications for practice—recommendations that the authors more fully explore in other sections of this book.

Professional Development and Institutional Norms

For a more fully enumerated discussion of the potential implications for professional development, see chapter 2 in which Dana Gross considers how colleges can provide more targeted and timely support to faculty program leaders. Further underscoring this need, despite the perceived differences between off-campus study programs and traditional on-campus courses, few of the faculty members interviewed for this chapter had received much professional development or formalized training to incorporate appropriate pedagogies or to consider the special implications for travel-embedded course design. A few interviewed faculty members noted having requested (and received) funds from their college to participate in workshops about global learning or intercultural pedagogy, but these examples proved to be the exception rather than the rule. Nearly all participants had benefited from attending an on-campus orientation or receiving a handbook of policies from their institution, but for the most part, such workshops or supplementary materials failed to address matters of teaching and learning explicitly. As a result, many of the faculty members interviewed engaged in a self-directed process of developing course elements and assignments to satisfy their formal and informal goals for students (e.g., disciplinary learning, independent thinking, cultural awareness). This high degree of autonomy is likely to result in highly varied student experiences—colleges that are concerned with offering students more consistent learning experiences should take note that more must be done to cultivate shared vision and shared pedagogical strategies across a campus.

Guided by the perspectives of the faculty members interviewed for this chapter, many liberal arts colleges have yet to articulate guidelines for teaching in off-campus study programs. Some of the findings presented in this chapter might serve as good starting points for future campus-wide conversations. Rather than leave all pedagogical and scheduling decisions to the sole discretion of a program leader, faculty members within a college might develop shared norms regarding the best uses of time in-country, how to balance workload expectations between reading and more experiential forms of learning, how rigidly to adhere to the lesson plan when a teachable moment arises, and how to purposefully incorporate interdisciplinary approaches. We expect that rich conversations would follow if prospective and seasoned program leaders thought through these topics together—not from a prescriptive angle about what an instructor must do but rather how instructors might navigate structures and opportunities to achieve course, major, and broader curricular goals. The use of case study examples—including some of the field-experiences of Carlin Metz, Jackson, and Godlaski—could serve as a starting point.

This chapter, moreover, encourages colleges to see the broader, and perhaps overlooked, benefits of leading an off-campus study program. Even though these off-campus study programs demanded considerable preparation and required individuals to spend time away from their campuses and sometimes their families, nearly 80% of respondents in the Faculty as Global Learners survey came back feeling "renewed" and "energized." Many faculty members who led an off-campus program reported making subsequent changes to the content and pedagogy of their on-campus courses upon returning, suggesting that there may be a spillover effect. Returning program leaders even described creating new courses outside of their home department as a result of their time away. Given these described benefits, colleges might reimagine the way in which program leaders are selected; for instance, leaders might be selected to help mid-career scholars avoid a post-tenure slump.

Limitations

The findings of this chapter reveal what a handful of faculty members who have led off-campus study programs see and believe. Speaking from their experiences at private liberal arts colleges, the faculty members consulted for this chapter explained how their programs foregrounded high-impact practices (for students) and became a site of pedagogical experimentation and innovation (for them). As readers, we must resist the temptation to equate the mere presence of a research-based pedagogical structure (or high-impact practice) with demonstrable evidence of student learning. The faculty members interviewed for this chapter described the perceived gains in students' self-efficacy, learning, independence, and maturity; it is important to draw a distinction between these beliefs and demonstrated student outcomes. Observations of teaching (Campbell, 2017) and the assessment of student work (Condon, Iverson, Manduca, Rutz, & Willett, 2016) would enhance the trustworthiness of these claims. Consistent with the goals of this collection, faculty perceptions, nonetheless, reveal important insights that deepen the ways in which we as scholars and practitioners characterize off-campus study programs in higher education.

CONCLUSION

The existing scholarly research on global learning in higher education has long been dominated by investigations of how students grow, change, and learn as a result of studying abroad. While few would dispute the centrality of students to the work of higher education researchers, leaders, and faculty members, the authors of this collection maintain that attending to the experiences and unmet needs of faculty members is critical to delivering a student-focused educational experience. Learning how faculty make sense of teaching in off-campus programs—and the ways in which they are shaped and supported by institutional contexts—reveals promising practices and opportunities to do better. By more closely examining the pedagogies and structures of off-campus study programs, we can see how these experiences complement traditional on-campus courses as vital and distinctive elements of a liberal arts education.

This chapter demonstrated how students and faculty are drawn to participate in off-campus study programs for similar reasons, including an innate curiosity about the world, a desire to experience other cultures, an interest in seeing academic concepts come to life in an experiential setting, a yearning to break out of their daily routines, or an eagerness to learn more about themselves. Leading an off-campus study program left a majority of faculty feeling renewed and energized. The Faculty as Global Learners survey and the continued research conducted for this chapter surfaced some of the longer term, positive effects of leading an off-campus study program. These benefits include faculty deepening their empathy for their students, experimenting with experiential project-based learning in their traditional on-campus courses, advising more students to study abroad, and broadening the use of international examples and anecdotes in their on-campus courses. Savvy colleges will realize that investing in, supporting, and celebrating faculty members as global learners is an essential component of internationalizing the college.

Using a qualitative case study approach, this chapter has analyzed the experiences of 11 faculty members at private liberal arts colleges who have led at least one off-campus study program. Their collective perceptions reveal what faculty members believe makes off-campus learning—at home or abroad—a distinctive learning opportunity for students. From flexible daily schedules to high levels of student-faculty engagement, off-campus study programs provide qualitatively different academic experiences than traditional on-campus courses. Time and again, study participants showed how leading an off-campus study program compelled them to (re)conceptualize their expectations surrounding academic rigor and to push students to think about their identities and recognize the influence of culture on their learning. Given that many faculty members relied on their own judgment and goals to shape students' learning off campus, this chapter signals a need for colleges to think more systematically about how to ensure that students benefit from a more consistent educational experience at home and abroad.

REFERENCES

Alexis, F., Casco, M., Martin, J., & Zhang, G. (2017). Cross-cultural and global inter-dependency development in STEM undergraduate students: Results from Singapore study abroad program. *Education, 137*(3), 249–256.

Anderson, C. L., Lorenz, K., & White, M. (2016). Instructor influence on student intercultural gains and learning during instructor-led, short-term study abroad. *Frontiers: The Interdisciplinary Journal of Study Abroad, 28,* 1–23.

Anderson Sathe, L., & Geisler, C. C. (2016). The reverberations of a graduate study abroad course in India. *Journal of Transformative Education, 15*(1), 16–36. doi:10.1177/1541344615604230

Andrade, L. M., Dittloff, S., & Nath, L. (2019). *A guide to faculty-led study abroad: How to create a transformative experience.* New York, NY: Routledge.

Andriano, B. R. (2010). *Study abroad participation and engagement practices of first-generation undergraduate students* (EdD dissertation). The George Washington University, Washington, DC.

Benham Rennick, J., & Desjardins, M. (Eds.). (2013). *The world is my classroom: International learning and Canadian higher education.* Toronto, Canada: University of Toronto Press.

Boyer, E. L. (1997). *Scholarship reconsidered: Priorities of the professoriate.* San Francisco, CA: Jossey-Bass.

Campbell, C. M. (2017). An inside view: The utility of quantitative observation in understanding college educational experiences. *Journal of College Student Development, 58*(2), 290–299. doi:10.1353/csd.2017.0021

Charmaz, K. (2014). *Constructing grounded theory* (2nd ed.). Introducing qualitative methods. London: SAGE Publications.

Chickering, A., & Gamson, Z. (1987). Seven principles for good practice in undergraduate education. *AAHE Bulletin, 39*(7), 3–7.

Condon, W., Iverson, E. R., Manduca, C. A., Rutz, C., & Willett, G. (2016). *Faculty development and student learning: Assessing the connections.* Scholarship of teaching and learning. Bloomington, IN: Indiana University Press.

Cuba, L., Jennings, N., Lovett, S., & Swingle, J. (2016). *Practice for life: Making decisions in college.* Cambridge, MA: Harvard University Press.

Davis, Y. (2014). *University faculty contribution to study abroad programs: What do we know about their motivation?* Ann Arbor, MI: ProQuest Dissertations Publishing.

Dunn, A. H., Dotson, E. K., Cross, S. B., Kesner, J., & Lundahl, B. (2014). Reconsidering the local after a transformative global experience: A comparison of two study abroad programs for preservice teachers. *Action in Teacher Education, 36*(4), 283–304. doi:10.1080/01626620.2014.948227

Ellinghaus, K., Spinks, J., Moore, G., Hetherington, P., & Atherton, C. (2019). Learning to teach in the field: Five professors tell how running an overseas study tour improved their classroom teaching. *Frontiers: The Interdisciplinary Journal of Study Abroad, 31*(1), 169–189.

Ellis, J. M. (2014). Pop culture, Twitter, and study abroad: Estonia as a case study. *Political Science & Politics, 47*(1), 204–208.

Feller, A. E. (2015). Where experience meets transformation: Pedagogy and study away. In N. W. Sobania (Ed.), *Putting the local in global education: Models for transformative learning through domestic off-campus programs* (pp. 52–72). Sterling, VA: Stylus Publishing.

Felten, P. (2013). Principles of good practice in SoTL. *Teaching & Learning Inquiry: The ISSOTL Journal, 1*(1), 121–125.

Finley, A., & McNair, T. (2013). *Assessing underserved students' engagement in high-impact practices.* Retrieved from https://leapconnections.aacu.org/system/files/assessinghipsmcnairfinley_0.pdf

Fitzsimmons, S. R., Flanagan, D. J., & Wang, X. A. (2013). Business students' choice of short-term or long-term study abroad opportunities. *Journal of Teaching in International Business, 24*(2), 125–137. doi:10.1080/08975930.2013.819710

France, H., & Rogers, L. (2012). Cuba study abroad: A pedagogical tool for reconstructing American national identity. *International Studies Perspectives, 13*(4), 390–407. doi:10.1111/j.1528-3585.2012.00478.x

Glaser, B. G., & Strauss, A. (1967). *The discovery of grounded theory: Strategies for qualitative research.* Chicago, IL: Aldine Press.

Gonsalvez, J. (2013). The pedagogy of short-term study-abroad programs. *Journal of Arts and Humanities, 2*(8), 1–5.

Goode, M. (2008). The role of faculty study abroad directors: A case study. *Frontier: The Interdisciplinary Journal of Study Abroad, 15*, 149–172.

Gross, D., Abrams, K., & Enns, C. Z. (Eds.). (2016). *Internationalizing the undergraduate psychology curriculum: Practical lessons learned at home and abroad.* Washington, DC: American Psychological Association.

Hutchings, P., Huber, M. T., & Ciccone, A. (2011). *The scholarship of teaching and learning reconsidered: Institutional integration and impact.* San Francisco, CA: Jossey-Bass.

Jasinski, L., & Davis, C. W. (2018). Reflections from Brazil: Improving international research experiences for graduate students. *Transformative Dialogues: Teaching & Learning Journal, 11*(3).

Johansson, C., & Felten, P. (2014). *Transforming students: Fulfilling the promise of higher education.* Baltimore, MD: Johns Hopkins University Press.

Jokisch, B. (2009). Making a traditional study-abroad program geographic: A theoretically informed regional approach. *Journal of Geography, 108*(3), 105–111. doi:10.1080/00221340903103318

Kuh, G. D. (2007). *Experiences that matter: Enhancing student learning and success: Annual Report 2007.* Retrieved from http://nsse.indiana.edu/NSSE_2007_Annual_Report/docs/withhold/NSSE_2007_Annual_Report.pdf

Kuh, G. D. (2008). *High-impact educational practices: What they are, who has access to them, and why they matter.* Washington, DC: Association of American Colleges & Universities.

Le, Q. V., Raven, P. V., & Chen, S. (2013). International service learning and short-term business study abroad programs: A case study. *Journal of Education for Business, 88*(5), 301–306. doi:10.1080/08832323.2012.697927

Malloy, M. N., & Davis, A. J. (2012). The University of Georgia avian biology study abroad program in Costa Rica. *North American Colleges and Teachers of Agriculture Journal, 56*(3), 24–29.

Malmgren, J., & Galvin, J. (2008). Effects of study abroad participation on student graduation rates: A study of three incoming freshman cohorts at the University of Minnesota, Twin Cities. *NACADA Journal, 28*(1), 29–42.

Merriam, S. B. (2001). *Qualitative research and case study applications in education: Revised and expanded from case study research in education* (2nd ed.). San Francisco, CA: Jossey-Bass.

Namaste, N. B. (2017). Designing and evaluating students' transformative learning. *Canadian Journal for the Scholarship of Teaching and Learning, 8*(3), 1–22. doi:10.5206/cjsotl-rcacea.2017.3.5

O'Meara, K., & Terosky, A. L. (2010). Engendering faculty professional growth. *Change: The Magazine of Higher Learning, 42*(6), 44–51. doi:10.1080/00091383.2010.523408

Rasch, D. C. (2001). *Faculty voices from the field: Perceptions and implications of study abroad* (Unpublished dissertation). Peabody College of Vanderbilt University, Nashville, TN.

Saldaña, J. (2016). *The coding manual for qualitative researchers* (3rd ed.). London: SAGE Publications.

Salisbury, M. H. (2011). *The effect of study abroad on intercultural competence among undergraduate college students* (Doctor of philosophy thesis). University of Iowa, Ames, IA.

Sandgren, D., Ellig, N., Hovde, P., Krejci, M., & Rice, M. (1999). How international experience affects teaching: Understanding the impact of faculty study abroad. *Journal of Studies in International Education, 3*(1), 33–56.

Schenker, T. (2018). Making short-term study abroad count: Effects on German language skills. *Foreign Language Annals, 51*(2), 411–429. doi:10.1111/flan.12339

Shulman, L. S. (1993). Teaching as community property: Putting an end to pedagogical solitude. *Change, 25*(6), 6–7.

Squire, D. D., Williams, T. E., Cartwright, M., Jourian, T. J., Monter, M., & Weath-
erford, A. (2015). Exploring gender through education abroad programs: A
graduate student case study. *Journal of Student Affairs Research and Practice,
52*(3), 262–274. doi:10.1080/19496591.2015.1035383

Vande Berg, M., Paige, R. M., & Lou, K. H. (Eds.). (2012). *Student learning abroad:
What our students are learning, what they're not, and what we can do about it.*
Sterling, VA: Stylus Publishing.

Wang, J., Peyvandi, A., & Coffey, B. S. (2014). Does a study abroad class make a
difference in student's global awareness? An empirical study. *International
Journal of Education Research, 9*(1), 151–162.

Young, G. E. (2014). Reentry: Supporting students in the final stage of study
abroad. *New Directions for Student Services, 2014*(146), 59–67.

APPENDIX A—INTERVIEW QUESTIONS

1. Can you start out by telling me a little about your past experiences leading study away or study abroad programs? Why
   did you want to get involved in this kind of teaching? What
   keeps you involved?

2. In general, talk me through the goals you have for the study
   abroad programs you lead and what you hope that your students will take away from these experiences? (What is your
   sense of how well these goals are achieved? How do you
   know?)

3. What kind of pedagogical strategies have you used in your
   study abroad program?

4. Can you give me an example of a moment during one of your
   study abroad programs where you felt like, from an instructional angle, everything worked very well? This might be a
   particularly effective assignment or a way of approaching a
   concept or topic that was very effective.

5. Can you give me an example of an unforeseen challenge you

faced as an instructor of a field-based program and how you overcame it?

6. Do you supplement your time abroad or off campus with on-campus seminars or group meetings? What kinds of things do you do or topics do you address before or after an off-campus experience to support student learning?

7. How would you characterize the differences, if any, between the teaching you do on campus and the teaching you do in off-campus programs?

8. How has leading a study abroad program changed the way you teach or the way you think about teaching or students?

9. What are your administrative responsibilities relative to the program—program planning and development, logistics, program review/assessment? How do you balance your instructional and administrative responsibilities? Have you ever felt that your administrative responsibilities have gotten in the way of your instructional goals?

10. Is there something else you think that I should know about your experiences related to teaching and faculty-led study abroad?

WELCOMING THE SURPRISING

Sensory Experience and the Sacred

L. DeAne Lagerquist

If you had been part of this class studying sacred places in Greece and Turkey in 2014, you might recall this moment about 10 days into our journey. We were leaving Delphi, headed for the hanging monasteries of Meteora, but we had stopped to wait for deliv-

ery of an item left behind in the previous night's hotel. It was an unplanned break in our itinerary. At the spot where the bus driver pulled off the road there were not any designated sacred sites: no temple ruins, no magnificent mosques, no Byzantine icons, not even the trickle of a sacred spring. Nonetheless, there was a subject worthy of a photograph. You see it here.

What do these photographs tell you about these students, their experiences, and what they learned that January away from campus? Imagine yourself joining them in this line. Feel your body striking a dynamic, balancing pose: arms up, fingers spread, legs bent. Compose your facial expression. Notice the breeze on your skin. Does it carry the salty smell of the gulf below, or is there a faint fragrance of the olive trees that cover the downward slope? Can you hear the quiet ringing of sheep bells? Are you able to see ancient Delphi, off to the northeast, above the modern village? Certainly, you are aware of your classmates' bodies and of their breath as you arrange yourselves, close to one another, near the mountain edge.

These photographs show my students making the most of a delay caused by one of their peer's forgetfulness. Together, without my prompting, they used their bodies to make that spot a sacred place. This was a temporary *temenos,* a space set apart for a specific purpose, often for a place of worship. I did not arrange stones to set it apart from the surrounding area or erect a marker to commemorate the spontaneous event. I merely took this photograph, a souvenir of that fleeting moment. Now it serves to remind me of them, of their good spirits, of their care for one another, of each one's individuality. Even though a photograph does not record smells, or sounds, or tactile sensations, this one does recall the sensory experiences I invited you to imagine, including viewing the ruins of Delphi that are outside the frame.

Beyond being a souvenir of a singular event, these photographs also point toward common features of study abroad and the part photography may play in students' learning. Study abroad is an embodied experience. Of course, all learning takes place in our bodies, but the conditions of travel make that truth more vivid in an off-campus program than in a classroom. Waking up to the call to prayer, flowing from one end of Izmir to the other, deepens one's understanding of Islamic notions of time beyond what is possible on a midwestern campus. When we are abroad, I'm more aware of, and responsible for, my students' physical well-being. I pay attention to what they eat, how much they sleep, their footwear, their propensity to motion sickness as the bus carries us along twisting mountain roads. To prevent the latter, I bring along ginger capsules. I tell students that bringing them all home—each one whole—is a condition of a successful program. Meeting this condition, however, does not in itself produce a successful class.

My students and I travel to Greece and Turkey to learn about sacred places. Studying abroad with students has taught me to acknowledge that sensory experience is integral to embodied learning and to invite students to make use of all their senses. A discussion may begin with each student naming something they heard or smelled or touched during a site visit. Or they might write about how multiple senses are engaged during the Orthodox Holy Liturgy: they see the frescoes and the elaborate vestments; they notice that worshippers' sense of time is not ruled by punctuality; they inhale incense and smoke from beeswax candles; they are aware of their own posture and the priest's movement in and out of the Holy of Holies; they observe worshippers kissing icons; they may taste the unconsecrated but blessed bread. After we attended a performance of the Sufi sema ritual, the dancers and pre-med students in this class led us in thinking about the body as a sacred place. Deliberate attention to sensory experience enriches the experience, promotes learning, and reinforces memory.

We take photographs in an attempt to capture something of this sensory, embodied experience. The high-quality digital cameras integrated into our phones make the effort all too easy. But the attempt will fail because a photograph, even one skillfully made, will always be one-dimensional and limited to sight. Worse, the act of taking photographs can be a distraction. I watched a student in an earlier group walk through the battlements of Thessaloniki clicking pictures without even looking at what was in front of her. I have scolded students for delaying the group by taking countless, comic selfies. In reaction I require students to read about the role of photography in tourism, to go one day in the month without taking any photographs, and to write a brief reflection about what they saw when their cameras were in their pockets instead of in front of their eyes. We also analyze their own photographs in comparison to purchased postcards of sites we have visited, noting both how the professional images inform their expectations and how the images they make differ in content, composition, and meaning.

These photographs I made have no commercial counterpart. Although the subject was self-consciously composed, it is really just a snapshot. As much as it shows, it is missing more. So, I'm inclined to forgo a claim that it captures anything. Better to suggest that it is a trace of an extraordinary episode of study abroad and to let it be a recommendation to be alert for the learning that arrives unexpected and unplanned.

READING LITERATURE ALOUD IN ITS HOME PLACE

Christine S. Cozzens

We're standing in a dank cell in Kilmainham Gaol, Dublin, where Charles Stewart Parnell—MP for Cork City and proponent of Irish Home Rule—was imprisoned in 1881 for agitating on behalf of land reform, a movement that would eventually transform rural Ireland. The tour guide finishes his account and nods to me. I have asked

permission to follow his explanation with readings of excerpts from Parnell's great speeches by a student on my Literary Ireland trip. Along with my 24 students, there are seven or eight other tourists in the group, several from Spain, a couple from Germany, and at least two other U.S. Americans. We've been doing these readings for several days now, and the students are getting used to it, but so far, they haven't had to read aloud in front of strangers. One of them reads Parnell's famous 1885 speech, including this famous passage: "No man has the right to fix the boundary to the march of a nation. No man has the right to say to his country 'Thus far shalt thou go and no further.'"

When she finishes, there's a thought-heavy silence in the cell, then a surprising round of applause. "That was stunning," says the young tour guide. "Why didn't I ever think of that?!" Perhaps he will add readings to his next tour. The U.S. Americans thank the student who read, and the others nod their approval. Did our simple reading add to their experience of the prison with its dense political history or help them understand Parnell a bit better? For the student reader, the moment will be memorable, something she will write about later. Not only did she put Parnell's famous words together with his time in prison, a measure of what he was willing to sacrifice to achieve his goals, but she also made that moment tangible and meaningful for classmates and strangers.

On the many student trips focusing on literature I've led to Ireland, perhaps the most distinctive feature is that the students read literature aloud, usually in public, in the places where it was born. I got the idea from a member of my department who long ago assigned passages from medieval English literature for his students to read aloud on a faculty-led trip to England. Like all the students going to Ireland with me for the first few days of each trip, I thought the practice sounded silly and embarrassing. But after trying it out a few times, I realized how wrong I had been. For the students who read and for their listeners—whether part of our group or simply members of the public who happen to be there—these unusual performances bring the words of great literature and oratory to life with startling power. Each performance gives the reader a chance to step outside the self and offers both readers and listeners a glimpse of the world of the past, the world of this unfamiliar place, the world of the creative work.

Many students have told me that they never really understood or appreciated a work of literature until they had the chance to read it aloud on-site. One said that she grasped the darkness and prescience of W. B. Yeats's "Easter, 1916" in a new way when she read it aloud at the mass grave of 14 leaders of the Easter Rising. Another found unexpected sympathy for the elegance and anachronism of the Anglo-Irish ascendancy class as she read the words of Elizabeth Bowen's novel *The Last September* on the lawn in front of a ruined Big House. For another student, Oscar Wilde's wit seemed more biting and yet sadder read aloud in front of the multicolored marble statue of him lounging on a rock in Merrion Square. My own understanding of these works deepens every time I hear one of these readings.

Though they need a bit of persuasion and cajoling at first, after a day or two of reading literature aloud in public places, the students begin to see that it is not onerous and is even kind of fun. They begin to claim certain readings at certain locations, competing for some of the more popular pieces: "Anna Liffey," Eavan Boland's ode to the Dublin's River Liffey and the gendered voice; "Pangur Bán," a poem about a monk and his cat that we read at Glendalough, a secluded monastery in the Wicklow Mountains; Yeats's "The Stolen Child" set in "the woods around Glencar" Waterfall. Very often three or four want to read Yeats's "The Wild Swans at Coole" by Coole Lake in Galway, and with luck there will be swans dipping and gliding in the background. By the time we get to Belfast, several readers are eager to remember Frederick Douglass's visit there in 1846 through the eloquent letters he wrote home about his experiences traveling around the island.

Each of these readings commemorates a creative act but also

marks the occasion of a reader bringing literature and history to life for a modern audience and experiencing the thrill of performance, if only for a moment. Fear of speaking in public, fear of mispronouncing Irish names and words, fear of misreading are not small obstacles to overcome. A student with severe dyslexia wanted to read some of the monastic poems when we were at Glendalough, so she got help memorizing them, freeing herself from the text. All of the readers have the sense that they are doing something unusual and important when they bring a work of literature to its home place.

The photograph included here captures a moment just after a student, Megan (holding our book of literary excerpts and seated next to Yeats's grave), had read Yeats's "Under Ben Bulben," a poem in which he imagines his own death, literally under Ben Bulben, the mountain in the background. Megan read the poem three times during our short visit, despite its length: once to the whole group in the church where Yeats's grandfather was rector; again at the grave for us, a few other tourists, and the current rector; and finally for herself and three friends.

As we walked out to the bus after Megan's reading, snow began to fall heavily. We had paid our homage and read our poems in the nick of time. By the time we rounded the bend in the road and looked back, Ben Bulben, the church, and Drumcliff churchyard were blanketed in snow.

BUILDING PARTNERSHIPS IN MWANDI, ZAMBIA

Verna Case

Davidson College's summer program in the village of Mwandi, Western Province, Zambia, began in 1995. Today, the program involves a course that focuses on cultural, environmental, economic, political, and social factors that affect health and health care in a community served by the United Church of Zambia

Mwandi Mission Hospital (UCZMMH). Students shadow hospital staff as a complement of the course.

First, some perspective: the Mwandi village has about 10,000 inhabitants, and the hospital's catchment area has roughly 28,000 residents. Subsistence farming and fishing are the basis for the local economy. Isolated from the rest of Zambia by inadequate roads, the health of Western Province's residents is impacted by poor water quality, frequent droughts limiting maize production, and infectious diseases (including HIV/AIDS).

Davidson began the Mwandi program to provide undergraduate students with the ability to have a medical experience abroad. When I began leading the program in 2000, I realized that the students would gain much more from their time in Mwandi if course learning outcomes were broadened to include understanding the many factors that affect health in this remote village. How could this shift in the program's goals be accomplished? The answer: engage the people of Mwandi as partners in the students' education. Like the African proverb, "It takes a village to raise a child," the success of Davidson's program hinges on the generosity of the Mwandi people who share their lives with us.

During the last 18 years, I developed strong relationships with Mwandi's hospital staff and community leaders. As the students engage in formal and informal conversations with these individuals, they learn to be keen observers, to ask informed questions, to listen critically, and to think holistically. Most of the students' time is spent with UCZMMH medical staff. On rounds, the doctor discusses clinical aspects of disease and challenges students with related questions. At other times, students help health care workers by taking patient weights, temperatures, and blood pressures and helping to dispense medication under the supervision of a pharmacist. By assisting in basic care duties, students form friendships that persist on social media for years. They also gain some understanding of challenges facing health care providers in a resource-limited hospital.

Hospital staff are not the only treatment providers in Mwandi. Many villagers seek medical treatment from traditional healers before they will go to the hospital. To understand the role of healers in the medical milieu, sessions with two traditional healers are a standard part of the program. The healers share information about the herbs they use in their treatments, the types of afflictions they can and cannot treat, and the path that led them to become a healer. In addition to using herbs, the two healers are spiritualists and discuss charms they make and use to protect their patients.

His Royal Highness, Senior Chief Inyambo Yeta is the Barotse Royal Establishment Reigning Prince. He began this role in 1977. Senior Chief Yeta also served as chairperson of Zambia's House of Chiefs and as a member of the Zambian Parliament. Residing in the Royal Court of Mwandi, Senior Chief Yeta graciously shares the history and culture of the Lozi people with the students. Based on his vast experiences as a traditional and national leader, he has an incredible understanding of Zambian political and economic issues. His global perspectives enable him to reflect on environmental and health concerns within sub-Saharan Africa and beyond. Senior Chief Yeta's long-term commitment to supporting health care is illustrated by his vision to convert a small rural health center into the Mwandi hospital in 1986.

In addition to meeting with the chief, students have the opportunity to talk with many other village leaders. Mwandi's mayor and members of the Royal Establishments' council (or Kuta) give students additional perspectives on the division of responsibilities between the government and Royal Establishment, particularly with respect to issues of health care. Because Christian churches form the core of Western Province society, church elders are some of Mwandi's most influential citizens. During our time in Mwandi, students have numerous opportunities to talk with church leaders and parishioners about the role that churches can play in the health of their congregations. Furthermore, church leaders provide students with insights about the roles mission hospitals play in Zambia.

As previously mentioned, Mwandi presents unusual opportunities for developing enduring relationships. As my network in the village continues to grow, it offers many new learning opportunities and keener insights for the students regarding the daily lives and struggles of Mwandi residents. A student who took advantage of one of these unique learning opportunities commented,

> I became involved with Kandiana, a housing facility for disabled elderly. I worked closely with Catherine, the caretaker, to clean rooms, wash soiled linens, give baths, and cook meals. I discovered how much Kandiana residents are affected by the policies of international donors and village leaders. The Mwandi program immerses students in the community to demonstrate that people live where global health policies end.

Opportunities for interaction with villagers also allow students to develop special, and sometimes lasting, relationships with particular individuals. Another student put it this way: "Dorothy taught me what it really means to have an open door in this life. To have an open door is to live compassionately, to live fully and gratefully, to live like Dorothy."

In summary, the microcosm of the Mwandi village provides an ideal environment for student learning. The long-standing partnership between the people in Mwandi and Davidson College is built on strong personal relationships and a commitment to many forms of education.

DEALING WITH STRONGLY VARYING STUDENT RESEARCH BACKGROUNDS IN STUDY ABROAD

James J. Ebersole

Supervising student research in study abroad semesters presents multiple challenges, including wide variation in student preparation. Here, I describe one strategy, successful in a semester in Tanzania, to help students, regardless of their previous research experience, progress in understanding how to do research.

My philosophy and approach include high expectations, strong support from me to meet those expectations, and guiding students to choose projects on their own. I choose individual projects over group projects, another legitimate option, because my experience on campus has shown that students learn most when they must develop their own ideas and make their own decisions in the field. While pushing students to excel in their projects, I also strongly believe that the substantial time that students spend on research projects should not detract from less structured, experiential, cross-cultural learning, which in my mind remains the core of study abroad. Fortunately, students can do both.

The Associated Colleges of the Midwest's semester program Tanzania: Ecology & Human Origins helps students "learn about the centrality, the methods, and the rewards of field work for knowledge in both the social and natural sciences" (ACM website) while experiencing cultural immersion in East Africa. Its unusual design combines natural and social science majors into one program. After introductory courses and preparation for research in the capital, the program spent four weeks in northern Tanzania where students conducted ethnographic research in Maasai villages or did natural science fieldwork in and near a national park.

In addition to variety in academic fields, students had widely varying research experience. Some had done several small-scale field projects in classes, often in groups; one or two had done larger projects; and others had no prior experience. This diversity required differentiated pedagogy to challenge the most experienced students while helping the less experienced learn about and feel encouraged in their first field research.

Both on campus and abroad, I approach student research using the proverb "Give a person a fish and feed them for a day; teach a person to fish and feed them for a lifetime." I want students to struggle with thinking through what makes an interesting research idea, a task that pushes them into intellectual discomfort. Students then develop, initially on their own, methods yielding data to address their idea. These are hard tasks, especially with limited background, so I provide support and feedback before frustration becomes counterproductive.

To help students develop research ideas, several months before the course I sent a document describing the process of choosing interesting and productive research ideas, with examples of previous strong projects from the program, a list of several journals to leaf through, and directions to search the literature on interesting ideas from classes. I emphasized that projects should, in most cases, address a larger theoretical idea with a specific study system rather than simply gathering data about a local system. One student, for example, rather than simply documenting how elephant damage to trees affects tree growth rates in Tarangire National Park, used these data to test the idea of overcompensation, that is, some species of plants may grow faster after moderate herbivory.

All students struggled with the challenges of developing an idea and wrapping a theory around it. Several of the most experienced students arrived with both tasks impressively well done. Others had preliminary ideas, whereas others said they don't read school emails in summer. In Tanzania, all students engaged actively in the process with lively discussions on possible topics, and more experienced students naturally helped others while brainstorming. The research neophytes grappled with, and grew in, understanding what makes an interesting research idea. Some of these students ended up with modifications of previous projects, but they learned through their struggle and intellectual discomfort.

Intermediate deadlines helped students stay on track while developing their ideas and writing their proposals. We also discussed previous, anonymized proposals, some excellent and some fair, and I pointed out strengths and weaknesses, so students could see how to move from fair to strong. The first deadline, early in the program, was one paragraph stating their research topic, which we workshopped as a class and in discipline-specific groups and to which they received my detailed feedback, both in writing and in one-on-one meetings. Students had subsequent deadlines for a carefully crafted hypothesis or question, methods, and the final proposal. We discussed the challenging task of setting research into a theoretical framework, and I provided introductions of published papers as models, with annotations pointing out how the authors introduced the theory behind their study. Peer reviews of proposal drafts gave everyone feedback on their ideas, and critiquing the ideas and writing of others helped students see their own proposal ideas and writing style with fresh eyes.

I encouraged students to aim high and in pre-course information included examples of undergraduate publications, so they could feel empowered, knowing that they could do publishable research. While encouraging them to aim for publications, I reassured them that not all strong projects would be publishable and that our main goal was learning how to do research.

After fieldwork was completed, intermediate deadlines, handouts with examples of how to move writing from adequate to strong, my detailed critiques on several drafts, and peer critiques helped students write strong papers. For projects submitted to peer-reviewed journals, I provided detailed advice on revisions and published examples to follow as analogues, so students could go as far as possible with the analysis, organization, and writing; I then made modest revisions before submission.

I hope and believe that all students, with ongoing support to discover their own answers, benefited greatly by wrestling with the creative process of developing an interesting idea, placing it into a larger context, and working out appropriate methods. Several told me they found the experience empowering and felt confident in developing research ideas and doing research on their own in the future. I hope that all are better prepared for future situations in which they must judge which questions/avenues are important and must determine on their own how to approach their goals.

CHAPTER 4

POOLING RESOURCES FOR OFF-CAMPUS STUDY PROGRAMS THROUGH INSTITUTIONAL PARTNERSHIPS

Benefits, Challenges, and Guidelines

Joan Gillespie

Higher education institutions who participated in a survey on strategic international partnerships, sponsored by the Institute of International Education (IIE) and Freie Universität Berlin (FUB), identified the top two "motivations" for developing partnerships as "extended opportunities for students" followed closely by "extended opportunities for faculty and researchers," each reason cited by more than 50% of respondents (Kuder & Banks, 2016, p. xiii). Third on the list was "global positioning," and the "use of synergies/pooling of resources" was fourth, representing 40% of respondents (p. xiii). The pooling of resources through collaboration addresses the economic reality of finite funding and staffing—a reality that dictates the extent to which any higher education institution pursues its mission-driven priorities. It can serve as a strategy specifically at small liberal arts institutions to support other campus initiatives and goals related to purposefully designed off-campus study programs. This chapter asserts that collaborative partnerships make a small college a larger one, with both educational and administrative benefits. By sharing know-how, funding, a faculty who offer a wide range of curricular choices, and a body of students who enroll in off-campus study, smaller liberal arts institutions engaged in a partnership can work toward their major goal of internationalization, creating opportunities that they could not create by themselves.

The IIE/FUB survey on international partnerships found several motivators besides those referenced above, touching on research quality and capacity, teaching quality and capacity, and funding. Kuder and Banks conclude, "This clearly indicates a great variety of reasons why higher education institutions decide to enter strategic partnerships and that, depending on the particular context, the partnerships will most certainly differ in structure and format" (2016, p. xiii). These many formats range from a modest plan for student exchange to the ambitious undertaking of a branch campus and joint degrees, from contracting with a third-party program provider to developing seminar-size, faculty-led student programs. While not all partnerships are motivated by faculty development, and not all models include faculty development opportunities, this chapter focuses on partnerships that embed opportunities for faculty in their program design.

The chapter begins by detailing how domestic and international partnerships at liberal arts colleges that include off-campus study intersect with other campus initiatives, specifically by (a) including diverse faculty and student populations in off-campus study; (b) providing requisite institutional support to faculty program leaders to advance their professional development, as described in chapter 2; and (c) offering a dynamic curriculum through place-based courses abroad. It reviews high-level characteristics of a successful partnership then makes recommendations for translating these ideals to action, including roles assigned to senior leadership, faculty members, and administrative staff. The primacy of intra-campus communication and collaboration underscores many points as the means to achieve the full benefits of partnerships. Caveats intended to manage expectations for institutions entering into a partnership also guide their ongoing work and may include ending a program or disbanding a partnership. The discussion is particularly directed to senior administrators and faculty who already are charged with the designated authority to plan and implement academic initiatives, including institutional partner-ships and off-campus study programs, and to those who aspire to centralize strategic international engagement with clear processes and protocols in order to further their educational mission.

A number of resources on strategic partnerships that advance institutional goals for students and faculty address agreements between U.S.-based institutions, particularly large public and pri-vate research universities, and non-U.S.-based higher education institutions or organizations (Banks, Siebe-Herbig, & Norton, 2016; Childress, 2018; Hudzik, 2015; Helms, 2015). These resources inform the section "Translating Concepts to Action in Establish-ing Partnerships" as they apply to liberal arts colleges. The section "Creating International Partnerships in the Liberal Arts" discusses the differences in academic cultures that liberal arts colleges nego-tiate in establishing a partnership with a non-U.S.-based higher education institution.

The past work of the Associated Colleges of the Midwest (ACM), a consortium of 14 private, residential liberal arts colleges, also informs this chapter, particularly on developing and man-aging a portfolio of off-campus study programs distinguished by the opportunities for faculty development. The decision by ACM leadership to close its international programs at the end of the 2018–2019 academic year serves as an example of the IIE/FUB sur-vey finding on international strategic partnerships; survey respon-dents were invited to comment on "the challenges . . . in developing and managing such partnerships" and identified "transition of leadership, followed by a change of priorities and different internal distribution of resources" (Kuder & Banks, 2016, p. xxiii) among the challenges. These circumstances were relevant to ACM and its decision to redirect resources to other initiatives. Nonetheless, several of the Faculty Voices in this study document the benefits of the ACM international programs to faculty members, students, and partners abroad and reinforce the profound value of collaborating across institutions to achieve mutual goals.

POOLING RESOURCES: FACULTY AND STUDENT DIVERSITY AND STUDY AWAY

An institution that uses global learning as a guide to structure its curriculum and co-curriculum also needs to consider how "to engage students who are underrepresented in study abroad and other global learning activities" (Whitehead, 2015, p. 10). The same consideration applies to faculty members who have been underrepresented in opportunities for international mobility (Bilecen & Van Mol, 2017, p. 1245). A portfolio of shared programs might engage faculty as program leaders, assistants, instructors, or research advisors, representing different fields and tenure status and who potentially can expand the demographic profiles of race, age, and gender of faculty leaders on campus-run programs.

Enlarging the program leadership pool directly addresses one of the needs that faculty program leaders identify in their own campus-run programs and simultaneously can contribute to the stability of a program. A familiar scenario at a liberal arts institution is a single department sponsoring an off-campus program for its majors that draws on a small number of departmental members to take turns leading the program. This scenario was voiced as a specific concern by faculty participants in the Faculty as Global Learners survey, introduced in chapter 1, who responded to Survey 11, Follow-up Questions for Faculty Members Who Lead Study

Away and Study Abroad Programs at Liberal Arts Institutions. One respondent wrote,

> I lead a study away program almost every year often times because other faculty cannot and we have a program that needs to have an interim abroad each year. (It) would be great to have . . . more faculty in my department so that we could spread out this responsibility more. (Gillespie, Glasco, Gross, Layne, & Jasinski, 2016)

In some cases, family or other personal commitments may make it impractical or impossible for all departmental faculty members to lead such programs. Adding new faculty lines to a department may be wishful thinking, unless one considers a partnership as a way to expand in numbers and expertise.

Other faculty participants in the study voiced concerns about finding a co-leader or identifying a mentee, particularly in the face of impending faculty retirements (Gillespie et al., 2016). The preference by some deans and department chairs to appoint only tenured professors to lead study away programs further reduces the pool of potential leaders. A partner institution might not only contribute co-leaders but also, in the case of mentees, cooperate on structuring a learning community for faculty leaders at all stages of their careers. Such partnerships particularly benefit those faculty who teach at institutions that do not currently sponsor campus-run study away programs, or, if they do, lack the administrative infrastructure to train and provide on-site support to a first-time or novice faculty leader. Absent a partnership, these faculty are unlikely to teach or lead such a program.

A partnership also promotes equal opportunity for faculty members by requiring a formal, transparent process for selecting leaders of programs that are controlled by the partner institutions and could be led by faculty representing a range of teaching and research interests. These policies are intrinsic to good management and are a step toward engaging a larger group of faculty members in study away opportunities. Guidelines for the selection process can start with an appointed group of institutional representatives charged with determining the responsibilities and qualifications for the call for applications, creating a realistic time line for reviewing applications and conducting interviews, and reaching consensus on the relative importance of a candidate's different merits that result in an offer to lead a program.

When faculty members who represent diverse populations serve as program leaders, the experience contributes to their success in meeting their multiple on-campus obligations, not only as classroom instructors but also as student research directors, student advisors, and mentors. As detailed in chapter 3, faculty leaders return to campus with new pedagogical methods that engage students in the active and transformative learning that is a hallmark of study away, along with new course content and a wider, even global, network (Ellinghaus, Spinks, Moore, Hetherington, & Atherton, 2019). As advisors, faculty members complement the work of an international or off-campus study office by making students aware of off-campus study options, particularly students who may not have considered the possibility (Gillespie, 2019; Twombly, Salisbury, Tumanut, & Klute, 2012). These students are among the many who benefit from a collaborative structure that facilitates a greater number of faculty to lead or teach in a program abroad.

A partnership or consortium that markets its programs and recruits students from the larger, more diverse population of multiple campuses not only advances the individual members' goals regarding student international mobility but also supports global learning and development for all students. Several faculty participants in the Faculty as Global Learners survey expressed this concern regarding the limited number and lack of diversity of students who are potential participants for their campus-run programs. In response to the survey question, "Describe one thing your current institution could do to enhance your ability to lead Study Away/ Study Abroad Programs," a respondent wrote, "Figure out a way to get more men and students of color to study abroad so my teaching can be more holistic and can get the richness of greater student perspectives" (Gillespie et al., 2016). In this book, Faculty Voices contributor Marcy Sacks, professor of U.S. history and African American history at Albion College, describes how she deliberately sought to enlist a diverse group of students for a short-term opportunity for faculty-student research. The challenge of enrolling a diverse student population in study away involves marketing and recruiting strategies, an institution's financial aid policies regarding study away, the training schedule and season for athletic teams, and campus culture. Partner institutions may work together to solve these competing priorities, to work toward international mobility for all students, and to target students from groups with consistently low participation in education abroad options.

POOLING RESOURCES: PROGRAM PLANNING

U.S.-based institutions working in a partnership can create opportunities for faculty, as well as administrative staff, to participate in the development, implementation, and assessment of innovative, multidisciplinary programs. The benefits of engaging a greater number of faculty and administrative staff in all stages of study away program planning are realized in the design of the curriculum and co-curriculum to advance global learning.

The preliminary stage of program development starts with faculty or academic administrative staff recognizing that a new or revised set of student learning goals requires new programming. Faculty members in a single department or working across departments might identify a disciplinary theme or project-based assignment for the majors that would be enriched through a place-based learning environment. Alternatively, faculty participants from different disciplines whose research interests converge in area studies, at a regional or national level, may frame their mutual interests as a structure for the program curriculum and co-curriculum to meet mutual student learning goals across disciplines. Deans, associate deans, or directors of education abroad may single out a discipline whose off-campus study options should be expanded and decide to investigate locations. Regardless of the impetus, a stable partnership offers structure for taking the next steps in program development through the designated institutional authorities.

The value of pooling resources for off-campus program development applies to the curriculum, which broadens in design in practical terms to represent the needs and interests of a greater number of students and in pedagogical terms to advance student learning. Cross-disciplinary study, a characteristic of the liberal arts, can guide students in making connections and making sense of an unfamiliar learning environment. Multiple options for experiential learning that involve international partners and engage students with their locale through fieldwork, community-based research, or internships, with relevant mentorship and reflection, require students to examine their cultural assumptions and biases and edge them to new perspectives.

The larger student population that is created through institutional collaboration on off-campus programs also increases the odds that a group of students select a program for the same reasons: the similarity of their personal and academic goals, self-awareness of their cross-cultural skills, and tolerance for ambiguity. Their shared purpose enriches the learning community for all students. Collaborative partnerships allow institutions to play to their own strengths while not having to offer specialized expertise in all disciplines or geographic locations. Faculty participants in the Faculty as Global Learners survey identified as a problem the limited pool of students for their courses because of the content. One faculty leader of a campus-run course wrote, "My course has difficulty finding students who wish to enroll in such a disruptive and challenging study abroad experience because so many other courses . . . don't question privilege, assumptions and bias among our students" (Gillespie et al., 2016). Students consider many factors in selecting a program—the opinion of returning students, the advice of an academic advisor or faculty mentor, cost, parental influence, and an expectation of academic and personal demands. One strategic advantage of collaboration is shared curricular offerings that have greater breadth and depth than a single college can offer.

Institutional partners also can draw on the shared expertise of professional staff in education abroad for guidance in program planning and logistical support during program development. Faculty respondents who were charged with many tasks and responsibilities because of staffing limitations during the planning, on-site phase, and return to campus identified a pressing need for this support (Gillespie, Glasco, Gross, Jasinski, & Layne, 2017). Theory and pedagogy relevant to off-campus study—for example, intercultural development, intercultural communication, experiential learning, and community-based learning—often fall within the purview of professional staff in education abroad. Whereas the experienced faculty leader knows how to apply this pedagogy to take advantage of off-campus opportunities, the new faculty leader needs the guidance of skilled staff members who understand the resources that ground an off-campus study program in sound theory and good practice.

The program support provided by professional staff is also essential to a well-run program because it frees faculty leaders to do what they do best: teach. As discussed in chapter 2, staff members in an office of education abroad are often best equipped to address issues of student health and welfare and minimize risk, two of the categories in which faculty felt least prepared (Gillespie, Glasco, Gross, Layne, & Jasinski, 2015). This support begins with advising students on programs and managing applications and admissions, responsibilities that some faculty participants in the Faculty as Global Learners survey note that they cannot take on because of time constraints or lack of previous experience. Once students are admitted to a program, education abroad staff can provide relevant logistical preparation, including predeparture orientation, assisting with visa applications, identifying on-site health care and coordinating health insurance plans, locating housing, and booking air and ground transportation, depending on the program location.

BUILDING A COMMUNITY OF PRACTICE ACROSS PARTNER INSTITUTIONS

Many faculty participants in the Faculty as Global Learners survey (Gillespie et al., 2016) expressed a need for a community of practice (Lave & Wenger, 1991). Such a practice would bring together faculty members leading study away programs to share ideas, resources, and knowledge during the planning stage and to debrief at the end of the program regarding decisions made or on-site challenges. A community of practice, in the context of this study of faculty and global learning, carries pedagogical value. Bringing together faculty leaders when they return to their campuses invites reflection, an essential step in learning, particularly the experiential and transformative learning that faculty program leaders describe as a benefit of leading study abroad (Gillespie et al., 2016; Savicki & Price, 2019).

A community of practice across similar institutions and disciplines invites faculty members in small academic departments to join with colleagues across campuses, expanding their cross-disciplinary network in the context of education abroad. This scenario applies in particular to faculty who may focus on a specific geographic region, such as the American Southwest or Southeast Asia, or a historical period, such as ancient Greece and Rome or post-colonial Africa, and whose teaching and research touch on the arts, economics, geography, history, language, literature, or sociological studies. A faculty member at a small campus may be the only one conducting research in a region or historical period, and her professional engagement with like-minded peers may be limited to annual national and regional conferences. In an institutional partnership that asks faculty representatives to plan and advise off-campus study programs, faculty members have the opportunity to establish working relationships with those whose interests coincide with their own and complement their expertise.

Another opportunity to formalize these contacts between or among faculty members at different institutions is through team teaching appointments on a study away program. When team teaching, faculty may share the excitement of interdisciplinary inquiry in upper-level classes, explore new pedagogies, and build an inventory of new teaching resources, among other possibilities. One faculty participant in the Faculty as Global Learners study, a male tenure-track professor in humanities, wrote of his team teaching experience on an off-campus program:

> I gained a renewed appreciation for slow, close reading of literary texts from my co-instructor. Finally, I came away with an interest in student cognition and its relevance to course design, again for the same reason. Overall, team-teaching across disciplinary lines was the most influential aspect of my study away experience. (Gillespie et al., 2016)

As an opportunity for faculty development, team teaching proved valuable to this faculty member not only during the off-campus semester but also when he returned to campus.

The benefits of establishing a community of practice among consortium members also applies to administrative staff and faculty who design and administer the policies for off-campus study at their institutions, particularly given the continually changing landscape of the field. As with a small academic department on campus, the office of off-campus study may have a staff of one or two, with a rotating cadre of part-time student interns. A consortium or partnership expands that department beyond the confines of the campus, without adding staff members, and it provides a forum for discussing good practice, for example, in response to an incident abroad; to garner opinions on a topic relevant to liberal arts colleges; or to share an idea. A central staff member in a consortium also can manage responsibilities that benefit the larger consortium and save costs that might otherwise be borne by a single institution. Examples of these responsibilities are many: organizing training for faculty program leaders across campuses; distributing surveys across member institutions on questions or issues relevant to them, then consolidating and sharing findings; and canvasing institutions on practices in academics, student life, and faculty recognition. A community of practice among staff members in education abroad serves the wider goal of creating professionals who are knowledgeable and skilled in the standards of good practice and who apply those standards to achieve the highest goals for student learning and development in the context of an off-campus program.

CHARACTERISTICS OF EFFECTIVE COLLABORATIONS

This section presents the conceptual framework for creating a partnership or collaboration, particularly for the purpose of off-campus study initiatives. It is written from the perspective of a U.S. institution of higher education forming a partnership with either another U.S. institution or an institution abroad, and the framework broadly applies to both models; however, in the case of international partnerships, additional considerations apply to working across borders and cultures. A conceptual framework for effective collaborations includes the following:

1. Support of top leadership: president or chancellor, board of directors.
2. Engagement of provost or dean, associate deans and faculty members with leadership positions.
3. Shared mission and alignment of goals, including strategic

goals for internationalization and students' global learning outcomes.

4. Potential for transforming the learning environment of both institutions through programs that are mutually beneficial, with depth and breadth of impact.

5. Agreement on initial programming and definition of program quality. (Eckel & Kezar, 2011)

Several principles are drawn from the writings of presidents of U.S. liberal arts colleges on the topic. Although a paucity of such testimony has been published, these sources speak to one of the key concepts: the involvement of relevant stakeholders in the process, starting with the president's leadership. Their agreement on common, fundamental characteristics also centers around the transformative potential and mutual benefit for the partners, shared mission and goals, and trust.

In celebrating the partnership that developed over more than 50 years between St. John's University and the College of St. Benedict, President Mary Hinton and President Michael Hemesath (2016) attributed their strength to the alignment of mission and goals:

> The real challenge of working in, and benefitting from, a partnership turns on truly integrating core parts of the institutions' missions. The place to start is philosophical, not practical, when considering such partnerships. And, yes, that philosophical starting point includes mission-central areas like academics and entails giving up some independence. (p. 60)

This statement underscores the necessary involvement of the president or chancellor, provost or dean, the board of directors, and senior level administrative staff and faculty members who define the institutional mission and goals in strategic planning (ACL, n.d., 1) and who, in turn, participate in the working relationship with a partner institution.

"Breadth of impact" is another defining feature of a success-ful strategic partnership, distinguished by institutions reaching out to several disciplines, departments, and administrative units and integrating faculty and staff members and students into the shared activities (Barnes, 2011, pp. 3–4). Hinton and Hemesath (2016) describe their institutions' "coordinated relationship" as an "integrated learning experience [that] combines a challenging lib-eral arts curriculum with extensive opportunities for international study, leadership, service-learning, spiritual growth, and civic and cultural involvement" (pp. 60–61). A recently formed partnership between three liberal arts colleges in the South likewise aspires to this "breadth of impact," engaging faculty and staff members in the planning and implementation of new opportunities designed to appeal to students from populations that have historically low rates of participation in off-campus study programs, including men, STEM majors, and students of color. Supported in part by an $850,000 grant from the Andrew W. Mellon Foundation, Cen-tre College, Rhodes College, and Sewanee: The University of the South are collaborating to offer new "student exchange" opportu-nities that span the institutions and broaden academic offerings through new on-campus courses, study abroad programs (includ-ing new programs in Africa and Russia), and off-campus intern-ships. A defining feature of this project, according to Centre Col-lege president John A. Roush, is its "collaborative nature" coming "at a time when colleges fear competition more than they seek to embrace partnerships. Students will benefit greatly through this collaboration, which is and always should be our paramount goal" (Strysick, 2018).

The Claremont colleges—now consisting of five undergradu-ate colleges (Claremont McKenna College, Harvey Mudd College, Pitzer College, Pomona College, Scripps College) and two gradu-ate institutes (Claremont Graduate University and Keck Graduate Institute)—represent another partnership model, as envisioned by founding member Pomona College to complement one another and to benefit from synergies across the campuses through shared facilities, faculties, and the "breadth of impact" described above. The joint science department of Claremont McKenna, Scripps, and Pitzer is one example of how these synergies offer international experience to faculty members. Science faculty appointments revolve on a three-year basis, and during their appointment to Pitzer, they qualify to teach on the Pitzer-sponsored summer program in health studies in Costa Rica (K. Mallory, personal communication, June 26, 2019). The Costa Rica program, as well as a summer program in Vietnam sponsored by Pitzer, are open only to students who attend one of the consortium colleges and who enroll in a Pitzer course specific to the location during the spring in preparation for the summer term.

Although a shared mission and goals provide the foundation of a partnership, a partnership might, in turn, drive stakeholders to reconsider their shared mission and goals, consistent with institutional identity. This evolution describes the St. John's/St. Benedict's partnership and meets the definition of a transformational partnership, offered in the context of international initiatives:

> Transformational collaborations . . . are those that change or transform entire departments, offices, and institutions, through the generation of common goals, projects, and products. Both sides emerge from the relationship somewhat altered. Transformational partnerships combine resources and view linkages as sources of institutional growth and collaborative learning. (Sutton & Obst, 2011, p. xvii)

A transformational partnership is distinct from a transaction, in which institutions may conduct business but are not otherwise changed by the partnership.

Hinton and Hemesath imply another fundamental characteristic of partnerships and collaborations: trust and communication. Smith College president Carol Christ (2014), describing the Five College Consortium in Western Massachusetts (Amherst College, Hampshire College, Mount Holyoke College, Smith College, University of Massachusetts Amherst) that offers a shared curriculum of specialized courses to students across the campuses, highlights this characteristic:

> This brings me to a critical point about partnerships: they depend upon the trust and communication developed through human relationships. In the Five Colleges, officers with the same jobs . . . meet regularly and frequently, in most cases once a month. . . . Because institutions always share somewhat different plans and priorities, projects inevitably hit rough spots and it takes trust and good communication to move beyond them. (p. 142)

These qualities that determine the success of domestic institutional partnerships apply to a range of activities, including the development and management of off-campus study programs.

A potential partnership between a liberal arts college and a non-U.S.-based institution requires that U.S. faculty and administrators study another conceptual framework—the traditional, culturally based educational philosophies and practices abroad that differ markedly from liberal arts education. Program leaders and faculty administrators who represent liberal arts education in the United States must be aware of these differences and understand their own practices as a disruptive "innovation" in the host country (Godwin, 2015). Faculty and students of both partners must negotiate these differences in teaching and learning, and the steps taken by program leaders to respect the differences, acknowledge the challenges of the experience, and manage expectations ultimately strengthen the learning opportunities.

TRANSLATING CONCEPTS TO ACTION IN ESTABLISHING PARTNERSHIPS

Institutional leaders who commit to exploring a partnership in off-campus study as a means to achieve student learning outcomes, to build capacity for faculty development, and to achieve the institutional mission also make a significant commitment of time and effort. This section presents one scenario that aims for an efficient use of these human resources by assigning leadership responsibilities to senior administrative leaders and faculty members to conduct an inventory of current partnerships, define the purpose of a new partnership, identify potential partners, and outline program quality. The guidelines apply both to domestic institutional partnerships and to partnerships between U.S.-based and non-U.S.-based institutions.

Exploratory Phase: Campus Leaders and Action Items

The president and other high-level administrators take the first step in exploring institutional partnerships by "taking into account all resources available—what kind and level of engagement would strengthen the international ethos of the institution and enhance the quality of education it offers" (Deardorff, de Wit, & Heyl, 2012, p. 461). The primary consideration in undertaking a program or portfolio of off-campus study is the right partner for such a venture, and high expectations of such a partnership are justified based on the robust connections between higher education institutions around the world. Using the measure of transformative potential, Sutton and Obst (2011) explain,

> More is expected of academic partnerships than in the past. There is increasing confidence that international collaborations—with carefully selected and strategic partners—can be an important ele-

ment of institutional growth. What happens outside institutions can change what happens within them. Resources can be shared or created. Joint projects can take institutions to new places. The partnership itself becomes a kind of bi-national academic unit. (p. xvii)

Although a partnership for a single purpose may serve as the initial stage in planning, the aspiration that the right partner will lead programming in many different directions is a valuable guide.

Once the president and board of directors agree on undertaking a partnership, the president's major responsibility is to identify the best candidates among administrative and faculty members to lead the initiative, beginning with the exploratory phase. Bryn Mawr president emeritus Jane Dammen McAuliffe (2014), in writing about international partnerships, argues from the practical point of view: "Most presidents will need to recruit faculty and administrative support for this work. The development of close connections with far-flung institutions, in particular, requires dedicated attention and experience as well as more time than most presidents can allocate" (pp. 152–153). In addition to relevant experience such as international work and the allocation of campus-wide resources, the president's appointee must be a recognized voice on campus. The informed discussion of various levels and models of engagement

> benefit[s] from having at least one international advocate situated at or near the top of the decision-making hierarchy. This increases the likelihood that the international agenda will be visible internally and externally, and puts internationalization on a par with other core activities and initiatives at the institution. (Rumbley, Altbach, & Reisberg., 2012, pp. 22–23)

Faculty members who are assigned to formal leadership roles guarantee the priority given to academics and student learning goals. Their essential contribution to higher education partnerships was identified in a study of good practice in the United States and abroad. The American Council on Education's (ACE) Center for Internationalization and Global Engagement (CIGE) initiated the study, in response to the 2011 Mapping Internationalization on U.S. Campuses survey, which found institutional international partnerships on the rise (ACE, 2012). The resulting report, "International Higher Education Partnerships: A Global Review of Standards and Practices," cited faculty engagement in identifying and working with institutional partners as one of the "Good Practices for Partnerships": "Active participation by faculty in decision making—particularly on academic matters—is important not only to gain their buy-in and support, but to tap their expertise and ensure the program remains on track" (Helms, 2015, p. 12). The ACE/CIGE review is an indispensable guide for administrators and faculty who are charged with establishing new partnerships or reviewing existing partnerships, both on the topic of faculty engagement as well as on the many considerations required by such an undertaking.

Faculty members bring value to partnership initiatives not only through their academic credentials but also through their connections on campus and across institutions and disciplinary fields. Faculty members are singled out as "the bridge between student learners and administration. In this capacity, they create curriculums, identify student learning goals, and deliver course content to students" (Holly, 2010, p. 114). Additionally, "faculty champions bring high levels of social capital to these ventures" (p. 114), building interest in the early stages of the partnership that supports program development from concept to action.

Table 21 sets out the parties and their tasks in this phase:

Identifying the specific program and possible partners begins with an audit or inventory of recent and existing collaborations (the "who") and programs (the "what"); this stage is a necessity at every institution but particularly at institutions where authority for international initiatives has not been centralized in a single office. The sources of information are several: faculty who may have international connections through research or teaching abroad, administrators who likewise have professional contacts, and students who may have participated with faculty in joint research abroad. McAuliffe (2014) encourages institutions to canvas their many constituents, beyond the administrative staff and faculty members on campus, to identify partners:

Table 21. Parties and Tasks During the Exploratory Phase in Off-Campus Program Partnerships

RESPONSIBLE PARTY	EXPLORATORY PHASE
President	Appoint senior administrator or faculty to lead partnership initiative, with appropriate committee or task force support
Provost or dean*	Direct feasibility study and audit of existing partnerships & programs; establish partnership criteria with Education Abroad; establish mission statement and goals for partnership; establish partnership approval process; draft policies and structures for managing partnerships
Academic departments/ faculty**	Identify academic needs for majors; propose cross-disciplinary curricular theme(s)
Office of Education Abroad	Identify gaps in current programming for students; establish partnership criteria with provost or dean
Finance	Prepare criteria for cost analysis of potential program
Legal	Review internal regulatory frameworks
Education Abroad Advisory Committee	Potential support for leadership initiative

Note: Adapted from Comprehensive internationalization: Institutional pathways to success (p. 65), by J. K. Hudzik, 2015, Abingdon, UK: Routledge; "Partnering for success," by L. Sternberger, 2005, International Educator, 14(4), p. 20; "The changing landscape of international partnerships," by S. B. Sutton & D. Obst, in S. B. Sutton & D. Obst (Eds.), Developing strategic international partnerships: Models for initiating and sustaining innovative institutional linkages (pp. xvii–xviii), 2011, New York, NY: Institute of International Education.
*Office appointed to lead partnership initiative.
**May overlap with Education Abroad Advisory Committee.

Most liberal arts colleges are already embedded in networks of international connections through faculty, alumnae/i, study-abroad sites, and the students we draw from around the world. Formalizing some of these connections by creating an international council of alumnae/i and parents builds a corps of institutional advocates and ambassadors in strategic locations around the globe. (pp. 152–153)

The idea of an international council suggests greatly expanding the reach of a liberal arts college far beyond the capabilities of staff and faculty members on campus.

Canvasing these various sources for the purpose of building a database of program models, the researcher would request detailed information to support an analysis of the potential of continuing or expanding the partnership. Among these details are

- program history and duration;
- program content and if/how it changed over time;
- partner contacts;
- student participation from home institution and partner institution;
- costs borne by home institution and by partner institution;
- external funding; and
- if the program has been discontinued, reasons for its closure.

A complementary set of data consists of an assessment of strengths and weaknesses, written by either staff or faculty members closely associated with the program on the home campus and at the partner institution; an analysis of student evaluations, if they exist; and a cost analysis.

On the basis of this data, the institution can begin to build a profile of potential partners. The "characteristics of strong potential partners" (Barnes, 2011, p. 5) for the University of Illinois–Urbana

Champaign when it embarked on a strategic plan to develop partnerships included

- similar scope of activities;
- historical and existing connections;
- mutual interest and commitment; and
- compatible administrative structures.

Barnes (2011) further notes, "Strong candidates for potential strategic partnerships will often share other institutional partners in common, providing a facilitated path for developing consortia of institutions with shared collaborative activities" (p. 5). These overlapping networks are particularly important in cultures and societies that value personal relationships in business negotiations, as individuals with existing institutional ties can make introductions and lay the foundation for open communication and trust—keys to a successful partnership.

PROGRAM DEVELOPMENT PHASE: GOALS AND STANDARDS

The Association for Consortium Leadership (ACL) compiled a checklist and performance indicators document with several categories "of possible measures of current activities that may be most helpful to building an effective and stable consortium" (ACL, n.d., p. 2), categories that also apply to partnerships for developing and managing off-campus study programs. Once stakeholders confirm that institutional missions and goals align, they can move forward in articulating the mission and goals for the consortium. Indicators specific to these two categories are similar, requiring that the consortium articulate a well-defined, focused mission and long-term goals; a strategic plan that incorporates the mission and goals; and a process for reviewing and revising annual goals and communicating them to relevant constituents (p. 2).

Another ACL category of good practice, assurance of program quality, necessitates agreement among the partners on what defines quality. The Forum on Education Abroad Standards of Good Practice set out a comprehensive framework for program quality that articulates the questions that teaching and administrative staff at higher education institutions should ask themselves in creating and managing an international program. The standards also provide a ready-made format for ongoing program assessment and evaluation. Not all standards and guiding questions apply to all international programs; however, certain basic questions regarding program quality do apply, regardless of the institutional sponsor and program scope.

Table 22 proposes a model for the roles of administrative staff and faculty members in the partnership initiative, placing the major responsibility in the provost's or dean's office during the program development phase. These details will vary, depending on the administrative structure of the home institution and the partner and available resources. However, the list represents the complexity of working across academic cultures and higher education systems.

Implementation and Assessment Phase

The implementation of a partnership requires ongoing support from the president's office and the commitment to a sense of shared purpose by the appointed representatives who operate in open communication and trust, with respect for the process. One detail that deserves to be singled out is creating an assessment process for the program and partnership, a pragmatic step that recognizes that some aspect of the Memorandum of Understanding may prove unworkable or unrealistic. Conversely, some feature of the partnership may prove more successful than anticipated and deserve more attention in the program. A review by both partners following the program's first run, matching program goals with

Table 22. Parties and Tasks During the Program Development Phase in Off-Campus Program Partnerships

RESPONSIBLE PARTY	PROGRAM DEVELOPMENT
Provost or dean*	Synthesize data from various sources; make site visits; assess potential partners per criteria; identify faculty champions; draft implementation plan
Academic departments/ faculty**	Outline potential curriculum based on student learning goals; make site visits; observe teaching practice and assess capabilities to teach curricular themes; advise provost or dean on strengths and weaknesses of potential partners
Office of Education Abroad	Propose potential partners based on data from various sources; plan and lead site visits; assess partner capabilities for academic and student life; advise provost or dean on strengths and weaknesses of potential partners; guide potential program through approval process
Finance	Conduct cost analysis of potential partners and program
Legal	Analyze regulatory frameworks of potential partners (labor law, contracts, banking, insurance, etc.)
Dean of students	Assess housing options at potential sites
Registrar	Analyze credit and grade conversion scales
Education Abroad Advisory Committee	Continuing support for initiative, as needed

Note: Adapted from "Partnering for success," by L. Sternberger, 2005, International Educator, 14(4), p. 20; "The changing landscape of international partnerships," by S. B. Sutton & D. Obst, in S. B. Sutton & D. Obst (Eds.), Developing strategic international partnerships: Models for initiating and sustaining innovative institutional linkages (pp. xvii–xviii), 2011, New York, NY: Institute of International Education.

*Office appointed to lead partnership initiative.

**May overlap with Education Abroad Advisory Committee.

actual costs, enrollment, and achievement of student learning, is essential to continued program planning and development. A scheduled review also can identify the areas of "demonstrable" and "measurable" mutual benefit (Barnes, 2011, pp. 3–4) to the institutions, pointing the way to additional programming. Table 23 presents the parties who continue to be engaged through the implementation phase.

Table 23. Parties and Tasks During the Program Implementation Phase in Off-Campus Program Partnerships

RESPONSIBLE PARTY	IMPLEMENTATION
President	Review recommendation from leadership; guide recommendation through final approval
Provost or dean*	Secure resources (staffing, financial aid, etc.); oversee management of partnership and program, per existing policies and procedures; develop program assessment plan; set regular calendar of communications, meetings
Academic departments/ faculty**	Advise students; participate in program management, per institutional policy
Office of Education Abroad	Coordinate with management team on marketing & recruiting, application and approval process, student pre-departure preparation; finalize on-site details with partner
Finance	Arrange financial transactions
Legal	Create Memorandums of Understanding (university, on-site providers for housing, travel, etc.)
Dean of students	Review housing contract with partner
Registrar	Confirm transcript process with partner
Education Abroad Advisory Committee	Approve program for credit transfer

*Office appointed to lead partnership initiative.
**May overlap with Education Abroad Advisory Committee.

An ongoing schedule of program review is embedded in good practice at an institutional level, and it addresses one of the challenges of sustaining a partnership: the inevitability that the mission and goals of an institution evolve and that administrators and faculty members who played central roles in program development may leave the institution and be replaced by individuals with different priorities. These changes affect the level of support for programs, requiring either that the missions and goals of the partnership be revised to accommodate the new profile of an institutional partner or that the partner withdraws. The ACL checklist builds into partnerships the consideration for both expanding or ending programs (n.d., p. 2), suggesting that consortium members consider the day when shifting markets, student and faculty demographics, and funding sources may open new possibilities for existing programs or compete with them. The checklist item may be read as a cautionary note: from the outset, members should plan both a development plan and an exit strategy for their programs, with measurable criteria to determine which direction to take.

The ACL checklist also includes leadership, staffing, financial resources, facilities, technology, equipment, internal and external relations, human resources, and legal counsel; all of these categories likewise apply to international programming. The exhaustive list is not optional; a partnership for managing an international program is an ambitious and complex enterprise that requires dotting all *i*s and crossing all *t*s. Preparation in all these categories is key to the achievement of program goals in meeting the institutional mission.

Although the literature does not mention the importance of a time line, it is a critical component at each of these stages—exploratory, planning, and initial implementation. Realistic deadlines will consider the academic calendar, the ongoing responsibilities of the senior administrators and faculty members who are involved in the initiative, and the necessity of accommodating the same time pressures of a particular partner. Depending on the experience of the partners in forming collaborations, it may require two to three years to bring an idea to fruition.

CREATING INTERNATIONAL PARTNERSHIPS IN THE LIBERAL ARTS

An international institutional partnership requires the same task list as a partnership between U.S.-based liberal arts colleges, with the complicating—and interesting—step of translating differences in academic cultures. In discussing the history of liberal education and prospects for its broader adoption, Peterson (2011) writes,

For much of the non-Western world, including countries that have a [liberal arts institution] transplant from an earlier era, liberal education is generally a foreign concept. . . . With no strong reason to understand the nature of baccalaureate education, there is also little incentive to understand the role of liberal education and its general education component in the curriculum. (p. 11)

This characterization applies to academic cultures not only in the non-Western world but in most of the world, where specialized, discipline-bound undergraduate education is the norm and the most common pedagogical practice is the lecture. Doubtless the differences present a challenge, but the challenge lies in finding common ground with a partner by identifying shared interests for student learning and faculty development opportunities. Gillespie et al. (2009) references the work of the Institute for International Liberal Education (IILE) at Bard College "as deep partnerships . . . to the extent that they engage our ethical, intellectual, and philosophical capacities, as well as our well-honed professional skills" (p. 507).

The joint academic programs between Bard College and the University of the Witwatersrand in South Africa and Bard and Smolny College of St. Petersburg State University in Russia demonstrate the necessity of agreement on program quality. These dual degree or dual credit programs include student exchange, faculty exchange, and shared curriculum. Gillespie at al. (2009) write,

Institutions are jealous of the capacity to award their degrees; they cherish and protect this right. Thus, by its very nature, dual accreditation assures a high level of academic co-ownership and administrative involvement. It requires the participating institutions to realize a common set of institutional goals and to apply formal assessment and evaluation criteria. Thus, it gives both institutions the leverage to insist on academic quality. (p. 507)

In a program of student exchange, a mutual benefit for institutional partners is that credit for courses taken at the partner is applied to the students' academic progress. This agreement requires discussion of many differences, among them, academic cultures, pedagogical practice, course loads, course content, grade conversion scales, faculty-student interactions, and student-student interactions. Setting goals, along with clear expectations, contribute to a common understanding of academic quality.

The global rankings systems that privilege faculty research and publications present another challenge to the liberal arts college, whose identity is built around teaching and community engagement (Brewer, 2010). Beloit College faced this challenge in its search for a partner in China:

> The desire for prestige makes the liberal arts college, which enters into rankings on a very different basis, an unnatural partner for many universities elsewhere in the world. . . . however, a partnership between institutions of different aims and characteristics can work, if the institutions understand the scope of such a partnership and can find opportunities for mutual benefit. (p. 85)

In the case of Beloit College and Henan University, mutually beneficial opportunities include Beloit students enrolling in a unique research course that requires their community engagement and Henan students enrolling at Beloit for a semester or a year. Two annual positions were opened to Beloit College graduates to teach English as a second language at Henan. The partnership likewise has had an impact on faculty; through funding from the Freeman Foundation, Beloit faculty visited Henan to observe the research course and subsequently developed courses and pedagogy on the basis of their observations.

Joint programming with an international partner also supports faculty development by creating a community of practice through mentoring, cross-departmental relationships, and team teaching.

An example described by Sutton (2018) is the International Summer School in China, jointly managed by Nanyang Technological University (Singapore), Nankai University and Tianjin University (China), University of Toronto, Australian National University, Stockholm University, and Bryn Mawr College. Faculty from different institutions co-teach students from partner institutions.

> Partnerships can enable faculty and staff with little prior international experience to gain the knowledge and experience they need to integrate global learning into their courses by working with partner faculty with similar interests and building on growing institutional knowledge of the partners and their countries. (Sutton, 2018, p. 19)

The value of such collaborations accrues to mentors and mentees and both members of a teaching team as they share pedagogical practice, disciplinary perspectives, and cross-cultural experience. Sutton explains, "Collaborative conferences, web chats, shadowing faculty already engaged with the partners, and visits to the partners are common mechanisms for getting started" (p. 19). It might be added here that the administrative staff or faculty leaders who were involved in the early stages of program planning and implementation could be instrumental in setting up these contacts and events.

International consortia also are potential venues for partnerships for liberal arts colleges, depending on the goals and membership requirements of the consortium. Three existing consortia—Universitas 21, a global network; Utrecht Network, a European-wide network; and the International Network of Universities—all share a commitment to internationalization but currently list only research universities as members. Their activities include student and faculty exchange programs, internationalization of curricula, joint courses, summer school, and joint research projects for their members.

An analysis of good practice within these consortia finds that they are typically managed through annual meetings of high-level administrators at member institutions, including presidents, vice presidents, and senior international education officers who set the agenda for consortium activities. Sternberger (2005) reports the following:

> a foundation of trust, communication, and commitment is at the core of any successful IHEC. . . . The development of systems for regular and timely dialogue across multiple venues and the careful and deliberate cultivation of relationships among institutional partners, are both a cause and effect of trust, communication, and commitment, and key to the success of any IHEC. (pp. 15–16)

Administrators at all levels are charged with building trust, developing relationships, and communicating with one another. Faculty and students are noteworthy additions to this list as drivers and participants in internationalization (Sternberger, 2005, p. 18).

Site Visits

One of the touchstones of program management is the site visit to potential program locations, an essential step in program development for partnerships and a rich opportunity for faculty development. "Professional development opportunities such as grants for teaching and research collaborations or travel to program sites, can help retain the faculty already involved in the activities of the partnership as well as draw new faculty and staff into the collaboration" (Helms, 2015, p. 12).

The site visit is a necessary cost of program development and management: meeting face-to-face with administrators, faculty, and other local providers for program details such as housing and field excursions; conducting test runs of excursions; touring the facilities and grounds; riding the public transportation that students will use. These on-site activities have no equivalent for learning, even in the digital age. This firsthand knowledge is critical to other stages of program development that require accurate, up-to-date information about the site, including advising students, selecting faculty leaders, and possibilities for the direction of the curriculum. In collaborative programs, these development costs can be shared among partners.

Once a partnership program is underway, annual site visits support ongoing program development and faculty enrichment. The value of site visits by Beloit College faculty members to partner institutions is a tangible outcome of the institution's ambitious process to internationalize the curriculum, a process that included faculty members and administrative staff in rethinking the institutional learning goals of off-campus study and establishing international institutional partnerships. Brewer (2010) writes of the site visits, "Critical to the curricular outcomes of these faculty development activities was a focus on how learning outside the classroom takes place, the particular challenges and opportunities for this learning in study abroad sites" (p. 91). These curricular outcomes were realized not only in revised or new courses on-campus, but faculty also drew from their learning and observations on-site visits to test the pedagogical practices of off-campus study, particularly experiential learning.

CONCLUSION

This chapter focused on the benefits to liberal arts colleges of creating partnerships with other higher education institutions and pooling resources to achieve positive outcomes for faculty development, student learning goals, and institutional goals for global initiatives. Both implicit and explicit in this discussion is the necessity of a centralized effort with strong, visible leaders who are committed to international initiatives and are charged with bringing together academic departments, administrative offices, and student support services to define the academic enterprise, set policies and protocols, agree on priorities, and make decisions about allocating resources. This intra-institutional collaboration provides a model for inter-institutional collaboration, while a shared mission and goals hold transformative potential for the liberal arts college.

REFERENCES

Association for Collaborative Leadership. (n.d.). *Checklist and key performance indicators for consortia.* Retrieved from https://trailsmt.org/wp-content/uploads/2017/06/ACLConsortiumChecklist-App_F.pdf

Banks, C., Siebe-Herbig, B., & Norton, K. (Eds.). (2016). *Global perspectives on strategic international partnerships: A guide to building sustainable academic linkages* (pp. xi–xxiv). New York, NY: Institute of International Education.

Barnes, T. (2011). Intentionality in international engagement: Identifying potential strategic international partnerships. In S. B. Sutton & D. Obst (Eds.), *Developing strategic international partnerships: Models for initiating and sustaining innovative institutional linkages* (pp. 1–6). New York, NY: Institute of International Education.

Bilecen, B., & Van Mol, C. (2017). Introduction: International academic mobility and inequalities. *Journal of Ethnic and Migration Studies, 43*(8), 1241–1255.

Brewer, E. (2010). Leveraging partnerships to internationalize the liberal arts college: Campus internationalization and the faculty. In P. L. Eddy (Ed.), *International collaborations: Opportunities, strategies, challenges* (pp. 83–96). San Francisco, CA: Jossey-Bass.

Childress, L. K. (2018). *The twenty-first century university: Developing faculty engagement in internationalization* (2nd ed.). New York, NY: Peter Lang.

Christ, C. T. (2014). The college without walls: Partnerships at home and abroad. In R. Chopp, S. Frost, & D. H. Weiss (Eds.), *Remaking college: Innovation and the liberal arts* (pp. 135–143). Baltimore, MD: Johns Hopkins University Press.

Deardorff, D. K., de Wit, H., & Heyl, J. D. (2012). Bridges to the future: The global landscape of international higher education. In D. K. Deardorff, H. de Wit, J. Heyl, & T. Adams (Eds.), *The SAGE handbook of international higher education* (pp. 457–485). Thousand Oaks, CA: Sage Publishing.

Ellinghaus, K., Spinks, J., Moore, G., Hetherington, P., & Atherton, C. (2019). Learning to teach in the field: Five professors tell how running an overseas study tour improved their classroom teaching. *Frontiers: The Interdisciplinary Journal of Study Abroad, 31*(1), 169–189.

Gillespie, J. (2019). Faculty roles in advancing student learning abroad. In E. Brewer & A. C. Ogden (Eds.), *Education abroad and the undergraduate experience: Critical perspectives and approaches to integration with student learning and development* (pp. 213–228). Sterling, VA: Stylus Publishing.

Gillespie, J., Glasco, S., Gross, D., Layne, P., & Jasinski, L. (2015). *Understanding faculty and student transformation in study abroad/study away programs.* Unpublished survey.

Gillespie, J., Glasco, S., Gross, D., Layne, P., & Jasinski, L. (2016). *Follow-up questions for faculty members who lead study away and study abroad programs at liberal arts institutions.* Unpublished survey.

Gillespie, S., with Becker, J. A., Billings, B., Bogdanov, S., Cavis, C., Haniff, F., . . . & Monakov, V. (2009). Creating deep partnerships with institutions abroad: Bard College as global citizen. In R. Lewin (Ed.), *The handbook of practice and research in study abroad: Higher education and the quest for global citizenship* (pp. 506–526). New York, NY: Routledge.

Godwin, K. A. (2015). The counter-narrative: Critical analysis of liberal education in a global context. *New Global Studies, 9*(3), 223–243.

Helms, R. M. (2015). *International higher education partnerships: A global review of standards and practices.* Washington, DC: American Council on Education, Center for Internationalization and Global Engagement. Retrieved from https://www.acenet.edu/Documents/CIGE-Insights-Intl-Higher-Ed-Partnerships.pdf

Helms, R. M., Brajkovic, L., & Struthers, B. (2017). *Mapping internationalization on U.S. campuses: 2017 edition.* Washington, DC: American Council on Education. Retrieved from https://www.acenet.edu/Documents/Mapping-Internationalization-2017.pdf

Hinton, M. D., & Hemesath, M. (2016). The true power of collaboration: From cooperation to partnership. *Liberal Education, 102*(2), 60–63.

Holly, L. N. (2010). Strategies for planning for the future. In P. L. Eddy (Ed.), *International collaborations: Opportunities, strategies, challenges* (pp. 107–116). San Francisco, CA: Jossey-Bass.

Hudzik, J. K. (2015). *Comprehensive internationalization: Institutional pathways to success.* Abingdon, UK: Routledge.

Kuder, M., & Banks, C. (2016). Current trends in strategic international partnerships. In C. Banks, B. Siebe-Herbig, & K. Norton (Eds.), *Global perspectives on strategic international partnerships: A guide to building sustainable academic linkages.* New York, NY: Institute of International Education.

Lave, J., & Wenger, E. (1991). *Situated learning: Legitimate peripheral participation.* Cambridge, UK: Cambridge University Press.

McAuliffe, J. D. (2014). The networked college—local, global, virtual. In R. Chopp, S. Frost, & D. H. Weiss (Eds.), *Remaking college: Innovation and the liberal arts* (pp. 144–154). Baltimore, MD: Johns Hopkins University Press.

Peterson, P. (2011). Liberal education in the global perspective. *International Higher Education, 62,* 10–11.

Rumbley, L. E., Altbach, P. G., & Reisberg, L. (2012). Internationalization within the higher education context. In D. K. Deardorff, H. de Wit, J. Heyl, & T. Adams (Eds.), *The SAGE handbook of international higher education* (pp. 3–26). Thousand Oaks, CA: Sage Publishing.

Savicki, V., & Price, M. V. (2019). Reflection as a tool in the educational continuum. In E. Brewer & A. C. Ogden (Eds.), *Education abroad and the undergraduate experience: Critical perspectives and approaches to integration with student learning and development* (pp. 165–180). Sterling, VA: Stylus Publishing.

Sternberger, L. (2005). Partnering for success. *International Educator, 14*(4), 12–21.

Strysick, M. (2018). *Mellon Foundation awards $850,000 collective grant to Centre, Rhodes and Sewanee* [Press release]. Retrieved from https://www.centre.edu/mellon-foundation-awards-850000-collective-grant-to-centre-rhodes-and-sewanee/

Sutton, S. B. (2018). Collaborative learning through international partnerships. *Peer Review, 20*(1), 16–20.

Sutton, S. B., & Obst, D. (2011). Introduction: The changing landscape of international partnerships. In S. B. Sutton & D. Obst (Eds.), *Developing strategic international partnerships: Models for initiating and sustaining innovative institutional linkages* (pp. xiii–xxiii). New York, NY: Institute of International Education.

Twombly, S. B., Salisbury, M. H., Tumanut, S. D., & Klute, P. (2012). *Study abroad in a new global century: Renewing the promise, refining the purpose.* ASHE higher education report. San Francisco, CA: Jossey-Bass.

Whitehead, D. M. (2015). Global learning: Key to making excellence inclusive. *Liberal Education, 101*(3), 6–13.

THE AFRICAN SKY IS BEST AT SUNSET

Debriefing to Reframe a Village Experience

William G. Moseley

Reaching that end-of-semester peace on a study abroad program, where the students have pushed through the challenging middle phase, is a bit like hanging on for an African sunset. Many people come out in the morning to see monuments and wildlife and then head home, never to return. Others stick around to encounter

the intense midday sun, as well as the fatigue, occasional hunger, and general irritation associated with uncomfortable conditions. While some call it quits during the hot noon hours, others make it through to see the glorious African sky at sunset—a time when people scurry about cities running errands, farmers head home and joke with neighbors, children play ball, and wildlife converge on water holes in national parks. It's worth the wait to not only see the glorious conclusion but understand and appreciate the full scope of African daily life.

My students had just returned from a four-day homestay in the village of Mochudi, a rural community in southern Botswana about an hour's drive from the country's capital, Gaborone. We were a little over two months into our semester-long Associated Colleges of the Midwest (ACM) study abroad program, so the students' grasp of the local language Setswana was beginning to improve. They had also traveled to some degree, having visited the vibrant metropolis of Johannesburg in January as well as the biologically diverse Okavango Delta in mid-March. As a seasoned study abroad instructor (Moseley, 2009), I thought my students were ready for a more intimate village experience. But many of them were also at that challenging midpoint of the study abroad emotional trajectory (Pedersen, 1995). They had moved beyond the initial euphoria of discovering a new place and people—yet to emerge with a more nuanced, balanced, and appreciative understanding of the place. In other words, several of them were in doldrums of the middle, that slightly depressed, angry state of struggling to adapt to a new culture, where just about everything seemed irritating and inefficient.

And so we began our debriefing in our usual classroom at the University of Botswana (UB). I had a series of question prompts to guide our discussion. What had it been like leaving the UB dorms (with their 20 something roommates) to spend four days and three nights with a rural family? What did they do and see during the day? What did they think of family life and rural activities? While several of the students were quite positive, a few openly expressed their displeasure with the visit. These students noted that it was hard just hanging out in a village with all of the downtime. Some had issues with the food and access to water. Others noted that it didn't seem like much was going on. And then one student more or less said that it seemed like rural people were lazy because they just sat around all of the time chatting. Why weren't people working more? Furthermore, the villagers had no respect for one's personal space and need for alone time.

My initial, internal reaction was one of surprise. I had put a lot of advance preparation into setting up this visit as it was a new addition to the program and something that I wanted to get right. I had collaborated with a local woman from the community who also happened to work at UB and was familiar with the concerns of U.S. students. She helped me recruit local host families whom I subsequently visited to interview, discuss expectations, and check out potential accommodations for our students. I had carefully prepared the village for the visit. What I didn't anticipate were the potential reactions of some of our students who simply had never experienced life in a small, rural community where the pace of life and focus on human relations was quite different. Although we had gone over a lot of appropriate contextual information in class on Southern African history, agriculture, animal husbandry, education, and health (Moseley, 2012), there was a difference between studying and debating these issues and actually experiencing them.

What ensued was the first of many discussions about how our own life experiences, or our positionality, often influences how we see and interpret the world around us. We discussed workaholic U.S. American culture and the sense that one always had to be doing something. We talked about the impersonal nature of many human interactions in the United States and the compunction to just get down to business rather than first acknowledging the humanity of the other person. Over time, these discussions gave way to a much more nuanced understanding of life in Botswana, especially in the weekly writing reflections that students would share with me.

> Gone were the shallow complaints about inefficient bureaucracy, the slow pace of life, or bad food from earlier in the term. Instead, the students showed a better ability to contextualize poverty, a greater appreciation for taking the time to get to know someone, or understanding Botswana on its own terms and in relation to the region, rather than just comparing it with American norms and practices. (Moseley, 2012)

Several students even went back to visit their host families in the village, indicating that this rural connection was one of the highlights of their study abroad experience in Botswana.

Indeed, that end-of-semester nuanced understanding, just like the African sunset, is worth the wait.

REFERENCES

Moseley, W. G. (2009). Making study abroad a win-win opportunity for pre-tenure faculty. *Frontiers: The Interdisciplinary Journal of Study Abroad, 18*, 231–240.

Moseley, W. G. (2012, December 11). Don't go soft on study abroad: A call for academic rigor. *The Chronicle of Higher Education*. Retrieved from https://www.chronicle.com/blogs/worldwise/dont-go-soft-on-study-abroad-a-call-for-academic-rigor/31082

Pedersen, P. 1995. *The five stages of culture shock: Critical incidents around the world*. Westport, CT: Greenwood Press.

PICTURE THIS

Cross-Disciplinary Travel in Cuzco, Peru

Kylie Quave and Chuck Lewis

CL: I believe a writing practice can enrich students' travel and study abroad experience, much as travel, in turn, offers an excellent opportunity to develop one's writing skills. I had taught both pre– and post– study abroad writing courses as well as an online interactive course for students studying in different locations around

the world all before I myself had the opportunity to teach a writing course while abroad with students. I finally had the chance to teach a writing course on travel and tourism in the Associated Colleges of the Midwest (ACM) Florence program in spring 2014, and the course I taught there had the students engaging with both photography and writing as modes of representation. That experience has since informed my teaching here at Beloit College, and it has also taken my research and publishing in new directions. In 2017, Kylie Quave, a colleague in anthropology and writing, asked me if I was interested in developing a pair of linked courses in Peru for a three-week summer program. We thought a collaborative pairing could be innovative, effective, and attractive for our students as well as rewarding and enriching for us.

KQ: I've been traveling to Cuzco since 2006 for anthropological and archaeological fieldwork, usually with several students whom I train in research methods. We've been laser-focused on empirical research such as reconstructing ancient diet or excavating 1,000-year-old houses. Busy field seasons have left little opportunity for informal learning and purposeful immersion into current social and political issues in Cuzco. I thought a collaboration with Chuck could yield pedagogical advantages. Our students would benefit from our complementary approaches: I had the local knowledge, while Chuck's expertise in writing and critical approaches to photography would be major assets as I pivoted to greater engagement with people and culture in the present.

CL: My course focused on writing, photography, and travel, but the collaborative integration and interaction of the writing and anthropology students brought a new dimension to their experience, as students in both classes engaged in virtually all activities together, shared common reading assignments, and responded to peers' multi-modal work in both classes. The creative and reflective focus of the writing students' work had more traction and range because of their anthropological reading and field engagement with Kylie and her students, who, in turn, benefited from playing image and text off each other around a series of creative and critical prompts.

KQ: In my course, we explored social inequality in Cuzco's past relative to current social, economic, and political challenges. Assignments included photography and writing in various configurations and formats for broader audiences. For example, anthropology students created a story using just four images. Subsequently, Chuck's students added 280-character (Tweet-length) captions to the photo stories without knowing the intent of the photographer. From this, I learned about how images can be misappropriated and misunderstood when traveling to an unknown place but also that multiple unexpected, yet accurate and valuable meanings could be created.

Chuck and our students showed me a different Cuzco that has changed my pedagogy and research already. As I read for the course and traversed the region with 15 students with a different set of objectives than I usually have, I took note of the conversations between market sellers, the identities of street performers, and the composition and comportment of the tourist crowds at archaeological sites. I observed where I formerly ignored. Coming from an empirical social science background, I had not considered the creative ways of writing that our students explored as they incorporated the rhythms of spoken word, recorded crowd sounds to immerse the reader, and found objects to accompany text and bring dimensionality to their stories. I had also not typically inserted overt reflections related to my identity into my public writing about Cuzco.

The day Chuck took the accompanying photo, we had traveled to a rural community in the Patacancha Valley to visit friends of friends, ostensibly to observe traditional weaving techniques. The community regularly received tourists, but as friends we expected a familiar and unrehearsed visit. However, we were treated to a ceremonious welcome into a home, with hired costumed dancers and musicians and a multi-course meal made from a whole alpaca butchered especially for us. The pelt of the slaughtered animal was proudly displayed at the entrance to the house and announced to be the source of our lunch. Following the locally sourced meal, we were encouraged to try on traditional clothing and to join the twirling dancers and musicians as they pulled us into their dizzying performance, clasping hands with our new friends. At the end of the visit, weavers invited us to purchase their creations.

It was disquieting to consume this elaborate display of living culture, particularly since we intended to pass through unobtrusively. We cautiously sought consent for the ways in which we participated. Students grappled with when to take photos and videos without objectifying our hosts. They disagreed on who should dress up and how and whether they ought to photograph the occasion. Some of them wrote about these ethical concerns.

I am a White, North American anthropologist. I feel the impulse to document these occasions and to participate in them fully, to the extent I'm invited. But we had urged our students to question these instincts, and now they were struggling to act thoughtfully and ethically as outsiders in a fabricated authenticity. As they navigated these questions, they had to be more purposeful in how and when they took photographs, which helped them to see that a picture is not a description but rather a transaction. I, too, learned this lesson by watching them that day and later reading their reactions. As an empirical social scientist, I do not merely document; I can see how I judge, filter, determine, interpret.

CL: Any photo I took that day is about as close to the living thing as that alpaca pelt. My course addressed both our desire for and the limits of photography as a "capture technology" for experience when traveling. There you will find only the skin of experience, but you won't taste the mint soup or breathe the woodsmoke and panpiped music in the air or touch the hands of the old women as we danced, as rough and gentle as avocados.

STRUCTURED FUN OR DOWNTIME?

Brian Caton

I have taught Asian and environmental history at Luther College since 2003. During my career there, I have led or contributed to study away programs several times. My research focuses on herders, their animals, and the state in 19th-century northern India.

I took the photo shown here during a course I led in January 2006 titled Reading Local History in India. This was my first study

away course. The course had the academic goal of acquainting students with a broad sweep of Indian history from the early modern period to the present, with a few forays into the more distant past. In addition, students were asked to think about the ways in which people preserve or reject the material past to produce narratives of a particular place. Some of the most successful work in this vein occurred during our visit to Amritsar, toward the end of the course, when we read about, discussed, and then visited the Jallianwala Bagh and, on a separate date, when we watched the border closing ceremony at nearby Wagah. However, it would be difficult for an instructor, and exhausting for students, were a study away course, even for three weeks, filled entirely by such formal learning. Transit time is a natural "downtime," but students use transit time differently: some sleep, others chat with their fellows, and still others take in as much visual information through the window as they can. Good practice dedicates other parts of the daily schedule to reflective writing and downtime.

As faculty who spend most of our time teaching on a fixed campus, we tend not to trouble ourselves with what students do during their downtime. In fact, we refer students who have difficulty organizing their downtime to various college agencies. Yet, as often the sole representatives of the college while on the study away course, we are compelled to do more to fill in students' extracurricular time. In courses traveling to some parts of the world, it is enough to turn students loose in their location and tell them to meet later at a particular time and place. In north India, some cities, like Udaipur, are familiar with and depend upon the positive experiences of foreign and domestic tourists. In other cities, Indians may view the foreign tourist as an intruder or an economic opportunity, and simply turning students into the streets for a few hours is asking for trouble. Meals can be good scheduled downtime, but for college students accustomed to a culture of "busyness," a meal lasting more than an hour may seem like a punishment. Some of these considerations can appear in pre-departure orientation, but one can never be sure how much of that information a student recalls while confronting the challenges of being on-site. How to fill scheduled time depends a great deal on the resources available.

We designed the itinerary of the course so that students would first land in Udaipur, for several reasons: the city treated tourists well; it had much of the material juxtaposition that fed course themes; and most of my wife's extended family live in or near the city. My wife's women and girl cousins were experienced and merciless bargain hunters and generously gave their time to the shopping needed to fit students with most of the clothes you see them wearing in the photo. My wife's men and boy cousins were resourceful in providing logistical aid, including transport and accommodation. We also decided to have our group visit Lakad-was, the ancestral village of my wife's maternal relatives, to give the students a more tangible sense of a smaller, decidedly rural, and poorer locality.

Our activities in Lakadwas focused on a formal class session; observation of the religious ceremonies of the central temple, housing a *bhairuji*, or local god; and a communal meal. The latter took most of the morning to prepare, so even though we took care of the class and the religious ceremonies, we still had to wait until the meal was ready. One of my wife's cousins, the man in the red-and-black shirt in the background of the photo, decided everyone should play *sitholia*, a ball game common to the region around Udaipur. The game starts with a stack of seven flat stones. One team's members try, one by one, to knock down the stack from a distance with the ball. Once the stack is knocked down, the team must work quickly to re-stack the stones and shout "*sitholia!*" before the other team hits them with the ball. Not everyone in our group was particularly skilled at the game, but nobody noticed how long it took before lunch was ready. Later in our stay in Udaipur, the students started playing impromptu games of *sitholia* with one another and with other younger children in the family in the court-yards of old houses and anywhere else they could find. They made plans to start an intramural *sitholia* club or tournament when they returned to campus. That never panned out, but they had found something in the local culture and wanted to make it theirs.

As faculty, we generally want two things out of our study away courses: get students outside the "bubble" of campus life and enough academic substance to persuade colleagues, parents, and administrators that students are not taking a guided tour. I doubt any of the students in 2006 remember any of the academic content of the course. They don't need it in their vocations: a bicycle mechanic, a restaurateur, an elementary school teacher, a flight attendant, a medical doctor, a mother of three, a sheep farmer. It's easy to overemphasize the academic side during the planning or execution of a study away course. Vast tracts of unstructured time can provide opportunity for exploration but can also permit students to turn inward. Structured fun, like *sitholia*, might place a limit on what students can do with their non-academic time, but it provides an opportunity for global learning that might prove more durable than the books and other staples of study away.

LESSONS FROM AUSCHWITZ

Education and Outreach

Amanda M. Caleb

Auschwitz is a place of horrors, one that exemplifies the need to bear witness. Not everyone can travel to Auschwitz, so it becomes the duty of those who can to share their experiences and testify to the inhumanity of the place. This need to bear witness and to educate others is nearly as dire now as it was 70 years ago, partic-

ularly given the rise in anti-Semitism in Europe (Henley, 2019) and the United States (ADL, n.d.) and the recent study by the Claims Conference (2018) that revealed that two-thirds of U.S. millennials did not know what Auschwitz was.

In thinking about these factors, I partnered with Stacy Gallin from the Maimonides Institute for Medicine, Ethics and the Holocaust, where I serve as an educational consultant, to brainstorm a study abroad opportunity that would be transformative for the individuals and broader community who could not travel with us. The impetus for this trip stemmed from a private donor who wanted to specifically support a trip for athletes and for the experience to have a large and lasting impact. Given that Division I athletes have a public platform, and given that student-athletes are both active learners and social change agents, this was a fitting group to bring. As an alumna of and former student-athlete at Davidson College, I thought of Coach Bob McKillop and the men's basketball team because of their popularity (thanks to Steph Curry) and the club's dedication to shaping future leaders, not just on the court. The decision to come on this trip was left in the hands of the student-athletes; notably this is one of the few study abroad opportunities they could have, and it came with no academic credit. Coach McKillop worked with me throughout the planning process, which was considerable given our different locations; we relied on weekly phone calls to address logistical issues (plane tickets from different cities) and emotional preparation (what the student-athletes should expect, how we could support them emotionally, etc.).

With these first components in place, we then reached out to Holocaust survivor Eva Mozes Kor and her nonprofit CANDLES Holocaust Museum and Education Center. CANDLES has been taking groups to Auschwitz with Eva since 2005, and the experience of going to a concentration camp with a survivor is life-changing. Partnering with CANDLES enabled us to travel with Eva and afforded the practical benefit of working with people who have extensive experience planning such a trip. We also hired a videographer to document the trip, with the intention of creating an educational video that extended the impact of this experience.

The trip was an intense three days. The first day we orientated the student-athletes to Kraków and introduced them to Eva, by way of individual conversations, a group meal, and a screening of her film, *Eva*. As we were walking in Eva's footsteps at Auschwitz, we spent day two at Auschwitz-Birkenau, where she was interned, and day three at Auschwitz 1, where she was liberated. Each day included a tour with a museum guide and with Eva, who explained the personal significance of each location. Standing on the Birkenau platform where she and her twin sister Miriam were ripped away from their mother, the student-athletes were moved to tears, and they turned to one another for support. Equally moving was their response to the Yad Vashem exhibit at Auschwitz 1, which focused on pre-Holocaust family films of individuals who would be murdered by the Nazis: student-athletes hugged one another and even me as we collectively processed the tragic loss of life and potential.

But the trip was not just about emotional responses: the student-athletes also cognitively processed the experience through daily journaling, both on-site and on the bus ride back to our hotel, and through nightly debriefing sessions, in which we discussed what they had learned, what they had experienced, and connections they could make in the world today. As the sole educator on the trip, one of my tasks was to guide the discussions, moving from academic insights, developed from what they learned and shaped by their majors, to personal reflections. Although the student-athletes and coaches only knew me for a short time, the intensity of the experience allowed them to feel comfortable to engage in meaningful discussions with me and their teammates. These nightly sessions revealed the student-athletes' transformation: although they knew something of Auschwitz from a pre-trip educational session, they did not know the individual stories, nor could they imagine the size and the overwhelming evidence of humankind at its worst.

The trip's impact was felt for months after we returned to the States, and our intention of reaching a wider audience was realized. Not only did we edit and release the documentary of the trip, which featured original music by student-athlete Cal Freundlich, but we also supported the publication of other accounts of the trip, including one written by me and student-athlete Patrick Casey in the *Davidson Journal*. The trip was mentioned in numerous press releases, on athletic websites, and even featured in a sermon at a Chicago church. I mention all these outlets to demonstrate how study abroad can be more than the experience itself and reach more people than just the participants—documenting the trip in many different ways allows for continued engagement with a wide audience about the lessons of Auschwitz.

For me, the lessons have been long-lasting, particularly what I learned as an alumna engaging with student-athletes. The experience felt authentic, in the sense that we were all learning and learning from one another, but without the pressure of grading and in the traditional roles of professor and students. I felt particularly connected to my alma mater by witnessing firsthand how the student-athletes responded to the experience; I have continued to think about a phrase my college field hockey coach told me 20 years ago: "It's not how you want to play on the field, but who you want to be as a person." The Davidson basketball players showed character and compassion in their interactions with Eva and their shared experience at Auschwitz. Having stayed in contact with several of them, I see how they have continued to grow and process the experience: for instance, Cal Freundlich and Kellan Grady have been active in speaking out against anti-Semitism. I was privileged in witnessing their intellectual and emotional growth; I am humbled by their continued dedication to education and justice.

REFERENCES

Anti-Defamation League. (n.d.). *Audit of anti-Semitic incidents: Year in review 2018.* Retrieved from https://www.adl.org/audit2018

Claims Conference. (2018, April 10). *Holocaust knowledge and awareness study: Executive summary.* The Conference on Jewish Material Claims Against Germany. Retrieved from http://www.claimscon.org/wp-content/uploads/2018/04/Holocaust-Knowledge-Awareness-Study_Executive-Summary-2018.pdf

Davidson Basketball Journey of Remembrance. (n.d.). Retrieved from https://www.youtube.com/watch?v=ThhJbX3drXw&t=3s

Henley, J. (2019, February 15). Antisemitism rising sharply across Europe, latest figures show. *The Guardian.* Retrieved from https://www.theguardian.com/news/2019/feb/15/antisemitism-rising-sharply-across-europe-latest-figures-show

CHAPTER 5

STRATEGIC LEADERSHIP FOR OFF-CAMPUS STUDY

How Colleges Reimagine the Place of Global Learning

Lisa Jasinski

Through the preceding chapters and reflective personal essays, this book has examined off-campus study programs at liberal arts colleges from many perspectives: the center directors who oversee programmatic offerings, the faculty members who develop and lead innovative courses, the professional staffers who disseminate best practices, and consortia and other partners who sustain models in cross-campus learning at home and abroad. This final chapter allows us to take the most comprehensive, and systemic, view by examining how private liberal arts colleges undertake efforts to produce dramatic and lasting institutional change in the related areas of global learning, study abroad, and internationalization. The examples considered in this chapter help us appreciate the role of senior administrators—often working in concert with faculty leaders and through established governance structures—who create and sustain supportive campus environments committed to the highest levels of excellence in global learning and faculty-led, off-campus study programs.

This chapter considers how some liberal arts colleges—led jointly by senior administrators and faculty advocates—have reinvented themselves in the arena of global learning by increasing student access to off-campus study, using strategic planning to formalize ambitious goals, leveraging donor support, adopting new curricular elements and graduation requirements, and crafting marketing messages to reflect underlying changes. These changes result in cultural changes. The chapter begins by identifying proven strategies that have contributed to institutional transformations across the higher education landscape and the importance of framing internationalization as transformative change. This framework provides an analytical tool to consider two case studies of institutions that are global learning "success stories in progress." The first vignette traces how Susquehanna University, in the span of a decade, went from being a college where less than a third of students studied abroad to one where *all* students now participate in a required off-campus, cross-cultural experience. The second case study charts Grinnell College's multi-year efforts to develop and operationalize a comprehensive internationalization plan; the plan has already resulted in reframing the college's commitment to global learning, the development of a new campus center, and the expansion of course-embedded travel opportunities for students. The chapter ends by identifying two facets of campus internationalization that remain most overlooked by colleges—aligning stated goals with reward and recognition systems and fulfilling a diversity and inclusion imperative. The chapter is intended to help better position senior administrators and faculty leaders to envision, plan for, and initiate transformative change on their own campuses.

GUIDING PRINCIPLES FOR INSTITUTIONAL TRANSFORMATION

Institutional change can be an elusive thing to measure or discuss, especially on a college campus. In some respects, colleges are places of continual renewal, innovation, and novelty. They are spaces marked by the frequent arrival and departure of students and other community members, the constant initiation of new programs, one-time special events, and seemingly endless construction and renovation projects. Metaphorically, liberal arts colleges might be seen as intellectual frontiers that both respond to and inspire new ways of thinking about academic disciplines, teaching and learning, and broader societal challenges. In other ways, liberal arts colleges can be seen as places of stasis and tradition. Shared governance processes have been derided as overly laborious, many academic calendars are marked by unchanging annual ceremonies, historic buildings may be in continual use for a century or more, and a long-serving tenured faculty member might spend much of their career exploring, and being rewarded for developing expertise in, a specific scholarly niche.

Change may be a challenging thing to perceive. To answer the question, What strategies lead to institutional change? the American Council on Education (ACE) and the W. K. Kellogg Foundation (WKKF) initiated the Project on Leadership and Institutional Transformation in 1994 to better support colleges engaged in what they described as "comprehensive or transformational change," defined as "a deep and pervasive type of intentional change that affects the institution as a whole rather than its discrete parts" (Hill, 2019). Through this initiative, ACE and WKKF selected 26 postsecondary institutions—of varying types and sizes—that were undertaking a comprehensive change agenda. Each participating campus had its own ambitious goal: for example, improving through assessment (University of Massachusetts Boston), developing campus community for quality teaching and scholarship (Centenary College), or creating a climate of social responsibility (Olivet College). No participating college explicitly pursued a project related to global learning or internationalization, but due to the ambitious nature of these efforts, at some campuses, projects inevitably impacted off-campus study programs, curricular elements, and strategies to prepare students to meet their obligations as global citizens. Although the envisioned outcomes were diverse, project administrators determined that institutions shared assumptions and values about the change process:

1. Support of top leadership: president or chancellor, board of directors.
2. Engagement of provost or dean, associate deans and faculty members with leadership positions.
3. Shared mission and alignment of goals, including strategic goals for internationalization and students' global learning outcomes.
4. Potential for transforming the learning environment of both institutions through programs that are mutually beneficial, with depth and breadth of impact.
5. Agreement on initial programming and definition of program quality. (Eckel & Kezar, 2011)

Assumptions and values were operationalized differently on the participating campuses—accounting for elements of the local organization and culture—yet these shared beliefs reveal defining characteristics of transformative change in higher education. Although colleges might find success implementing comparatively modest change using other means, transformative change by its very nature seems to hinge upon collaboration, communication, transparency, and inclusion. Over five years, representatives from ACE and WKKF worked closely with campus leaders to chart milestones and to reflect on lessons learned throughout the change process.

Five Core Strategies for Transformational Change

Eckel and Kezar (2011) expanded upon the findings of the ACE and WKKF project in their book, *Taking the Reins: Institutional Transformation in Higher Education.* Upon reviewing the results of change processes at more than two dozen colleges and universities, they identified "five core strategies" necessary for achieving change on this broad scale. These strategies included (a) senior administrative support, (b) collaborative leadership, (c) flexible vision, (d) staff development, and (e) visible action (p. 78).

Some examples of the first strategy, *senior administrative support,* included focusing campus attention on the change, allocating necessary resources, and creating administrative structures to support campus goals. As a second strategy, *collaborative leadership* referred to the involvement of other individuals, beyond senior leaders, in all aspects of the change initiative, from conception to implementation. Collaborative leadership calls upon the larger tradition of shared governance to guide decision-making in academia, understood as a "delicate balance between faculty and staff participation in planning and decision-making processes paired with administrative accountability" (Olson, 2009). Eckel and Kezar (2011) defined *flexible vision,* the third strategy, as "creating a picture of the future that is clear and succinct but that does not foreclose possible opportunities that might emerge" (p. 76). In the long run, Eckel and Kezar found that achieving the ideal level of specificity in the vision provided a "road map" for change while allowing enough leeway to those involved in the change process to evolve and "think differently" (p. 80). A sufficiently flexible vision allows ample guidance to keep the initiative focused while enabling those involved in the change process to collaborate on developing the vision, consistent with the second strategy.

The fourth strategy, *staff development,* refers to programmatic efforts like workshops and orientations to help employees acquire the skills and knowledge necessary to carry out the change initiative. Readers who seek information about promising opportunities for faculty and staff development related to off-campus study programs are advised to consult chapter 2 of this book for additional information. The final strategy identified from schools that participated in the ACE and WKKF transformation initiative is *visible action* and refers to demonstrable, symbolic, and highly publicized outcomes related to the change agenda. Visible actions or "small wins" preserve a sense of momentum in long-term change efforts. By analyzing more than 20 participants in the initiative, Eckel and Kezar determined that when one of these five strategies was absent, the likelihood of institutional transformation was diminished. Taken together, these interrelated five strategies proved critical to achieving a primary characteristic of transformative change: helping people think differently.

Transformative Change and Internationalization

Transformative change processes take on a special significance in the current higher education climate, one that is marked by significant shifts in student enrollment, political skepticism, economic pressures, and technological advances (Grawe, 2018; McGee, 2015; Pierce, 2017). In an age of tight budgets and increasing competition for top students, liberal arts colleges seek to deploy their limited resources intentionally without compromising the quality of academic offerings. At all small private colleges, global programs offer high strategic value, demand considerable resources, and exact a substantial opportunity cost.

Global learning initiatives, plans for campus internationalization, and policies governing off-campus study for students have often been developed without sufficient faculty participation or consent (Childress, 2018; Green, 2002, 2005). Examining case studies from universities around the world, Hudzik (2015) found that in spite of institutional differences, faculty participation remained a key component in the successful internationalization of an institution. Colleges have used a variety of means to generate high levels of faculty participation. As Childress explained (2018), Duke University and the University of Richmond, for instance, sought to build interest by "engag[ing] a critical mass of faculty throughout the institution, spanning many disciplines" and not just a handful of "committed internationalists" (p. 5). By framing internationalization and global learning as a shared commitment in a formalized internationalization plan—not a boutique interest among a select few—these colleges raised shared visibility and investment. These institutions followed up with incentives so that an "internationalization plan became a living document on a campus" (p. 65). For off-campus study programs to achieve the aims championed broadly by liberal arts colleges—to be student-centered, accessible, and dedicated to excellence in disciplinary and interdisciplinary learning—campus leaders and faculty members may find success in drawing on the broader lessons identified through the Project on Leadership and Institutional Transformation as well as the specific strategies adopted by Susquehanna University and Grinnell College.

LEARNING FROM CASE STUDIES

Within higher education, case studies serve as instructive tools. Case studies illuminate the key events, processes, and decisions that contributed toward a positive outcome (often with the benefit of hindsight). Rather than explain exactly how to achieve the desired result, case studies reveal why certain decisions or strategies were effective in a specific context. The question of praxis—the act of putting theoretical principles into practice—is inevitably one of calibration and customization. Even when institutions might appear to share many common characteristics or attributes, an approach must be suitably adapted to local contexts and cultures to be successfully implemented. Many roads can lead to the same destination. Modeled on Childress's approach (2018), this chapter considers two case studies hinged upon the actions of individual change agents as well as systems and cultures in a campus environment to increase and improve global learning.

Selection of Case Studies

The campuses profiled in this chapter—Susquehanna and Grinnell—demonstrate how motivated stakeholders within private liberal arts colleges have elevated the status and place of global learning. With the support of senior campus leaders, the faculty of Susquehanna University adopted curricular changes that substantially and materially changed the undergraduate experience. Grinnell College also expanded course-embedded travel opportunities for students while undertaking a more holistic reimagining of how campus units can pursue global learning as a shared strategic goal. It should not be inferred that either college has done this perfectly or that every stated goal has been achieved as initially envisioned. Although each college has achieved notable progress worthy of recognition, these "success stories in progress" serve to remind us that campus transformation can be a slow, iterative, and, at times, even a recursive process.

The pairing of these two institutions is intentional. Both Susquehanna and Grinnell are co-ed, private, residential liberal arts colleges enrolling approximately 2,000 undergraduate students and located in rural communities. These colleges are also marked by differences in selectivity, resources, student diversity, governance structures, histories, and campus cultures. Institutional characteristics and student demographics are summarized in Table 24.

Susquehanna is a religiously affiliated college with a regional reputation—60% of students come from Pennsylvania (2% are international students). With an endowment valued at $161 million in 2017, Susquehanna admitted 68% of applicants. By several measures, Grinnell College is one of the nation's elite and most

Table 24. Institutional Characteristics and Student Demographics of Susquehanna University and Grinnell College, 2018–2019

	Susquehanna University	Grinnell College
Institutional characteristics		
Student enrollment	2,238	1,712
U.S. News & World Report ranking (Best National Liberal Arts College)	135	11
Total endowment (2017)	$161.2 million	$1.9 billion
Acceptance rate (fall 2017)	68%	29%
Selectivity rating	Selective	Most selective
Student-to-faculty ratio	12:1	9:1
First-year retention rate	85%	95%
Six-year graduation rate	72%	87%
Tuition and fees	$47,290	$52,392
Student demographics		
% of White students	80%	51%
% of international students	2%	18%
% of Pell-eligible students	26%	20%
% of students who study abroad	100%*	55%

Note: Data gathered from the U.S. Department of Education Scorecard, *U.S. News & World Report*, and Susquehanna University and Grinnell College websites.

*100% of Susquehanna University students complete a cross-cultural experience (international or domestic).

selective institutions. According to recent estimates, Grinnell's endowment was valued at nearly $2 billion (2017). Grinnell's reputation is further distinguished by its ability to enroll talented students from across the United States and abroad (20% of students are international) as well as high first-year retention (95%) and six-year graduation rates (87%) in 2017.

Grinnell demonstrates that a postsecondary institution can be both diverse and elite. According to the U.S. Department of Education College Scorecard, roughly half of Grinnell students identified as White (51%) in 2020. Although the racial and ethnic diversity of the Susquehanna student body has increased in recent years, 80% of undergraduates identified as White by the same methodology. Perhaps surprising to some readers, students who attend Susquehanna and Grinnell come from families, on average, with strikingly similar family socioeconomic profiles. According to the Equality of Opportunity Project (now called Opportunity Insights; Aisch, Buchanan, Cox, & Quealy, 2017), the median family income of a Susquehanna student was $122,300, slightly higher than that of a Grinnell student ($119,700). Susquehanna, however, enrolled a higher percentage of Pell Grant eligible students: 26% compared to 20% at Grinnell. Susquehanna has been singled out for achieving considerable socioeconomic diversity among its students (Leonhardt, 2014).

Both Susquehanna and Grinnell operate under a home school tuition/tuition exchange model, wherein students are permitted to apply institutional scholarships or grants to offset the costs of studying abroad for a semester or year. High-need students may also apply for additional funds to cover other program costs such as airfare, passport and visa fees, and the like. At both institutions, the cost of short-term off-campus programs that occur during a break period is not covered by annual tuition; Susquehanna estimates the average cost of a short-term off-campus study program to be $5,000. Websites at both colleges indicate that financial aid may be available to students with demonstrated need who seek to study abroad or away.

Research Methodology

To develop each case study, several resources were consulted, including campus websites, industry publications (e.g., *Inside Higher Ed*), publicly available data about enrolled students and institutional characteristics (e.g., U.S. Department of Education Scorecard), and conference presentations. In addition, campus personnel involved in change processes were interviewed by phone. Citations are included for direct quotations, but for the purposes of readability, other information is paraphrased and presented in summarized form. Draft case studies were reviewed by campus personnel to limit factual errors and mischaracterizations.

CASE STUDY #1: SUSQUEHANNA UNIVERSITY— ACHIEVING CROSS-CULTURAL EXPERIENCES FOR ALL

Beginning with the graduating class of 2013, Susquehanna University became one of the only postsecondary institutions in the United States to require an off-campus, cross-cultural immersion experience for all students. Susquehanna demonstrates how a small institution with modest financial resources realized the ambitious goal to make study away experiences a reality for all students, regardless of financial means, ability, or area of study.

Impetus for Change

Student responses to Susquehanna's 2003 administration of the National Survey of Student Engagement (NSSE) ultimately initiated a process to reimagine curricular requirements, institutional values, and campus culture. On the survey, students reported infrequently engaging in discussions with diverse others and, overall, scored poorly on other questions regarding dealing with difference. Despite the university's goal to prepare students to engage with other viewpoints to acquire the skills to succeed in an increasingly diverse world, survey results indicated that students were failing to avail themselves of opportunities to step outside their comfort zones. The NSSE results sparked initial conversations, among concerned faculty and staff members, about how the university might structure experiences to ensure that future students would have cause to experience cultural differences, at home or abroad.

Key Features of the Change Process

In 2003, Susquehanna University president L. Jay Lemon launched a year-long strategic planning process to coincide with the development of a self-study required by the Middle States Commission on Higher Education (MSCHE) for the institution's reaffirmation of accreditation. Among the objectives for this broad-scale planning process were addressing the root causes contributing to students' NSSE responses (Manning, 2016). The university president's endorsement of this period of institutional reflection and goal setting signals the presence of *senior administrative support*, one of Eckel and Kezar's essential strategies for institutional change. In addition, the added impetus of an approaching review by the MSCHE allowed Susquehanna to align its desire to bring about changes to the student experience with an external time line. At roughly the same period, the faculty began a process to identify common student learning outcomes for the entire university.

The first step in this process began in 2003 when the university president appointed the dean of the business school to convene a planning group to brainstorm ways to increase students' interactions with diverse others. Working over a period of years, this group of faculty, staff, and administrators explored many different ways that Susquehanna might address perceived shortcomings in how students engaged with diverse others and difference more generally. This structure exhibited two characteristics identified by Eckel and Kezar. First, by appointing a dean to work with a group of faculty and staff members, the process adopted a *collaborative leadership* model; other members of the Susquehanna community were invited to participate in open fora and to share their ideas with the appointed members of the planning group. Second, although the planning group was provided general guidelines to focus their work, they received a loose charge that allowed them to benefit from a *flexible vision* of success. The planning group members were permitted leeway on how the university might improve the student experience. While entertaining various alternatives, such as required volunteerism, internships, or other forms of experiential learning, group members continually returned to the merits of required off-campus study. The ability to shape and refine goals during the change process allowed the campus to align multiple, concurrent, mutually informing campus-initiatives.

Formal governance structures and university policies contributed to key milestones throughout the four-year process to reimagine how future Susquehanna students might engage with difference. The change process followed documented institutional norms of governance beginning with the appointment of a planning group, a faculty-led process to devise common learning goals, and, ultimately, an all-faculty vote to approve a new curriculum in 2007. Working in parallel to these processes, influential and informal networks of like-minded individuals played important roles. On the Susquehanna campus, a group of approximately 15 to 20 committed study abroad advocates among the faculty and staff helped build shared buy-in for an off-campus study requirement. While this group did not hold explicit decision-making authority, its members met regularly for lunch and used informal encounters to maintain momentum for the process that resulted in the approval of the new curriculum and ongoing planning. Many group members had recently received tenure and were eager to put their stamp on the institution.

Some of these affiliated members served on formal committees or the president's planning task force; their regular communication with others helped achieve a sense of alignment. Another affiliate-group member was later appointed university provost, all but ensuring that study abroad remained among the senior administration's top priorities. Building on a unique feature of Susquehanna's governance structure, whereby two faculty members and two students are elected to serve on the university's board of trustees, affiliated faculty sought out this service opportunity and used their influence to build support for off-campus experiences among these campus advisors. By serving on committees empowered to adopt new policies, to draft curricular requirements and learning goals, and to shape university practices, members of this loose affiliation were essential to the adoption of a cross-cultural experience requirement.

It is important to recognize that piecing together elements of a change process with the benefit of hindsight can make the elements appear more orderly, intentional, and linear than they appeared at the time. A faculty member involved in aspects of this change agenda described it as "diffuse" in that "you couldn't draw a straight line between goals and outcomes." He also stated that sometimes the progress came in "fits and starts," periods of intense activity and intermittent lulls.

Adopted Policies and Practices, Curricular Elements, and Organizational Units

By the time the members of the class of 2013 matriculated to Susquehanna, the faculty had ratified a new general education curriculum, university-wide learning goals, and a comprehensive assessment program. At this time, faculty had begun to shape cross-cultural experiences. The adopted student learning goals included exploring different beliefs and values—two goals that could be achieved through project-based learning and community-based research. Two distinctive characteristics of Susquehanna's cross-cultural experience are that (a) students may fulfill the requirement either at home or abroad, and (b) no students can seek an exemption. The curriculum included several new "Connections" requirements with designated courses on diversity, interdisciplinarity, and a cross-cultural experience (paired with pre- and post-coursework). Susquehanna students can fulfill the university's cross-cultural experience requirement by participating in one of three Global Opportunities (GO): GO Short, GO Long, or GO Your Own Way. The university describes the opportunities in the following way:

The GO requirement is flexible so that it can accommodate students' needs. Students may participate on a Susquehanna GO Short Program (2–6 weeks during winter or summer break, led by Susquehanna faculty/staff), a GO Long Program (a traditional semester study away program), or a GO Your Own Way (two or more weeks in an internship, volunteer work or independent research in a cross-cultural setting) to fulfill their GO requirement. Students should consider their personal, professional and academic goals and discuss their GO options with their faculty advisor and the GO Office. (Susquehanna University, n.d.)

The requirement has been in place for nearly a decade, and credit-bearing GO Short programs have proven to be the most popular option for students; more than half of all students (55% to 60%) fulfill their GO requirement this way. These experiences often include travel over the summer or during winter break to destinations around the world, including Morocco, New Zealand, France, Iceland, Jerusalem, Cuba, Hawaii, and New Orleans. Students who choose a GO Long program participate in one of more than 80 approved semester or year-long study abroad programs. Students enroll directly at an international university and may participate in other program elements, such as internships and/or homestays. Susquehanna devised GO Your Own Way to meet the needs of individual students, especially those who might find it challenging to study abroad otherwise. Personnel in the Global Programs Office can work one-on-one with students to develop a customized solution, taking into account the student's physical or mental health conditions, unique family circumstances, and academic goals, to provide a level of inclusivity that is rare within more conventional approaches to study abroad. As a general practice, the GPO staff use a strengths-based approach to identify ways to "rule students into study abroad instead of ruling them out" based on their GPAs or other factors. Rather than focus on the challenges facing individual students, staff engage in creative experiences designed to build upon students' abilities and interests.

In order to facilitate the new curriculum and the cross-cultural experience requirement, Susquehanna has made additional changes across the campus. For instance, the university's curriculum committee developed a screening, approval, and assessment process to ensure that all faculty and staff-led programs meet the stated goals. The university expanded *staff development* for faculty and staff members who lead GO programs. At the same time, the university is continuing to work to formalize common elements across GO programs and use more consistent approaches to improve students' intercultural learning. The Global Programs Office grew in size to meet student demand and to expand support programs, such as a pre-departure webinar for students and their families to review important policies and calibrate their expectations for off-campus learning. In addition, the university examined its financial policies and allocated resources to help students with demonstrated need fulfill the GO requirement—a considerable challenge given that the implementation of the new curriculum coincided with the global financial crisis. Susquehanna has received considerable press for these achievements and often appears in national lists of colleges and universities with the highest rates of study abroad participation. All of these changes represent *visible actions*, meaningful and visible indicators to the campus community of the significant changes afoot.

Emerging Impact on Campus Culture and Remaining Challenges

It has now been roughly a decade since Susquehanna adopted its university-wide learning goals, a new general education curriculum, a cross-cultural experience requirement, and a more systematic approach to assessing gains in student learning. One unintended (but welcome) outcome of these changes has been notable growth in student diversity. The collected impact of these changes has resulted in a "paradigm shift" (Manning, 2016). Senior students now report higher levels of interaction with difference than first-year students on the NSSE survey, suggesting that changing student demographics and the launch of the GO programs have coincided to achieve the university's intended aims.

Another way that the adoption of a cross-curricular requirement has impacted Susquehanna has been the large number of faculty and staff participants who lead GO programs. Individuals from a variety of disciplines and departments have served as program leaders, demonstrating that expanding opportunities for students can also result in deepening the global experiences for faculty and staff. At the same time that the new requirement has produced positive gains, Susquehanna has faced challenges to achieve a sustainable staffing model for off-campus study programs. During the global recession, the university slowed the rate by which tenure-track vacancies were filled, resulting in a slight reduction in the pool of available program leaders. Although job candidates and recent hires often express enthusiasm for leading GO programs during the hiring process, many early-career faculty members choose to wait a few years before taking on this added professional responsibility. As many of the faculty members who were part of the original cohort of program leaders a decade ago begin to step back from their involvement—for various reasons ranging from personal choice to shifting professional interests—it is important that the university develop a process to bring a new generation of tenured (and pre-tenure) faculty program leaders into the fold to ensure that the program offerings can continue. The university recently reallocated instructional time to pilot a new program to evaluate student portfolios, and it continues to navigate the way it addresses the added work associated with assessing artifacts that students create pre- and post-program. In hindsight, the dean of Global Programs regrets not anticipating these challenges. Knowing what he knows now, Manning would have advocated for additional personnel and other resources to ease the implementation of the requirement in both the short and long term.

CASE STUDY #2: GRINNELL COLLEGE—REPOSITIONING INTERNATIONALIZATION FROM MARGIN TO CENTER

Whereas Susquehanna developed a new curricular requirement to facilitate student engagement with diverse others, Grinnell College sought to elevate the status of global learning in a more holistic sense. While Grinnell's efforts remain a work in progress, there are many signs that the initiative has had much success, including the creation of a new campus center, expanded course-embedded travel opportunities for students, and generous support from donors.

Impetus for Change

In 2008, then-President Russell Osgood formed Grinnell's first presidential task force on internationalization planning. Continuing this tradition, in the summer of 2014, Osgood's successor, President Raynard Kington, formed a second group called the Global Grinnell Task Force. This second group was tasked with taking stock of changes since the previous report, conducting an assessment of international engagement at the college, leading a discussion of student learning goals, and making recommendations for an internationalization plan. The task force was presented with an opportunity to build upon a preexisting foundation to expand the scope and visibility of global learning:

> Grinnell has a long tradition of thinking globally and linking the campus to institutions in other parts of the world. . . . Yet the college lacks an explicit articulation of what our students should learn about the world and a forward-looking plan that will enable Grin-

nell to align its resources with a focused international strategy. Grinnell's many discrete initiatives to promote faculty research and teaching, attract international students, send students abroad, and foster intentional connections between the experiences of our students and world developments would strongly benefit from a more deliberate, integrated approach. (Global Grinnell Task Force, 2016, p. 6)

At Grinnell, internationalization was understood to have many facets, of which study abroad played an important part. This rationale for the task force's work acknowledges the college's intent to bring greater coherence to what were previously seen as "discrete initiatives." By forming a task force, Grinnell recognized an opportunity to refine and sharpen existing efforts.

Key Features of the Change Process

Much like the change initiative undertaken at Susquehanna, Grinnell's internationalization efforts also benefited from strong *senior administrative support*, given that the group was launched and task force members were appointed by the president. President Kington requested "periodic reports and presentations" to keep him apprised of the task force's progress. The task force was co-chaired by a senior faculty member and a senior administrator (the vice president for academic affairs and dean of the college), and the additional 14 members represented other campus units, including other faculty members, student affairs, alumni relations, career services, financial aid, and admissions. Kington charged the task force to "lead a campus-wide discussion about student global learning goals and assessment" (Global Grinnell Task Force, 2016, p. 7). Between the diversity of perspectives included on the task force and the expectation of outreach, Grinnell modeled Eckel and Kezar's (2011) strategy of *collaborative leadership*. Members of the task force met with and surveyed the faculty and staff, spoke with the Student Government Association, and offered regular communication to the board of trustees, thus ensuring that many perspectives were included in the task force's final recommendations.

Eckel and Kezar (2011) found that a *flexible vision* for change contributed to transformative change in higher education. In many ways, the work of the Global Grinnell Task Force offers a compelling example of how this principle might be operationalized; the group began with a broad charge, embarked on a period of self-analysis and data gathering, articulated long-term goals, and then posed action steps. The task force divided its work into two phases, each lasting approximately one academic year. In the first phase, the group engaged in "information gathering, consultation, and strategic thinking." Before rushing to implementation strategies, the task force spent the better part of a year exploring different approaches. In the second phase, the members of the task force "centered on refinement of recommendations and plans for implementation." At this stage, task force members divided into five subcommittees to focus their energies more pointedly on topics, including the international dimensions of the curriculum or off-campus study. Subcommittees shared updates frequently to ensure coherence across elements.

Opportunities for learning and professional development were woven throughout the task force's work. Recall that Eckel and Kezar (2011) underscored how *professional development* supports campus transformation by helping faculty and staff to acquire new knowledge, skills, and perspectives. Grinnell allocated more than $30,000 for task force members to travel to Washington, D.C., to participate in the Internationalization Laboratory hosted by the American Council on Education's (ACE) Center for Internationalization and Global Engagement (CIGE) (Global Grinnell Task Force, 2016, p. 8). At CIGE, task force members interacted with their counterparts at other postsecondary institutions engaged in concurrent international planning processes; a program representative from ACE later visited Grinnell to offer additional support. By drawing on national resources and allowing the task force members to learn from their peers, the change process strengthened participants' expertise and exposed them to alternative ways of facilitating global learning on campus. Looking back on it with the benefit of hindsight, the co-chairs of the group were grateful that they did not rush this process. They agreed that two years allowed an appropriate amount of time to review and gather data from stakeholders, to adequately vet implementation strategies, and to build a sense of buy-in across the campus. While the process was energy intensive, the group was not overly fatigued by the end.

Adopted Policies and Practices, Curricular Elements, and Organizational Units

In 2016, the Global Grinnell Task Force concluded its work by issuing three overarching recommendations in a final report:

1. [The Task Force] argues for the incorporation of international goals and priorities in the college's statements of mission and identity and communications for external audiences.
2. [The Task Force] recommends a stronger, more integrative structure to lead, sustain, and evaluate international education.
3. [The Task Force] recommends the definition of strategic partnerships for sustained investment where the college's multiple international priorities converge. (p. 2)

Each of these overarching recommendations was accompanied by student learning outcomes (i.e., "students will understand their home or home country in global terms") and administrative action steps (i.e., establish international student enrollment goals, adopt a home tuition model that allows students to use existing financial aid for study abroad). Reflecting the influence of *collaborative lead-ership*, the task force's recommendations spanned the campus and required broad participation to achieve stated aims.

The task force called upon the college "to build a vibrant, highly visible physical presence for the college's international program-ming and activities into the renovation and construction of a new academic space" (p. 10). Following this recommendation, the Grin-nell Institute for Global Education (GIGE) was created to replace the long-standing Center for International Studies. A $5,000,000 gift from a donor endowed the institute's operations, and it occu-pies a prime location in a recently renovated academic building. The previous Center for International Studies had a faculty direc-tor, and the institute appointed a faculty and staff member to serve as co-directors. The new administrative structure was perceived to offer several advantages, enabling the institute to promote coherence across international initiatives and expand the reach of programming. The senior director of global initiatives brings specialized professional knowledge regarding best practices in study abroad program administration and intercultural learning, oversees the institute's budget, supervises six staff members, and supports the institute's fundraising and marketing initiatives. A rotating faculty co-director, appointed as assistant vice president and senior global officer, supports the institute by maintaining the global studies curriculum, planning campus events and symposia, and recruiting faculty to lead off-campus study programs while continuing to teach, do research, and engage in university service. The faculty co-director has played a significant role in expanding global faculty-directed student research projects. Previously, all of these duties would have fallen to a faculty director and other mem-bers of a professional staff; the new model allows for two senior leaders to share the responsibilities and benefit from complemen-tary skills. Together, the co-directors have collaborated to create an effective and proactive support system for Grinnell's many international programs and partnerships. To celebrate its launch, the institute hosted several widely publicized events, including a multi-day event entitled "Globalizing Knowledge: Collaborations through the Liberal Arts" that brought together partners from India, France, the Netherlands, the United Kingdom, and China. Publicity materials for the 2019 event announced, "Grinnell is entering a new era in how it engages with the world."

Another important *visible action* that has resulted from the task force is the expansion of course-embedded travel opportunities through the recently launched Global Learning Program (GLP). GLP courses enroll first-year students and offer an interdisciplinary and comparative focus, considering topics such as global migration or food culture and identity, and includes travel to multiple countries. Students in the global migration GLP course participated in a trip to the U.S./Mexico border and a three-week tour of Europe (visiting Spain and Greece) to examine migration in different geographic contexts. In its first year, the college offered two seminars, each capped at 15 students; the program may grow in time. A $4,000,000 gift from a donor and a private foundation defrayed participation and travel costs—enrolled students are responsible for paying a $400 supplement. The hope is that students who participate in the GLP as first-year students will avail themselves of additional opportunities to study abroad later in college. Students who participated in the inaugural seminars were 10% more likely to study abroad than those who did not (Redden, 2017).

Emerging Impact on Campus Culture and Remaining Challenges

Although Grinnell has been implementing the task force's recommendations for only three years, the impact has already been felt. Significant gifts secured through the college's comprehensive fundraising campaign have accelerated the creation of the Institute for Global Engagement and launched highly visible, course-embedded travel for first-year students through the signature GLP. The college's marketing efforts emphasize Grinnell's commitment to internationalization while extolling the benefits of comparative international study to better prepare graduates to navigate careers on a global scale. An on-campus symposium event brought higher education thought leaders to Iowa to imagine the future of the liberal arts.

The college has made notably slower progress toward the task force's third overarching goal: to define "strategic partnerships for sustained investment where the college's multiple international priorities converge" (p. 2). In 2016, the task force recommended that Grinnell concentrate its international activities in select "nodes" or geographic regions in which there were strong alumni connections, preexisting university partnerships, and overlapping faculty expertise. Early efforts to implement this strategy surfaced a common tension facing many small institutions—a desire to offer students and faculty truly global experiences while achieving cost (and energy) efficiencies. To focus the college's activities in specific regions inevitably means limiting opportunities elsewhere and perhaps precluding other worthy projects. Faced with the sure-to-be-unpopular prospect of denying otherwise compelling proposals, senior administrators have instead taken a more fluid approach to administering this objective.

The theme of the 2019 GIGE symposium was collaboration, and for several days, the panelists and attendees considered innovative approaches to international partnerships. Representing a shift from the task force's original vision of designating a limited set of partners and restricting the college's offerings to these zones, the college will instead identify strategic "areas of emphasis" while acknowledging that these areas might change over time. To capitalize on an emerging interest in the Global South, for instance, Grinnell will sponsor its next faculty and staff development seminar in Ghana and South Africa in hopes of fostering future programs and partnerships in Africa. Although the prospect of concentrating efforts in a particular region may offer strategic appeal, in practice, restricting a college's programming and focus may limit the ability of global learners to meet their goals.

Another related action step that has proven challenging to implement is reducing the financial burden of study abroad while not hindering student choice. A stated "weakness" of past policies, identified by the task force, was that "full portability of financial aid is a very expensive practice, and in recent years Grinnell has expended upwards of $3,000,000 annually to maintain it" (p. 18). One factor that contributed to these mounting costs was Grinnell's decision to offer students considerable choice in semester or year abroad programs, including expensive programs in Western Europe and Japan. While the college might contain expenses by limiting students' choices to less expensive programs, there is a desire to support students' goals and ambitions by allowing full access to the world's top academic programs. An expanded faculty advisory committee will work with GIGE to achieve a financially sustainable study abroad portfolio that balances a responsible stewardship of finite resources without compromising quality or choice. Indeed, one of the most significant challenges that institutions face is allocating limited resources in accordance with values. To meet this challenge, Grinnell will continue to engage stakeholders from across the campus to develop an approach that reflects these multiple perspectives and interests.

CONFRONTING PERSISTENT CHALLENGES: OPPORTUNITIES FOR STRATEGIC LEADERSHIP

At a national level, there remains considerable work to do to strengthen faculty-led off-campus study programs and internationalization efforts at liberal arts colleges. Two of the most persistent challenges include aligning stated campus values with recognition criteria and attending to issues of diversity and equity more fully. When articulating future frameworks and undertaking sustained change processes, senior academic leaders are advised to be more attentive to these important, and all too frequently overlooked, considerations.

Align Stated Values and Rewards

While institution-wide strategic plans might espouse the value of internationalization, schools and departments undercut such goals by failing to reflect such activities in their tenure and promotion criteria (Peterson, 2006). Perhaps the single most meaningful thing that a college can do to elevate the status of off-campus study programs is include them in tenure, promotion, and annual evaluation criteria (Childress, 2018). A report released by ACE determined that at most colleges and universities, there is little alignment between broadly expressed goals to internationalize a campus (e.g., a campus strategic plan) and the criteria to evaluate faculty contributions (e.g., departmental promotion standards) (Helms, 2015). Still, many faculty members voluntarily invest considerable time and effort to internationalization efforts, even when such activities are not specifically rewarded by their university's recognition systems (Gillespie, Glasco, Gross, Jasinski, & Layne, 2017; Nyangau, 2018). Although a faculty member's intrinsic motivation or personal commitment to global learning might serve as an incentive to lead off-campus study programs, relying exclusively on the goodwill of individual faculty is a precarious long-term strategy.

Despite the call to expand tenure and promotion guidelines to include "globally focused criteria," a follow-up report from ACE in 2017 revealed that, by and large, institutions have been slow to respond. Fewer than one in 10 institutions reward faculty members for their international engagement, either as a consideration in promotion and tenure review or as a condition of hiring (Helms, Brajkovic, & Struthers, 2017). Even among the handful of institutions that explicitly credit international contributions in tenure and promotion criteria, only about one-third explicitly value "study abroad program development, direction, and delivery" (p. 14) and only two schools in the 100 that were analyzed by ACE included "curriculum internationalization and pedagogy" in their tenure and promotion criteria.

Standards for promotion and tenure have the greatest influence on the behavior of pre-tenure, early-career faculty members. As such, college leaders should be particularly attuned to the ways that the newest arrivals on campus are acculturated, supported, and mentored in the area of global education. Helms (2015) argued that explicitly valuing involvement in off-campus study programs "gives junior faculty license to bring this work to the top of the list of competing priorities, and ensures that spending time on these activities will not hurt their tenure prospects" (p. 1). Failing to elevate and reward off-campus program participation sends an implicit message that such pursuits are less valuable than other forms of teaching, research, and service.

Engaging pre-tenure faculty as program leaders. Some liberal arts colleges prohibit early-career faculty members from leading off-campus study programs, an approach that has been criticized by Moseley (2009). Speaking from his own experiences as a pre-tenure faculty member at Macalester College, Moseley argued that the policy, though well intentioned, yielded too many unintended consequences. For Moseley, mentoring international undergraduate research projects not only bolstered his publication record during the initial years of his appointment, but also site-based teaching also helped him refine his student-centered teaching practice. Moseley reasoned that, rather than limiting their participation in off-campus study programs, academic departments and colleges should provide greater support, mentorship, and encouragement to pre-tenure faculty. While helping faculty members develop their professional practice, expressly valuing participation in off-campus study programs can yield significant long-term benefits for a college. Leading off-campus study programs can help early career faculty members build their institutional investment. From a practical standpoint, colleges may find untenured faculty members to be a pool of promising program leaders—many are energetic, have the freedom to travel due to limited familial commitments, or, like Moseley, already possess strong international relationships to facilitate site work. Like all leaders of off-campus study programs, pre-tenure faculty members benefit from robust institutional and staff support to facilitate the many administrative and logistical demands of taking students abroad.

In addition to formal policies that restrict program leadership to tenured faculty members, informal practices can influence the participation of early career faculty members in off-campus study programs. This is especially true of the critical role that mid-level leaders, namely department chairs, play in guiding pre-tenure faculty through the many and sometimes competing demands they face as new professionals in the academy. When an early career faculty member expresses an interest in leading an off-campus study program, chairs should encourage this interest and leverage available resources to facilitate participation. For instance, when developing a course schedule, a chair might help limit the number of new course preparations for an early career scholar, thus allowing them the sufficient time to develop new field-based and experiential opportunities for students. A chair might allocate one-time funds to enable a new faculty member to attend a professional development workshop related to off-campus study. Or, when negotiating a start-up package with a new hire, a chair might structure travel funds to allow the individual an opportunity to conduct research abroad while also networking with prospective partners for an off-campus study program (e.g., nonprofit organizations). Such arrangements need not be resource intensive; rather, chairs can leverage their resources more effectively. In total, these small gestures signal to pre-tenure faculty that the department and the institution remain equally committed to advancing shared strategic goals while also investing in a faculty member's growth as a scholar, instructor, global learner, and leader.

Opportunities for senior leaders. Given the nature of shared governance, most senior academic leaders lack the positional authority to revise tenure and promotion standards at the department or program level. Senior leaders can, however, encourage and incentivize departments, programs, and schools to revise their guidelines. Leaders can circulate memos, provide sample language, and allocate resources to support efforts to align university-wide goals and departmental policies. Senior leaders can enlist faculty champions and provide examples from peer and aspirant universities to support broader conversations. Leaders might, in turn, celebrate successes and encourage other programs to follow early adopters. When tenure and promotion criteria affirm the value of teaching in off-campus study programs, senior leaders can ease the practical demands on faculty members. Senior leaders can remove structural barriers that discourage faculty participation, chief among them insufficient financial resources to support faculty travel and research abroad, burdensome reimbursement procedures, and certain administrative tasks. Finally, colleges should not overlook the role of international and area studies centers to provide valuable teaching resources to faculty to incubate new international initiatives (Childress, 2018). A broader discussion of ways to better support faculty program leaders is included in chapter 2.

Attending to Issues of Diversity, Inclusion, and Equity

A second area where senior leaders should devote more attention is to address persistent inequities and long-standing patterns of underrepresentation and exclusion in off-campus study programs. In many ways, Susquehanna has made considerable progress on this front by developing a range of off-campus study opportunities, especially individualized opportunities to meet the needs of students whose personal circumstances might otherwise prevent them from off-campus study programs.

Expanding student access. Although more students study abroad today than ever before, the percentage of U.S. students who study abroad during their undergraduate program remains relatively small: estimates range from 2% (Twombly, Salisbury, Tumanut, & Klute, 2012) to 16% (IIE, 2019). Students at private, residential colleges are among those most likely to participate (Twombly et al., 2012). In the last decade, the number of U.S. American college students who study abroad has increased by about 30% (IIE, 2019). During the same time period, the percentage of students of color who studied abroad increased from 18.1% to 29.2% (Redden, 2018), although 70% of study abroad participants identified as White (IIE, 2019). Women have long outnumbered men by nearly a 2:1 margin in study abroad participation, a gap that continued to widen, according to the 2019 Open Doors report completed by IIE. Historically, students majoring in the humanities, social sciences, and fine arts have studied abroad with greater frequency than their STEM and business major counterparts (Twombly et al., 2012). Signaling a positive change, IIE in 2019 reported that STEM majors now account for 25.6% of all study abroad participants, up from 17.5% a decade ago (Redden, 2018). Students from lower-income families and those possessing fewer advantages of social and cultural capital remain slightly less likely to study abroad compared to more affluent or otherwise advantaged peers (Paus, Collins, Okay, & Picard, 2007; Simon & Ainsworth, 2012; Twombly et al., 2012).

Some colleges have removed structural barriers that prevented all students from participating in study abroad. Many small liberal arts colleges, including Colorado College, Davidson, Grinnell, Wellesley, Williams, and Sarah Lawrence, have sought to enhance student scholarships and global initiatives through major fundraising campaigns—the success of these campaigns indicates a willingness among donors to support such initiatives. For some students, financial barriers may be more perceived than actual (Van Der Meid, 2003). For many students, the decision to participate in an off-campus program hinges upon encouragement from their families and faculty mentors (Paus et al., 2007; Simon & Ainsworth, 2012).

From access to inclusion. While expanded financial resources and improved advising help increase student access to study abroad, there remain opportunities to promote equity and inclusion in global programs. Inequitable student participation undercuts the effectiveness of global learning, because "when global learning involves only some students, it limits global awareness, perspective, and problem solving for all" (Doscher & Landorf, 2018, p. 7). Liberal arts colleges might strive to increase the number of students who study abroad but also to materially increase the quality of the student experience. An important element of program quality is the need for colleges to make a concerted effort to build inclusive off-campus study programs. In the simplest of terms, an inclusive climate might be measured by

> feelings of inclusion and belonging across [students from] racial and ethnic groups, the extent to which students interact substantially across difference, where and what students learn about race, appraisals of institutional commitments to fostering inclusive environments, and characterizations of the supportiveness of classrooms and other spaces. (Harper & Davis, 2016, p. 32)

More than reducing or eliminating barriers that limit student participation in off-campus study programs, Harper and Davis (2016) maintain that colleges must support, encourage, and attend to racial and other differences. Although climate surveys can reveal whether students feel affirmed, respected, and safe on their home campus, colleges must take added steps to ensure that off-campus study programs are examined and included within systemic attempts to promote equity and inclusion. Practically speaking, there are acute challenges to maintaining a supportive atmosphere when programs take place away from campus.

Increasing the diversity of faculty program leaders and international education professionals. Another strategy that colleges can use to encourage diverse students to participate in off-campus study programs is to increase the racial, gender, and disciplinary diversity of faculty and staff members who are involved in these efforts. A recent survey conducted by the Diversity Abroad Network exposed the need for colleges to reexamine hiring and retention efforts. The survey included responses from 500 individuals who work in the field of international education (broadly defined); nearly all participants worked for four-year colleges or universities in the United States. A majority of survey respondents (65.3%) described their work as primarily administrative in nature, including "outbound student exchange and services" (Lopez-McGee, 2018, p. 19). In addition, a majority of survey respondents (70%) who recruit and support students to study abroad identified as White. In the survey sample, nearly eight out of 10 international education professionals responding were women, suggesting a strong gender imbalance among international education professionals. While it is important to note that this survey does not necessarily represent the full spectrum of international education professionals, the demographics of survey respondents suggests a gap between those responsible for recruiting and supporting study abroad students and the more diverse student populations they serve.

Respondents to the Diversity Abroad Network survey offered suggestions of how their institutions could better support diverse students who study abroad. A majority of survey respondents (78.4%) agreed or strongly agreed that their organization "supported diverse and underrepresented students throughout the education abroad process" (Lopez-McGee, 2018, p. 30). At the same time, less than half of survey respondents believed that their institution "actively involved all levels of faculty and/or staff in institutional efforts to increase the diversity of students, faculty, and staff who have access to international opportunities" (p. 7). Respondents called upon their institutions to provide resources and other forms of support for diverse students who study abroad, including low-income students, students of color, and LGBTQIA+ students. In particular, respondents wanted more tools and resources to support student learning before, during, and after studying abroad, as well as mental health, physical health, and safety resources in-country.

Although there is no database of the faculty members who lead off-campus study programs at U.S. colleges, the Faculty as Global Learners survey described in chapter 1 found that 85% of survey respondents identified as White (Gillespie et al., 2017). Academic leaders are encouraged to learn about the demographics of program leaders on their own campuses and determine what, if any, barriers or practices may contribute to these patterns. Faculty of color often report carrying a higher advising, mentoring, and service load than their White peers (Gasman, Kim, & Nguyen, 2011; June, 2015). Senior leaders, in collaboration with faculty and staff, should work to determine whether any of these factors have contributed to faculty participation in leading off-campus study programs. Ensuring that faculty members are appropriately recognized and rewarded for their contributions will help reduce these structural inequities.

Opportunities for senior leaders to improve diversity and inclusion in off-campus study. Colleges and senior leaders can take steps to alter the misperception that global learning is only for "some" members of the campus community. Participating in off-campus and international study may pose special challenges to students whose gender and sexual identities, abilities, religious beliefs, and/or racial and cultural identities may make them susceptible to discrimination abroad. In some parts of the world, students (and faculty program leaders) may not be privy to the same legal protections they receive in the United States. For undocumented students, participating in off-campus study programs may remain an elusive dream. For students struggling with serious physical and mental health conditions, their needs may require unique knowledge and expertise among faculty leaders and the professional staff who collaborate to create off-campus study opportunities. Indeed, international education professionals reported that they think their institutions should be doing more to ensure that the most vulnerable members of the campus community are sufficiently protected and supported while studying abroad (Lopez-McGee, 2018). As a foray into this work, senior leaders and other stakeholders might first determine the nature of unmet needs on their campus and then collaborate to develop resources and responsive policies together.

In order to offer off-campus study programs with greater appeal for students with historically low rates of study abroad participation, colleges might convene focus groups or informal conversations to identify potential topics, geographic locations, or instructors that might entice students to participate. Using this information, colleges might then reverse-engineer their program offerings to provide more relevant opportunities. This is not to say that colleges should always be at the mercy of students' desires or adopt a consumer mindset; it is only to suggest that adopting a more open, transparent, and student-centered program development process could serve a college's strategic interests better than the status quo.

A college's pool of prospective off-campus study program leaders is largely shaped by the diversity of its faculty as a whole. Since diversifying a college's faculty is inherently a long-term process that may take decades, what can colleges do in the short-term? If and when diverse program leaders cannot be identified from the full-time faculty, Agnes Scott College has found success recruiting junior and senior students to serve as program assistants, who play the role of an "intermediary between students and faculty." Efforts are made to recruit program assistants from all walks of life, and they are trained to share student concerns (anonymously) with the faculty program leader throughout a program. Davidson College regularly invites alumni with specialized expertise on a topic or a region to serve as co-program leaders, an arrangement that is described by Amanda Caleb in her essay in this collection. By engaging diverse alumni as program mentors, small colleges might begin to make strides toward long-term diversification goals.

CONCLUSION

For decades, the preponderance of research on the impact and value of study abroad had focused, justifiably, on college students. This book argues for a more comprehensive consideration of the people, structures, and programs comprising the off-campus study ecosystem. Students stand to be the ultimate beneficiaries of a sustained analysis of how these individuals (and their often-overlooked contributions) guide and support student learning. To put a college on a trajectory to better serve the needs of all global learners, defined broadly to include students and faculty, the case studies in this chapter demonstrate how dedicated faculty champions have engaged with senior leaders to achieve strategic and systemic change. While colleges regularly espouse the benefits of study abroad to prepare graduates to succeed in a globalized world, it is essential that such rhetorical claims are matched with supportive practices and explicit tenure and promotion guidelines to elevate the value of off-campus study programs. Colleges must also give due attention to making off-campus study programs accessible and inclusive.

In the foreword to this collection, Milton Reigelman, a lifelong advocate for study abroad, traced the evolution of off-campus study programs at liberal arts colleges over the past four decades. As the inheritors of a storied and ever-changing tradition, today's liberal arts colleges are in a unique position to shape the future. Examples from Grinnell and Susquehanna reinforce how senior administrators and faculty leaders share a collective responsibility to offer students high-value academic experiences at a manageable cost, to forge global partnerships that enhance the curricular offerings of small private colleges, and to formally recognize the contributions of faculty members who are integral to the whole enterprise.

REFERENCES

Aisch, G., Buchanan, L., Cox, A., & Quealy, K. (2017, January 18). Some colleges have more students from the top 1 percent than the bottom 60. Find yours. *The New York Times*. Retrieved from https://www.nytimes.com/interactive/2017/01/18/upshot/some-colleges-have-more-students-from-the-top-1-percent-than-the-bottom-60.html

Childress, L. K. (2018). *The twenty-first century university: Developing faculty engagement in internationalization* (2nd ed.). New York, NY: Peter Lang.

Doscher, S., & Landorf, H. (2018). Universal global learning, inclusive excellence, and higher education's greater purposes. *Peer Review, 20*(1), 4–7. Retrieved from https://www.aacu.org/peerreview/2018/Winter/FIU

Eckel, P. D., & Kezar, A. (2011). *Taking the reins: Institutional transformation in higher education*. American Council on Education/Praeger series on higher education. Lanham, MD: Rowman & Littlefield Publishing.

Gasman, M., Kim, J., & Nguyen, T.-H. (2011). Effectively recruiting faculty of color at highly selective institutions: A School of Education case study. *Journal of Diversity in Higher Education, 4*(4), 212–222. doi:10.1037/a0025130

Gillespie, J., Glasco, S., Gross, D., Jasinski, L., & Layne, P. (2017). *Faculty as global learners: The transformative impact of leading study away and study abroad programs.* Paper presented at Elon University Symposium on Integrating Global Learning with the University Experience.

Global Grinnell Task Force. (2016, July 5). *Global Grinnell Task Force: Final Report.* Grinnell, IA. Retrieved from https://www.grinnell.edu/sites/default/files/documents/GlobalTaskForce_FinalReport.pdf

Grawe, N. D. (2018). *Demographics and the demand for higher education.* Baltimore, MD: Johns Hopkins University Press.

Green, M. F. (2002). Joining the world: The challenge of internationalizing undergraduate education. *Change: The Magazine of Higher Learning, 34*(3), 12–21.

Green, M. F. (2005). *Measuring internationalization at research universities.* Washington, DC: American Council on Education.

Harper, S. R., & Davis, C. H. F. (2016). Eight actions to reduce racism in college classrooms. *Academe*, 30–34.

Helms, R. M. (2015). *Internationalizing the tenure code: Policies to promote a globally focused faculty*. Washington, DC: American Council on Education.

Helms, R. M., Brajkovic, L., & Struthers, B. (2017). *Mapping internationalization on U.S. campuses: 2017 edition*. Washington, DC: American Council on Education. Retrieved from https://www.acenet.edu/Documents/Mapping-Internation-alization-2017.pdf

Hill, B. (2019). *Strategies for successful change: Lessons from the American Council on Education and W. K. Kellogg Foundation Project on Transformational Change*. Retrieved from https://www.clir.org/pubs/reports/pub85/strategies/

Hudzik, J. K. (2015). *Comprehensive internationalization: Institutional pathways to success*. Abingdon, UK: Routledge.

Institute for International Education (IIE). (2019). Fast facts. *Open Doors report on international education exchange*. Retrieved from https://www.iie.org/Research-and-Insights/Open-Doors/Fact-Sheets-and-Infographics/Fast-Facts

June, A. W. (2015, November 8). The invisible labor of minority professors. *The Chronicle of Higher Education*.

Leonhardt, D. (2014, September 8). Top colleges that enroll rich, middle class, and poor. *The New York Times*. Retrieved from https://www.nytimes.com/2014/09/09/upshot/top-colleges-that-enroll-rich-middle-class-and-poor.html

Lopez-McGee, L. (2018). *Survey of diversity and inclusion among international educators*. Berkeley, CA: Diversity Abroad. Retrieved from https://www.diversitynetwork.org/page/Research_Reports

Manning, S. (2016, Spring). Global opportunities for cross-cultural learning at Susquehanna University. *Diversity & Democracy*.

McGee, J. (2015). *Breakpoint: The changing marketplace for higher education*. Baltimore, MD: Johns Hopkins University Press.

Moseley, W. G. (2009). Making study abroad a win-win opportunity for pre-tenure faculty. *Frontiers: The Interdisciplinary Journal of Study Abroad, 18*, 231–240.

Nyangau, J. Z. (2018). Motivations of faculty engagement in internationalization: An agenda for future research. *FIRE: Forum for International Research in Education, 4*(3), 7–32.

Olson, G. A. (2009, July 23). Exactly what is "shared governance"? *The Chronicle of Higher Education*. Retrieved from https://www.chronicle.com/article/Exactly-What-Is-Shared/47065

Paus, E., Okay, J., & Picard, J. (2007). *Global education for all students: Innovation & integration in expanding learning abroad*. South Hadley, MA: Mt. Holyoke College. Retrieved from http://www.teaglefoundation.org/Library-Resources/Fresh-Thinking/Global-Education-for-All-Students-Innovation-In

Peterson, N. J. (2006). Still missing the boat: Faculty involvement in study abroad. In M. Tillman (Ed.), *Study abroad: A 21st century perspective*. Stamford, CT:

AIFS Foundation.

Pierce, S. R. (2017, January 31). Hope and denial are not strategies. *Inside Higher Ed*. Retrieved from https://www.insidehighered.com/views/2017/01/31/how-colleges-should-rethink-their-strategic-planning-processes-essay

Redden, E. (2017, May 8). Studying the borderlands: First-year Grinnell students travel to Germany, Greece, Mexico, Spain and the U.S. Southwest for comparative class on migration, borders and refugees. *Inside Higher Ed*. Retrieved from https://www.insidehighered.com/news/2017/05/08/comparative-class-grinnell-focuses-migration-and-border-policy-us-and-europe

Redden, E. (2018, November 13). Study abroad numbers grow. *Inside Higher Ed*. Retrieved from https://www.insidehighered.com/news/2018/11/13/study-abroad-numbers-continue-grow-driven-continued-growth-short-term-programs

Simon, J., & Ainsworth, J. W. (2012). Race and socioeconomic status differences in study abroad participation: The role of habitus, social networks, and cultural capital. *International Scholarly Research Notices, 2012*, 1–21. doi:10.5402/2012/413896

Susquehanna University. *Parent, family, & supporter's guide to study away*. Retrieved from https://go.susqu.edu

Twombly, S. B., Salisbury, M. H., Tumanut, S. D., & Klute, P. (2012). *Study abroad in a new global century: Renewing the promise, refining the purpose*. ASHE higher education report. San Francisco, CA: Jossey-Bass.

U.S. Department of Education College Scorecard. (n.d.). *Student body information*. Retrieved from https://collegescorecard.ed.gov/

Van Der Meid, J. S. (2003). Asian Americans: Factors influencing the decision to study abroad. *Frontiers: The Interdisciplinary Journal of Study Abroad, 9*, 71–110.

PROMOTING INCLUSIVITY IN ACADEMIA

A Case Study in Taking Underrepresented Students to Research Archives in the United States

Marcy Sacks

A few years ago, l invited two African American students to join me in applying for an off-campus research opportunity consisting of three weeks of intensive, primary source investigations at the

Massachusetts Historical Society and other Boston-area libraries. My initial inclination in deliberately recruiting students of color was straightforward: few humanities academics hail from under-represented populations. Consequently, students of color rarely envision themselves in humanities professions or in the more general arena of intellectual production.

As a professor of African American history, I spend virtually every teaching day addressing the role of racial discrimination in the creation of exclusivity, whether it be residential, educational, economic, or social. But despite the stated mission of many institutions of higher learning to increase access and success for under-represented populations, my own profession has generally failed to achieve this. Academia comes nowhere near reflecting the U.S. population writ large. By offering this chance to students of color, I sought a specific—albeit small—way to make inroads into the intractable whiteness of my world.

I selected two especially promising underclassmen as my co-applicants, approaching the entire pursuit with conventional goals that mirrored my own experience of conducting research as an undergraduate and subsequently pursuing a PhD and becoming an academic. But the students' very different conception of what we were doing exposed the value of diversity: they expressed much different objectives than I had ever imagined. They thereby helped me develop a far more expansive understanding of the transformative power of this undertaking that I had not understood or recognized. To wit, one student wrote in his narrative that he wanted to be a role model for other kids in his Detroit community. In all of my years of involving students in my research projects, I had never before encountered a student who identified an altruistic outcome for the work itself (as opposed to the product of the research). For him, undertaking an intellectual endeavor like this one represented a fundamental reimagining of the possibilities available to young people from his world. He was raised to see sports as his only ticket to upward mobility, and he wanted other boys (in particular) to realize that non-sports options existed. He viewed his participation in the research program as a way to offer a new path to other kids even more than how he might benefit.

Our application was funded, and our team joined two other groups in the Boston Summer Seminar where my students had their first-ever experience in the rarified spaces of research archives. Over three weeks, they transformed from wide-eyed novices to confident scholars; their growing belief in their own intellectual legitimacy was palpable. When one of the two students graduated this past May, he pulled me aside to thank me. "You were the first person to believe I was smart," he told me. While it is devastating that no mentor ever told him this before he arrived at Albion, his participation in the research program helped to convince him of his abilities. He has just begun a graduate program in literature and dreams of becoming a writer.

This past summer I again traveled with two African American undergraduates to East Coast archives. Unlike our previous experience with an external funder, this time, we secured backing through my own institution's summer research program. Our initial application was denied on the grounds that the students had not adequately identified the significance of the project or the anticipated outcomes. Not unexpectedly, the committee evaluated our proposal in traditional ways, demanding a polished narrative with language reflecting a preexisting familiarity with academic conventions. Eventually, the proposal was accepted but only because we reconstructed it to more explicitly conform to customary standards about the project's worth (where it fit within the literature of our field) and hoped-for results (continuation of the work via a senior thesis and eventual presentation at a research conference). Yet the actual value of the project came not in the formal outcomes of written papers but in the students' own reimagining of themselves as members of an intellectual community. Neither student aspires to careers in academia, but both now have greater recognition of their own worth as full-fledged, equal members of society. Nowhere in traditional grant applications is that identified as a worthy outcome unto itself. And this is troubling.

Those of us in academia function—perhaps unwittingly—as gatekeepers. Despite our expressed commitment to diversity, we nevertheless replicate the exclusivity of the intellectual arena and persist in recreating the academic world in our own image. We demand that students conform to our expectations and norms rather than consider how our institutions ignore or dismiss the things that they find meaningful. By doing so, we imply that their absence in our elite circle is a fault of theirs, not ours. If we continue to value only things that reproduce our own experiences, we will neither increase participation nor grasp the genuinely transformative potential of intellectual inquiry.

I was struck and disheartened by the overwhelming whiteness of the students involved in Albion's summer program. Although our student population is now remarkably diverse, nearly all of the researchers were white. Either our many students of color cannot imagine themselves conducting this type of work, and therefore they do not even apply, or they perhaps apply but do not adhere to the conventional expectations of what has academic and intellectual merit. If we restrict our own spaces—including and especially the intellectual ones—to others in our own mirror image, then our understanding of what has value and why will continue to stagnate. We must obligate ourselves to reimagine what has worth; in doing so, we have the power to transform people's lives, including our own.

To that end, I am now pursuing two distinct actions. First, I have made changes in my own approach to collaborations with students by explicitly reaching out to freshmen in an effort to help them imagine the idea of academic work at an earlier stage of their college careers. Albion's Student Research Partners program funds research assistants; this year I have been careful to title my projects in such a way that might appeal to a diverse array of students and encourage them to apply.

More broadly, I am coordinating with the members of relevant committees on campus to begin discussions of the ways in which we inadvertently diminish access to intellectual pursuits in our gatekeeping efforts. I hope to encourage a more expansive view of what has value and worth. While it is too early to determine if these efforts will bear fruit, it behooves us all if we genuinely seek to promote inclusion and truly value diversity to consciously recognize the impediments we are creating toward those goals. The first step on the path to breaking barriers is to identify their very existence.

THE H1N1 OUTBREAK IN CHINA

A Unique Research Opportunity

Shiwei Chen

In 2009, I took five students from Lake Forest College to China to conduct field research with an ASIANetwork Freeman Student-Faculty Fellows Grant. Our goal was to achieve a better understanding of China's economic transition through analyzing three-pronged cases in industry, social order, and education. Before we

left for China, our team prepared a variety of interdisciplinary approaches to facilitate our fieldwork in remote Hebei Province, including personal interviews, on-site investigations, observation of business activities, collection of firsthand materials, and round-table discussions with Chinese people. However, a few days before our arrival in Shanghai, the first case of the virus H1N1 was documented. The public health emergency put an end to our carefully laid plans, but it gave us a unique chance to reformulate our project: how the Chinese government handled the pandemic.

I made the decision to redirect our research with the memory of the SARS (Severe Acute Respiratory Syndrome) outbreak in 2003, when China came under heavy international criticism for its ineffectiveness at handling emergencies. The SARS outbreak was not only a health crisis but also a social-political issue, revealing that in the opaque one-party system, which had been masked by economic success, the government's failure to handle a crisis could raise doubt that China was ready to join the 21st century. This painful lesson made the prevention of the spread of H1N1 virus especially significant for the Chinese government to demonstrate itself as a responsible actor on the world stage. In spite of its unfortunate impact, H1N1 provided our team with a unique opportunity.

My research team and I moved swiftly from Shanghai to Beijing, a city where I had lived and worked for many years. I arranged through my personal contacts to investigate the working model of China's new disease prevention protocol, the government's measures to control disease, and the reactions of ordinary Chinese. Our fieldwork began with a number of interviews with professionals. The first person we talked to, a doctor at the Department of Pathology of Peking Union Medical College Hospital, had been working with Beijing's Ministry of Health (see photo). The doctor explained how the H1N1 virus was different from the regular flu and the public health safety measures the Chinese government had implemented to combat its spread, starting with a public information campaign even before the first case was reported in China. The Ministry of Health was also coordinating with the General Administration of Quality Supervision, Inspection and Quarantine (GAQSIQ), which instructed anyone with flu-like symptoms to report them immediately. Internationally, the ministry had contacted doctors in both the United States and Mexico to find out more about the illness and successful prevention.

We also spoke with a journalist at the Guangming Daily in Beijing about the media's role in the public information campaign. Since the SARS outbreak in 2003, the Chinese government has allowed the press greater freedom to report on disasters and public health issues to give the public confidence in dealing with crises and quiet previous criticism from Western media about whether the Chinese government keeps the public informed.

Next, I introduced our students to my former colleague at Peking University, a professor of history who had lived through the turbulence of the Cultural Revolution and the growth of the market-based economic system. He was in a unique position to see the current H1N1 virus crisis from the perspective of age and wisdom. He summarized the government's mishandling of SARS in 2003: local authorities did not report the illness to avoid the perception of their own failures; government cover-ups, denials, and irresponsibility led to avoidable deaths and fear throughout the world and in China; and newspapers, following government orders, suppressed details of the outbreak. Finally, overcrowding in the major urban centers and a weak infrastructure for disease prevention allowed the illness to spread rapidly.

To understand how the middle class viewed the threat of the virus and what the government was doing to protect the population, we spoke to a successful businessman about the economic and international policy implications. Our questions concerned the political and economic ramifications of the H1N1 virus outbreak during the global economic slump. He told us the practical reasons why the Chinese government would want to deal so stringently with prevention, as some of the same conditions that allowed the spread of the SARS virus in 2003, such as a weak health care infrastructure in overcrowded urban centers, still existed.

Lastly, we went to Renmin University in Beijing and heard the opinion of two students, a sample of people a generation younger than the others we interviewed. They were not afraid of contracting the H1N1 virus and said they would willingly quarantine themselves if they noticed any influenza-like symptoms. They knew the information about the virus through the public information campaign. China, the students articulated, a country that for much of its history has been considered an introvert, was slowly reversing that trend and now reaching out to take its place in the international arena.

The six people we talked to by no means define the views of the roughly 1.31 billion people living in China, but they offer a cross section of the personal opinions of the residents of Beijing, a perspective that no newspaper or government spokesperson could. Weeks of travel and multiple interviews revealed just how important the H1N1 epidemic and the events surrounding it are to China as it moves from its past into its future. The research provided our team with a comprehensive and in-depth understanding of China's increasing ability to handle crises in the changing global balance of power with China's ascension to the top of the international economic ladder. Even though the H1N1 virus epidemic was not over when we left for the United States, we gained a great deal of knowledge about China's approach in containing its spread.

The 2009 field trip to China that I conducted with five students was a great success. Students returned home safely with a plethora of cherished memories enriched by their interviews. As a faculty director, I also acquired considerable administrative skills from managing the program at a critical historical juncture, all of which enabled me to be in a unique position and derive important and permanent ways to help Lake Forest College's off-campus programs for the future.

FLORENCE AND CHICAGO

Material Culture and Cities as Texts

Linda D. Horwitz

In 2015, I taught a course entitled Rhetorical Florence in the Associated Colleges of the Midwest's Arts in Context program, which looked at art, architecture, and public spaces to understand how Florence tells the story of its past. This material culture approach was a necessity as neither I, nor my students, had the historical

foundation or language skills in either Italian or Latin to do mean-ingful discursive textual analysis. Rhetorical Florence improved our understanding of rhetorical theories and built up our rhe-torical skills by analyzing the physical structures built during the Renaissance that remain today. It also gave me experience teaching on-site and provided me with Florentine examples so that later in a similar course on Chicago I had a rich repertoire of references for the rhetorical skills I was teaching.

I had visited Florence before, but living in Florence for six months as a professor was an incredible gift. I spent most of my time walking, reading the city as a rhetorical text. Rhetoric is about choices; human-built environments, just like written texts, are cre-ated through human choices. Those choices reveal values, beliefs, attitudes, and worldviews—what we call culture.

My students' first assignment was to create a map of their com-mute from their Florentine family's home to the classroom. We evaluated the maps by having other students find their way based on them. The assignment was intended to introduce basic visual concepts, inspire my students to look around, create a record of their experience abroad, and illustrate that choices make mean-ings. The students discussed their use of permanent versus tem-porary landmarks as well as the differences between iconic, index-ical, and symbolic signs. They noticed not only marble fountains and famous statues but also how the bridges, churches, and paved squares functioned to delineate neighborhoods of the city. They also noticed how the bronze map in the centrally located Piazza della Repubblica offered a bird's eye view of the world they were inhabiting, thereby transforming the confusing twisting streets into a manageable and meaningful space.

One landmark that appeared on most students' maps is the *Col-onna dell'Abbondanza* (Column of Abundance) in the Piazza della Repubblica. It marks the point where the *cardus* and *decumanus* of the original Roman Forum met. It was the central market before the new market was built in 1551. The current column is original, built in 1431, but the statue of the Roman goddess Abundance is a 1956 copy of Poggio's copy of an original by Donatello, which broke in 1721. The Roman goddess reminds us of Florence's origin as a Roman city and of the Renaissance interest in the Roman Republic. It also prompts the current inhabitant to see that this square was not always home to fancy boutiques, expensive cafés, and a turn-of-the-century carousel. What is no longer visible is how the old market was turned into the Jewish Ghetto in 1571; during that period, the statue of Abundance was an ironic marker.

Like Florence, Chicago has its own goddess up on high at an important intersection in Chicago's financial district. We call ours *Ceres,* after the Roman goddess of agriculture and fertility. She stands not on a column but on top of the Board of Trade Building. The Art Deco–style building was the tallest in Chicago when it was completed in 1930. According to the Chicago Architecture Center, *Ceres,* a faceless metal statue with "straight lines on her garment" and "machine-made appearance," is "the quintessential Art Deco ornament for this completely stylized structure."

Florence's Abundance is a Renaissance sculpture atop a Renaissance column created when this style was all the rage. Chicago's Art Deco *Ceres* above an Art Deco building was also created using the latest style. In both, the artists were referencing antiquity yet using contemporary styles and materials to portray the connection between agriculture and commerce. In both cases, an agricultural market was symbolically blessed by the presence of a goddess of agriculture. Yet the differences are also noteworthy. Abundance originally reigned over an actual market where people bought and sold food; Chicago's *Ceres* reigns over the world's oldest future and options exchange, where people buy and sell nothing tangible. Instead, they buy and sell future interests in agricultural goods.

This *Ceres* is an apt portrayal of Chicago because, though the city is surrounded by the farmlands that serve as the nation's breadbasket, Chicago does not actually grow anything; instead, Chicago processes, packages, and distributes agricultural products. A faceless aluminum Art Deco *Ceres* represents Chicago's abstraction from the process of working in the fields, even as we are reliant on agriculture for our success. It represents Chicago as a metropolis: the urban center of the Midwest, where people wear suits and deal in financial options and futures but whose fortunes, just like the farmer, still depend on the good graces of Ceres. She also personifies Chicago at its hundredth anniversary (1933). Instead of looking backwards as the city did with the neoclassical architecture of the 1893 Columbian Exposition's "White City" architecture, Chicago in the 1930s wanted to be seen as modern and innovative.

Being in Florence allowed me to see my native Chicago with new eyes. This experience elevated my teaching and scholarship by expanding my rhetorical analysis to include material culture. Material rhetoric's way of bringing along its history while speaking in the present tense to current audiences offers a clear advantage in today's classroom. I now teach a Rhetorical Chicago course that alternates being taught on-site in the city and on our suburban campus. We use rhetorical tools and theories to investigate the art, architecture, and public spaces that explain major events of Chicago's history in order to come to a better understanding of Chicago's ever-evolving culture. Whether my students are creating maps or analyzing three-dimensional structures, exploring Chicago as a rhetorical text has made rhetorical theories and skills relevant and engaging. Learning Florence through its physical symbols and historical built environment gave me a new language to teach my students.

REFERENCES

Chicago Architecture Center. (2018). *Chicago Board of Trade Building.* Retrieved from http://www.architecture.org/learn/resources/buildings-of-chicago/building/chicago-board-of-trade-building/

Contributors

Nancy K. Barry is Professor of English at Luther College in Decorah, Iowa. She recently directed the London portion of the Associated Colleges of the Midwest semester in Florence and London, along with several month-long courses on theatre in London. She has served as Director of Advising at Luther College and has written a one-woman play, *Lessons from Cancer College*.

Amanda M. Caleb is Associate Professor of English and Director of Medical and Health Humanities at Misericordia University. She specializes in 19th- and 20th-century intersections of literature, medicine, and science, with a special focus on the ways that individual accounts of illness influence health care practices and policies. She has published articles on topics ranging from accounts of illness in the Victorian period to British eugenics to dementia and the role of narrative medicine to stigma reduction of mental health illness and opioid addiction.

Verna Case, Beverly F. Dolan Professor of Biology, has served Davidson College since 1974. She chaired the Department of Biology at Davidson for 16 years and was Associate Dean for Teaching, Learning and Research for four years and Associate Dean of Faculty for the last three years. Dr. Case teaches a global health course and leads a month-long summer program in Mwandi, Zambia.

Brian Caton is an Associate Professor and Chair of the Department of History at Luther College where he teaches courses related to South Asia and environmental history. His research interests in South Asia history include modern South Asia, social and political history of Punjab, and veterinary medicine and animal breeding.

Shiwei Chen is Professor of History at Lake Forest College and Visiting Faculty Director of the Associated Colleges of the Midwest Shanghai program (2017, 2018). At Lake Forest College, he has also served as the Chair of Asian Studies and Director of the Beijing Program, the college's off-campus program.

Christine S. Cozzens is Charles A. Dana Professor of English and Director of the Center for Writing and Speaking at Agnes Scott College. She teaches a variety of writing courses, including the nonfiction sequence in the creative writing program and Irish literature and film. She has led more than a dozen student trips to Ireland. Her essays about travel, writing, and other subjects have appeared in *The New York Times*, *The Boston Globe*, and *The Baltimore Sun*, among other publications, and her blog *The View from Here* about Irish literature, culture, and landscape has thousands of readers.

James J. Ebersole is Professor of Organismal Biology and Ecology at Colorado College where he teaches a variety of courses on ecology, botany, and biostatistics. He has led field semesters in Tanzania and Alaska and about a dozen month-long courses in the Canadian Arctic, Namibia, Spain, Tanzania, and Patagonia. He has coauthored papers with undergraduates on topics ranging from interactions of baboons and impala to Maasai relationships with domestic dogs.

Joan Gillespie is an instructor in Northwestern University's graduate program in higher education administration and policy. She was Vice President and Director of off-campus study programs for the Associated Colleges of the Midwest and held senior positions at IES Abroad. She has published and presented papers on international program quality standards, assessment of student learning and development abroad, and undergraduate research in off-campus study.

Dana Gross is Professor of Psychology at St. Olaf College. As Associate Dean of Interdisciplinary and General Studies (2013–2019), she worked closely with the Office of International and Off-Campus Studies. She is co-editor of *Internationalizing the Undergraduate Psychology Curriculum: Practical Lessons Learned at Home and Abroad* (APA Books, 2016) and has led January-term courses for undergraduates in India and China.

Linda D. Horwitz earned a MA and PhD in Communication Studies as well as a certificate of Women's Studies from Northwestern University. She has been teaching at Lake Forest College since 2003, where she is an Associate Professor of Communication. She is an advocate of study abroad, having had the opportunity to study and/or teach in England, India, the Netherlands, Greece, and Italy. Her current research is on rhetorical approaches to remembering the Holocaust, civic pedagogy, public memory, and the rhetorical construction of cities.

Lisa Jasinski is Special Assistant to the Vice President for Academic Affairs at Trinity University. At Trinity, she led three academic service-learning programs to the Eastern Caribbean island of Dominica for pre-service teachers. While a doctoral student at The University of Texas at Austin, Lisa researched the implications of federal affirmative action policies in universities in southern Brazil. In 2020, she served as a Fulbright Specialist to Finland.

L. DeAne Lagerquist, Professor of Religion, joined the St. Olaf faculty in 1988 and credits leading off-campus study programs to Greece, Turkey, and India with expanding and enriching her teaching and research. She previously served as field supervisor for the Global Semester, a program that included courses in Egypt, India, Hong Kong, and Korea.

Chuck Lewis is Professor of English and Director of the Writing Program at Beloit College, where he teaches courses in literature, creative writing, and expository writing. His most recent publications focus on late 19th- and 21st-century American fiction.

Emily Margaretten is a cultural anthropologist and has directed semester-long study abroad programs for undergraduate students in Tanzania and Botswana. Her research and teaching interests focus on topics relating to sub-Saharan Africa, urban anthropology, global health, gender and sexuality, and transnationalism and migration.

Susan Jaret McKinstry, Helen F. Lewis Professor of English at Carleton College, studies and teaches 19th-century British literature (with focus on the Pre-Raphaelite Brotherhood), intermedial arts, narrative theory, and creative writing. She co-edited *Feminism, Bakhtin, and the Dialogic* (1991); has published articles on Dante Rossetti, William Morris, Jane Austen, Emily Brontë, Emily Dickinson, T. S. Eliot, Ann Beattie, and others; and writes and publishes poetry. She co-directed Carleton's Andrew Mellon–funded interdisciplinary initiative Visual Learning (2009–2012) and has led off-campus programs for students and alumni to London, Ireland, Scotland, and Florence.

William G. (Bill) Moseley is Professor of Geography and Director of the Program for Food, Agriculture & Society at Macalester College. His research interests include tropical agriculture, food security, political ecology, environment, development, and Africa.

Professor Moseley's research, teaching, and development work have led to extended stays in Botswana, Burkina Faso, Burundi, India, Lesotho, Niger, Malawi, Mali, South Africa, and Zimbabwe.

Kylie Quave is Assistant Professor of Writing and Anthropology at The George Washington University. She has conducted anthropological archaeological research in Cuzco on the local impacts of imperialism and colonialism (11th to 18th centuries). She previously taught at Beloit College, including the course discussed in this publication.

Milton Reigelman, Cowan Professor of English Emeritus at Centre College, has been Centre's Humanities Division Chair, Associate Dean, Vice President for Planning and Resources, Director of the Center for Global Citizenship, Special Assistant to the President and Acting President. After acquiring an AB in philosophy at The College of William & Mary and working for *The Washington Post*, he studied at Johns Hopkins University and the Universities of Pennsylvania and Iowa, served in Army Intelligence, was a Fulbright Professor in Warsaw and Kiev, and has directed Centre's study abroad programs in Strasbourg and London several times.

Marcy Sacks is the Julian S. Rammelkamp Professor of History at Albion College, Michigan, where she has been teaching for the last 20 years. Her most recent book, *Joe Louis: Sports and Race in Twentieth-Century America*, was published by Routledge in 2018. Outside of her professional endeavors, she is a competitive marathoner.

Michael A. Schneider is Professor of History and Asian Studies at Knox College in Galesburg, Illinois. His research and publications focus on cultural internationalism in 20th-century Japan. He has served twice as resident director for ACM/GLCA Japan Study and led numerous student and faculty groups in East Asia.

Claudena Skran, Professor of Government, Lawrence University, earned her DPhil in International Relations from Oxford University and first went to Sierra Leone as a Fulbright Scholar in 2005–2006. An expert on refugees and international humanitarian aid, she has since taken more than 150 students to West Africa as part of a community-engaged field experience.

Stephen Volz has been teaching African history at Kenyon College since 2004. He first became interested in Africa as a Peace Corps volunteer in Botswana during the late-1980s, and his research frequently brings him to the region of southern Africa. His own off-campus study experience as an undergraduate was in Germany, and he regularly encourages and advises Kenyon students on their off-campus study plans.

Acknowledgments

Joan Gillespie, Lisa Jasinski, and Dana Gross

Our experiences leading off-campus study programs challenged each of us to reimagine many fundamental assumptions about teaching and learning. By traveling with and learning from our students, each of us came to more fully appreciate learning as an emotional, transformative, academic, and lifelong endeavor. We begin by offering our sincerest thanks to our students for providing us with the ability to do work that is rewarding and meaningful; it has truly been our privilege to learn from you.

Inspired by our firsthand experiences leading off-campus study programs, we began a broader scholarly exploration about faculty members who have also engaged in this practice. We came together with two other researchers, Prudence Layne and Sarah Glasco, during "Integrating Global Learning with the University Experience: Higher Impact Study Abroad and Off-Campus Domestic Study," a research seminar facilitated by the Center for Engaged Learning, Elon College, North Carolina (2015–2017). For two years, our research team collaborated to conduct and analyze the findings from a multi-institution survey of more than 200 faculty members representing 28 small private liberal arts colleges. We appreciate that our faculty colleagues at the Associated Colleges of the Midwest, the Associated Colleges of the South, and

Elon University took our survey seriously and shared their personal stories with great candor, humor, and humility. We wish to offer our most special thanks to Prudence and Sarah, two Red Star Rock Stars for life, for their contributions to our team and their many insights about off-campus study programs.

The seminar leaders at Elon—Mick Vande Berg, Amanda Sturgill, Neal Sobania, and Nina Namaste—helped us refine our research goals, encouraged us to share our work in progress, and doled out hugs when needed. During our annual seminar meetings, Jessie Moore, Director of the Center for Engaged Learning, led graciously, offered wise guidance and positive encouragement, and provided delicious meals. The other participants in the seminar gave generous constructive feedback and helped strengthen our project.

Over the past few years, we have benefited from the encouragement and suggestions from our professional colleagues during academic conferences. We wish to thank those who attended our presentations and stopped by our posters at the Forum on Education Abroad, Association of International Education Administrators, Association for the Study of Higher Education, Association of American Colleges & Universities (AAC&U), and elsewhere. Your questions encouraged us to examine our data more closely and sharpened our thinking. In particular, we wish to offer special thanks to Dawn Whitehead, Senior Director for Global Learning and Curricular Change at AAC&U, and Hilary Kahn, Assistant Dean for International Education and Global Initiative, Director for the Study of Global Change, and Senior Lecturer at Indiana University Bloomington.

Given our interest and belief in the value of liberal arts colleges, we could not imagine a better partner for this volume than Lever Press and our editor, Beth Bouloukos. The insightful suggestions and encouragement from the anonymous readers made this a better book. At Michigan Publishing, the guidance of Amanda Karby and the sharp editorial eye of Alja Kooistra helped us bring our ideas to the page with greater clarity. Developing this volume has provided us with the opportunity to continue to learn from and be inspired by the excellent work being done by colleagues across the country, especially Milton Reigelman and the 18 authors who contributed the Faculty Voices essays. We hope that our book, in some small way, contributes to the good work you are all doing at liberal arts colleges across the country.

At last, we also wish to thank our spouses and families for their unwavering support during the lifespan of this project. Thanks for holding down the fort when we were away at "research camp" in North Carolina and patiently waiting for us to finish our Sunday night conference calls. You all get a red star.